THE NORTHROP STORY

Also by Richard Sanders Allen

REVOLUTION
IN THE SKY

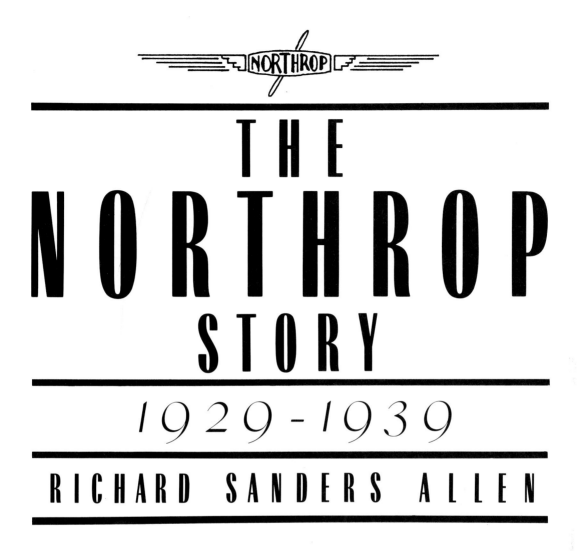

THE NORTHROP STORY

STORY

1929-1939

RICHARD SANDERS ALLEN

ORION BOOKS/NEW YORK

Frontispiece: *A forty-six-year contrast. Prior to enshrinement in the National Air and Space Museum, TWA's restored Northrop Alpha mail plane poses with modern jetliner.* Walter Boyne collections

Copyright © 1990 by Richard Sanders Allen

Published by Orion Books, a division of Crown Publishers, Inc., 201 East 50th Street, New York, New York 10022.

ORION and colophon are trademarks of Crown Publishers, Inc.

Manufactured in the United States of America

Library of Congress Cataloging-in-Publication Data

Allen, Richard Sanders, 1927–
The Northrop story, 1929–1939 / Richard Sanders Allen,—1st ed.
p.   cm.
Includes bibliographical references (p.
1. Northrop, John Knudsen, 1895–1981. 2. Industrialists—United States—Biography. 3. Aircraft industry—United States—History.
4. Northrop Corporation—History.   I. Title.
HD9711.U6N673   1990
338.7'62913'0092—dc20
[B]   90-7094
CIP

ISBN 0-517-56677-X

Design by Jake Victor Thomas

10 9 8 7 6 5 4 3 2 1

First Edition

To my son
Richard Stanley Allen

CONTENTS

INTRODUCTION

The Armchair Aviator

Except for a brown-and-white spaniel, he lives alone in a beat-up trailer in one of the canyons above Burbank. Not too much smog, but the bright California sun doesn't get in there before noon. He has a few hives out back and sells a little honey, but mostly occupies his time just puttering around. Thick glasses, not much hair, a friendly chuckle, and a lopsided grin; he has to be pushing eighty. He calls himself an "armchair aviator."

"Yes," he muses, "there were airports all up the valley. Open fields then. . . ." He ticks them off: "L.A. Airways, the National Guard Field, Grand Central, Lockheed, United Airport, North Hollywood; and a couple more over to Alhambra. Seemed like everybody and his brother was out building and flying airplanes. Every time you'd hear an engine, you'd run outside, squint your eyes, and try to figure out: 'What ship is that?'

"The airline planes, the big Fords and Fokkers with their three engines, were easy. What a roar! And besides the Lockheeds—cigar-shaped—there were lots of little biplanes: Wacos, Travel Airs, American Eagles, and Alexander Eaglerocks. Good times, lots of money, men and women all of 'em learning to fly, just for the fun of it.

"We kids used to go down to Grand Central and spend the day—just to watch airplanes. We'd keep little scribbled notebooks—I've still got one—with things like 'August 16, 1929: Saw an Emsco midwing, Al Wilson's Curtiss JN-4. Bobbi Trout with her Golden Eagle Chief!' My dad took me down to Clover Field to see the start of the first Women's Air Race, to Cleveland. Somebody—maybe it was Will Rogers—called it the Powder Puff Derby, and the name stuck. Oh, those were great days. When I wasn't in school, it seems like I spent most of my time at one airport or another, just watching airplanes.

"My favorites? You don't have to ask. The Northrops, of course. They were building them down at United Airport, and I was there, hanging on the fence, when they put the 'flying wing' and that first Alpha on show. They were all streamlined and shiny, polished up so's you could hardly look at 'em without smoked glasses. The 'wing' was an odd one. Never saw anyone ride in the second cockpit. We called it 'the bat.'

"And that Alpha! An all-metal airplane! Lots different from the old wind-in-the-wires, splinters-and-rags trainers we saw flying around every day.

"Here, I'll show you!" Animated now, he rummages in the trailer and emerges with a battered scrapbook, held together with a knotted rubber band. On the cover is a stained decal, a stylized red gull in a circle: Northrop's first logo.

Inside, on loose brown pages, his forefinger stabs the pasted clippings, the faded old black-cornered photographs, the mouse-nibbled cards and programs of long-ago aviation events.

He points out an Alpha mail plane. "TWA flew 'em," he says. "That used to mean Transcontinental & Western Air."

Another page. "There's Frank Hawks and his *Texaco Sky Chief* Northrop Gamma. You had to stopper your ears when he revved up that big Cyclone engine! Seven hundred horses! And there's Russ Thaw and Jackie Cochran and Roscoe Turner and Howard Hughes. Nobody remembers Hughes used to be a crack racing and test pilot. They *all* flew the Northrops!"

Farther on are page after page of low-wing military aircraft with striped tails, all emblazoned with big stars. "Northrop A-17s," he breathes reverently. "Used to see 'em out at March Field. Best attack plane we had before the war—World War Two, that is. . . .

"Me? No, I never flew." He gestures ruefully at his myopic eyes. "I was in insurance up north for years. Came back here in '75. Northrop went on to big things while I was gone—Army and Navy contracts, Black Widows, Flying Wings, Scorpion and Tiger fighters, missiles . . . way more'n I can keep track of. But I remember the Northrop airplanes of the '30s. That was the beginning, and they were great!"

Those early Northrop aircraft were indeed prime examples of the growth years of aviation—successively stronger, bigger, and more powerful. Though comparatively small in number, they pioneered all-metal aircraft construction techniques in the United States. The Northrops were mail carriers and record breakers and flew in regions where no aircraft had ever ventured. Among them were test ships, training planes, and light bombers. Some were failures, but others achieved huge successes. These famous aircraft, developed under John K. Northrop, led to our present age of aeronautical jet power and atomic energy.

This is their story.

THE
NORTHROP
STORY

BEGINNINGS

There was a lot of activity in the back of Rusk's Garage on State Street. It was only three blocks from the Santa Barbara waterfront, and the thin young man often directed his steps in that direction. With the cap that covered his shock of sandy hair pulled low to deflect the California summer sunshine, the stroller would time his visits carefully. Slowly pacing by, he'd peer into the dim recesses of the building. No doubt about it, they were building an airplane in there.

The year was 1916 and the young man was John Knudsen Northrop, who'd had his twentieth birthday the previous November. He'd been born in Newark, New Jersey, but had no ties with the East. His father, a carpenter and building contractor, had tried Nebraska and then set up shop in Santa Barbara in 1904.

Young Jack Northrop was fortunate in the choice of location. The Santa Barbara school system was modern and progressive, and Jack put his full energies into study. He took naturally to math, physics, and chemistry. A loner, Northrop was particularly curious about how things worked, and he excelled in courses in mechanical drawing.

Jack's earliest contact with aviation came as a teenager. He went down to Los Angeles and watched a man fly. It was Didier Masson, a Frenchman and early exhibition pilot, who coaxed his primitive pusher, a wood-and-fabric contraption, up and around a field. Masson flew low and slow, propelled by a diminutive engine that belched fumes of castor oil. The boy from Santa Barbara was enthralled.

Young Northrop became an excellent draftsman. His career at Santa Barbara High School was to be the sole extent of his formal education. On graduation he began to do some home building with his father and worked on automobiles part-time at Rusk's, the garage in which the airplane was being built. Since he needed a job, Northrop eventually

A Loughead-built HS2L flying boat of World War I. Northrop at right next to Allan Loughead. Malcolm Loughead in gun port and Anthony Stadlman second from left.

Using stress analysis learned in high school, Jack Northrop designed the 71-foot wings of the Loughead brothers' F-1 seaplane.

mustered enough determination to go back into the shop and ask for one.

The fledgling airplane builders were the Loughead brothers, Allan and Malcolm, and they proposed to construct a ten-passenger flying boat. With financial backing from Bernard R. Rodman, a Santa Barbara machine-shop owner, the Lougheads began production in the old garage. In addition to Northrop, their handful of employees included a Czech-born ex-barnstormer from Chicago, Anthony Stadlman, who was made shop superintendent.

Cockpit of F-1, in 1916 the world's largest flying boat.

Shy young Northrop was put to work on the flying boat, first on the design of the hull and then on the wings. In high school, by intense study, the towheaded new employee had managed to learn stress analysis. With no training other than theory and common sense, Northrop proceeded to design and stress the huge (71-foot) wings of the Lougheads' F-1 flying boat, at the time the world's largest seaplane.

Drafted in World War I, Jack Northrop spent nine months in the Signal Corps, but was released to return to Santa Barbara when the Loughead brothers built two Curtiss HS2L flying boats under a Navy contract. The brothers spent $5,000 in an effort to better the design, and Northrop, now a "project engineer," spent long hours of study and self-training with it.

Fascinated with streamlined, drag-eliminating forms and lifting bodies, Northrop devised a primitive wind tunnel. Shapes to be tested were hung in a wide glass tube. A worker was presented with a good Havana cigar and told to puff away to his heart's content, blowing smoke into the glass receptacle. Alert Jack Northrop would sit and watch the cigar smoke flow around the various suspended shapes of his own design, quickly sketching and making notes.

With the end of the war, the Loughead brothers hoped to continue in the airplane business. Northrop's work served to convert the old F-1 seaplane into a landplane, which was used for passenger-hopping, motion-picture work, and a long-distance flight attempt.

In July 1919, Northrop joined Allan and Malcolm

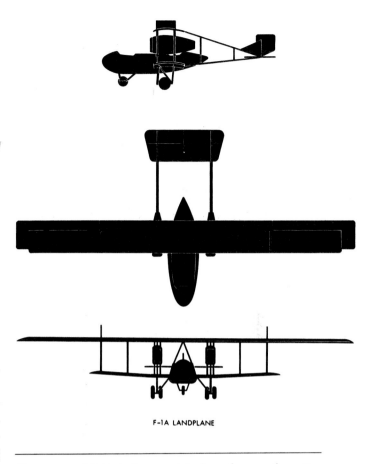

F-1A LANDPLANE

Three-view of F-1A indicates original seaplane configuration before conversion to landplane.

In a brave attempt at long-distance flying, the F-1A of 1918 takes off from a rough field at Goleta, California.

Innovative little S-1 had folding wings and an air-brake arrangement.

Loughead and Tony Stadlman in a four-way agreement for "the development, construction and use of aircraft and aeronautical appliances of all kinds," in which ideas were to be pooled and acted upon by joint effort.

There was much talk of postwar expansion in aeronautics, and the Loughead Aircraft Manufacturing Company's bid for "a poor man's airplane" was the Loughead S-1, designed by Jack Northrop.

The S-1 was a distinct departure from pioneer and wartime aircraft. Northrop's experiments resulted in a unique cigar-shaped, streamlined fuselage that was of monocoque (French for "single shell") construction, in which strength comes from the outside skin rather than internal bracing. Northrop, Stadlman, and the Lougheads devised and patented a process to make monocoque fuselage shells (U.S. Patent #1,425,113, August 8, 1922). For the S-1, they used a 21-foot-long concrete mold. In this were placed three thicknesses of spruce plywood strips, alternately laid, and well saturated with casein glue. Once the strips were in position, the mold was covered and a rubber bag

Concrete mold in which monocoque wooden shell of the S-1 Loughead sport biplane of 1919 was formed.

was inflated inside. Pressure was maintained for twenty-four hours. The half shells produced could be joined, making clean, smooth, bulletlike fuselages.

Although their friendship had cooled, years later Tony Stadlman compared Jack Northrop to the chief bonding ingredient: "He was the glue that held that first company together . . . a remarkable young man."

When it came to wings for the little S-1 sport plane, Northrop decided to study bird flight. He and the workmen dumped barrels of dead fish in a vacant lot near the Santa Barbara waterfront. Unperturbed by the odor and glad of the privacy, the designer-engineer spent hours watching the flight of squalling gulls as they swooped down to feed.

Why not, he mused, have an airplane that would be simply a "flying wing"—a lifting body, internally controlled, with all the qualities of flight? If a powerful motor was used, it would not be necessary for the wings to push, flutter, and flap. It was something to think about—for the future.

From the observations on the fish dump also came Northrop's sketches for the lower wing of the S-1. It could be turned from horizontal toward vertical to act as an air brake—a forerunner of the flaps on modern aircraft. Since the airplane was intended for "every man's garage," the single-place biplane's wings could be folded for easy storage. The whole plane weighed less than 800 pounds and could be landed at such low speed that the airbrake wing position was seldom used.

Unfortunately, there were hundreds of surplus wartime two-place training planes, Curtiss Jennies and Canucks, on the market for as little as $350, brand-new and still in their crates. Despite its advanced design and novel features, nobody wanted the Loughead S-1 single-place sport plane. Not even the prototype was sold.

Poor timing spelled the end of the innovative S-1, the Loughead company operations at Santa Barbara, and Jack Northrop's job. The principals went their separate ways. Allan Loughead sold real estate. His brother Malcolm went to Detroit, where he successfully marketed his patented hydraulic automobile brake. The family name was changed to Lockheed, making the pronunciation more obvious. Tony Stadlman and Jack Northrop, after jobless periods, were hired by Donald Douglas.

Jack was broke and hungry. His first work at the Douglas Company's plant in Santa Monica was a week in the carpentry shop. He built truss-type wooden ribs for the U.S. Army's World Cruisers, which were to circumnavigate the globe in 1924. Given a chance in the engineering department, he was appalled to find that his first assignment was to design a fuselage fairing to be attached by clips to metal tubing. In all his work with the Lougheads, Northrop had never done anything of this sort. After fiddling around all morning, he got sick and went home. When he returned the next day, expecting to be fired, the new "engineer" happily found that somebody else had taken over the fairing design and he was reassigned to designing aluminum gas tanks, a job with which he was familiar.

Northrop put in three years with Douglas, "under happy circumstances," and was never again caught with a design problem which his brain refused to address. He studied and mastered everything that came across the drawing boards at Douglas and much that didn't. He worked on conventional two-seater biplanes, both commercial and military, including the Navy's Douglas T2D, and could not fail to see the tremendous possibilities for cleaning up the designs. The elimination of parasite drag, unnecessary struts, and bulky flying wires—anything that did not contribute to lift— seemed imperative to Northrop.

Donald Wills Douglas was primarily the promoter-salesman for his company and its airplanes. Design was left largely to individuals and, later, to teams. Northrop knew he had Douglas's approval, but still felt the lack of a formal engineering background. During a lean period, Douglas missed out on a military contract and felt he had to cut back on costs. He wired Santa Monica: "Let all engineers go except Art Mankey and Northrop." Such oblique praise went a long way toward cementing lifelong associations.

While working for Douglas and even later, Jack Northrop could not resist taking on a few moonlighting jobs for his friends in the airplane business. Al Menasco, who built engines, needed and appreciated Northrop's advice on how best to wed a powerplant to an airframe. In 1925, the wing of Claude Ryan's little M-1 monoplane was redesigned with significant weight reduction by Northrop and Douglas engineer Art Mankey. The Ryan, built in San Diego for Pacific Air Transport's mail routes, was a forerunner of the small firm's most famous airplane—Lindbergh's *Spirit of St.*

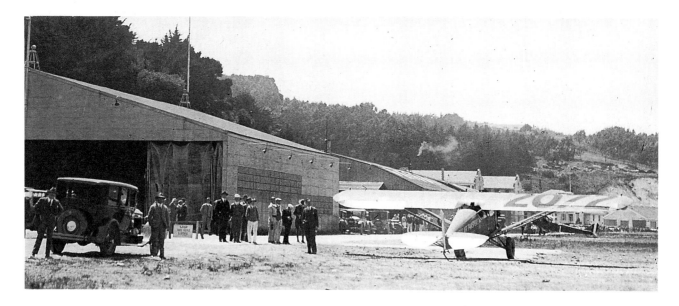

On the side, Northrop redesigned the wing of T. Claude Ryan's M-1 monoplane, shown here flying for Pacific Air Transport out of San Francisco's Crissy Field.

Louis. Then too, up in San Francisco there was Vance Breese, who was trying to get into aircraft manufacture. Northrop made no small contribution to the design of the Breese-Wild passenger mono-plane, built for another mail contractor, Varney Air Transport. (Later, in a new career, Vance Breese would become a much-sought-after test pilot; he made the first flights in a number of Northrop-designed aircraft.)

The Breese-Wild cabin monoplane of 1926–27, to which Jack Northrop contributed design work.

In the fall of 1926, working nights and weekends at home, Jack Northrop began planning his own airplane, roughing out the details on paper. He sketched a large wooden monocoque fuselage with a single cantilevered wing, capable of carrying a pilot and four passengers. One of the new radial Wright Whirlwind engines should be able to pull something like this along at a pretty good clip, he figured.

It was a radical design, and Northrop felt that Douglas wouldn't be interested. Instead he went back to Allan Loughead and they started up a new Lockheed Aircraft Company. Loughead and a friend, William Kenneth Jay, got financial support and Tony Stadlman came back to superintend con-struction. John K. Northrop was a cofounder of the company as well as its chief (and only) engineer. It was almost like the old days in Santa Barbara,

but the new "factory" was a small warehouse in Hollywood.

It was there that Jack Northrop's "dream ship" took shape. They called it the Lockheed Vega after one of the brightest stars in the firmament, and it was an airplane far in advance of its time. There was some argument about the cantilever wing. Allan Loughead contended that no one would buy an airplane with a wing that had no visible means of support. Northrop knew that Anthony H. G. Fokker, the Dutch designer, had had success with just such a wing on airplanes built in both Holland and the United States. He persevered, and the Vega, first of a famous line, made its initial flight on the Fourth of July in 1927.

Northrop had a private pilot's license and did a certain amount of solo flying for his own edification. Unlike many of his contemporaries, he never had an overpowering desire to be a "daring aviator."

Ready to fly the Northrop-designed second Lockheed Vega to New York. Ken Jay (left) and Jack Northrop (right) with ferry pilot Reuben C. Moffat and party.

For the most part, he "went along for the ride" and to learn what he could do to improve the airplane.

Test flights with the Lockheed Vega brought Northrop into contact with Edward Antoine Bellande. Stocky, Mississippi-born Eddie Bellande was an ex-barnstormer, skywriter, and crop duster who had come to roost in southern California. On the second proving flight of the Vega, in which Northrop rode, Bellande told the designer-engineer that the new ship had "a bit of a wobble." It needed a bigger tail fin and less rudder. With trust in Eddie's judgment, Jack made the correction on subsequent models. The Vega became one of the

Wooden monocoque fuselage shells and diaphragm ribs for Lockheed Vegas at the factory in Burbank, California.

classic aircraft of aviation history, admired, wanted, and flown by nearly every famous aviator of its day.

Success for the Vega took a little time. There was internal dissension in getting the Lockheed company off and running. The cofounders were often in disagreement. Jack Northrop was, as usual, thinking far ahead, this time considering construction material. Yes, the Vega was a big step forward for

The wing-rib shop at Lockheed's factory. Jack Northrop's father, a former carpenter-builder, toils at right.

aviation. No more of the box-kite, wind-in-the-wires business. With the aviation boom induced by Charles A. Lindbergh's solo flight to Paris in May 1927, whole new industries were starting. The introduction of the clean, fast Vega was just as right in timing in 1927 as that of the little S-1 had been wrong in 1919. But just suppose, thought Northrop, just suppose that a *metal* airplane on the lines of the Lockheed Vega could be developed and flown? Something, say, made of light aluminum alloy, internally braced?

Despite his part in the development of the wooden monocoque fuselage and the clean cantilever wing, Jack Northrop was now thinking of metal shapes for aircraft. And there was always in the back of his mind the scientific possibility of a true flying wing.

2
THE FLYING WING
(1929)

oved to Burbank, in California's San Fernando Valley, the infant Lockheed Aircraft Corporation had built only six airplanes by mid-1928, all under the direction of chief engineer John K. Northrop. Though the output was small, the buyers included newspaper publishers George Hearst and Bernarr Macfadden, Western Air Express, Captain George H. Wilkins, and well-to-do Santa Monica sportsman Harry J. Tucker, whose *Yankee Doodle* set transcontinental speed records. In his year and a half as designer of the first Lockheed Vegas and the parasol-wing Air Express model, Northrop also laid out a low-wing version of the monocoque-fuselaged craft, a single-float outrigger-pontoon seaplane for the possible use of explorer Wilkins.

Jack Northrop had hired an assistant, a young California Institute of Technology graduate named Gerard F. Vultee, whose first job at Lockheed had been to double-check the chief engineer's stress analysis. Jerry Vultee was to take the unfinished seaplane and fashion it into the first of a series of Lockheed low-wing airplanes, the Explorer, Sirius, Orion, and Altair, which would compete with Northrop's later designs.

With Vultee established and the Lockheed company settling down to mass production, Northrop felt it time to make his departure. June 1928 saw his last appearance at the drafting tables of Lockheed's little brick office and factory in Burbank. Together with the company's treasurer, Ken Jay, Northrop entered on a new venture that promised freedom to develop some radically new concepts in

---

Ken Jay and Jack Northrop discuss the tractor-engined version of Experimental No. 1. *with Eddie Bellande.*

---

aircraft design. Jay would promote the financial backing.

The money came from George Hearst, eldest son of the well-known publisher William Randolph Hearst. Their *San Francisco Examiner* had entered the original Northrop-designed Lockheed Vega in the Dole Race to Hawaii in 1927.

Despite his father's ambitions, George Hearst felt more at home in airplanes than in newspaper city rooms. He learned to fly in the mid-1920s and expressed a desire "to fly everything that was built." The first Vega for the Dole Race was purchased in George's name, but was flown by Jack Frost and Gordon Scott, with the name *Golden Eagle*.

That first Lockheed Vega disappeared in the Pacific during the ill-starred race to Hawaii. But when Jack Northrop and Ken Jay approached George Hearst the following year asking for backing to build a still more radical prototype airplane, they found a willing investor.

George Randolph Hearst and his mother-in-law, Ada Wilbur, along with Northrop and Jay, formed The Avion Corporation. This company, with only a handful of employees, started operations in a rented shop at 4515 Alger Street, off San Fernando Road on the edge of Los Angeles.

What they built in 1929 was the *Avion Experimental No. 1*, a small all-metal flying laboratory to test the novel structure and unconventional arrangements that came from Jack Northrop's thought and planning.

Though called by the press a "flying wing," the unique airplane was actually a monoplane with a broad cantilevered wing. The two open side-by-side cockpits were placed in the thick, multicellular wing itself, as was the four-cylinder inverted engine that Northrop's friend Al Menasco had been experimenting with. This was referred to as a "British" Cirrus Mark III power plant, adapted for use in an inverted position. An air tunnel from the front cowl to the trailing edge of the wing cooled the 90-hp engine. The newly developed Alclad reinforced duralumin skin not only provided covering for the plane but added structural strength as well. For aerial stability, *Experimental No. 1* had twin booms extending to the rear, with twin fins and rudders and a horizontal stabilizer-elevator between.

After nearly a year's work the Avion prototype was completed and an experimental license applied

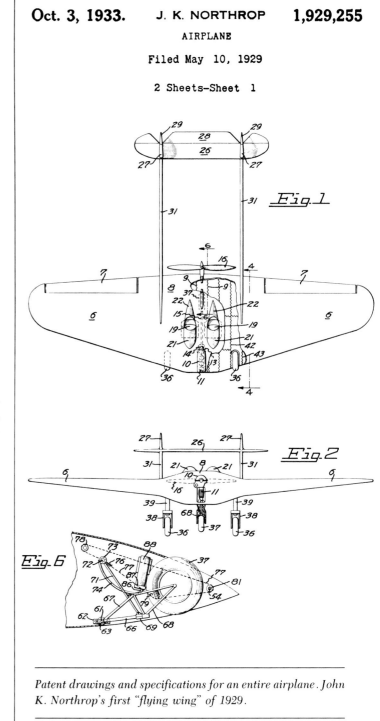

Patent drawings and specifications for an entire airplane. John K. Northrop's first "flying wing" of 1929.

for. The entire design of the airplane received a United States Patent (#1,929,255), filed May 10, 1929.

While The Avion Corporation's experimental ship was taking shape in the rented shop on the Los Angeles River bottoms, Al Menasco came by occasionally to confer on the installation of his engine.

with engine maker Pratt & Whitney and propeller manufacturer Hamilton (also a builder of airplanes, its plane being of corrugated metal).

Bill Boeing liked what he saw at the Avion shop. Though originally a lumberman, he could see that the future of aircraft lay in all-metal design. What Northrop had here not only was fabricated of the new aluminum alloy, but was a giant step forward in interior cellular construction; it was a highly streamlined airplane of great strength, lift, and efficiency.

By the autumn of 1929, United Aircraft, at Boeing's urging, bought out The Avion Corporation from George Hearst and Mrs. Wilbur. With fresh financing, a new company, Northrop Aircraft Corporation, was established, and the "factory" was transferred to a hangar at United Airport in Burbank. As of January 1, 1930, Northrop Aircraft became a division of the United Aircraft & Transport Corporation. With the Northrop "flying wing" under the giant wing of United, the new company's future and expansion seemed assured.

Quietly trucked out to Muroc Dry Lake in the Mojave Desert, the *No. 1* was test-flown for months by Eddie Bellande, the same pilot who two years earlier had made the initial flights with Northrop's Lockheed Vega. Eddie, flying from the left cockpit, cautiously eased the ship up off the lake bed and flew patterns over the barren test area. The airplane appeared to have normal flight characteristics, and her maximum speed was 25 percent better than that of any known plane of similar capacity and power. Not a tail-dragger, the Avion was flown for the most part with a reverse tricycle landing gear—two sizable wheels forward and a steerable tail wheel aft, all under the thick lifting wing. "A three-point landing is no trouble at all," boasted Eddie Bellande.

Jack Northrop himself described his new brainchild:

"The design, when completed, turned out to be about as queer a looking machine as we could wish to see. Those who have been associated with it for a year and a half have begun to get used to the appearance, but a newcomer is generally at a loss for words of comparison, and it is suspected that we very rarely hear the true opinion of those who see the machine, as it generally is muttered under one's breath." This was certainly a modest appraisal.

The experimental ship was flown from both

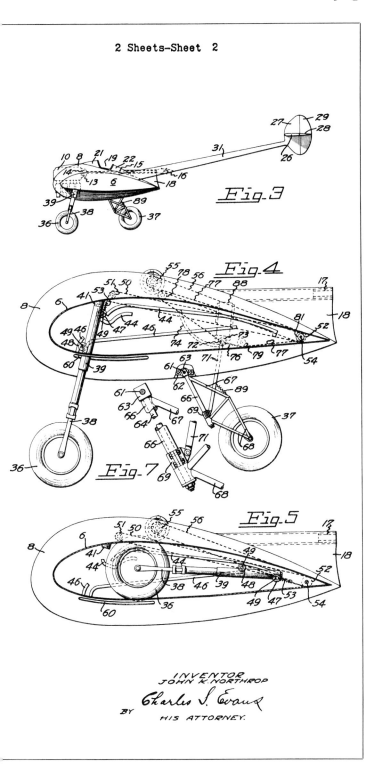

2 Sheets—Sheet 2

Fig. 3

Fig. 4

Fig. 7

Fig. 5

INVENTOR
JOHN K. NORTHROP

Charles J. Evans

BY   HIS ATTORNEY.

One day he brought along William E. Boeing of Seattle's Boeing Airplane Company, just to take a look at the little "flying wing." Boeing was by that time the chairman of the board of United Aircraft & Transport, one of the nation's major aviation holding companies. Its manufacturing units included Boeing, Sikorsky, Stearman, and Vought, together

The Avion Corporation's unique "flying wing" drones over the second Northrop "factory" and Al Menasco's engine shop at Burbank's United Airport.

Muroc Dry Lake and United Airport in Burbank, at first with a pusher propeller between the twin booms at the end of a shaft behind the engine. Later, a tractor propeller was installed ahead of the wing, and equally good performance was attained. Both the fixed and a retractable tricycle landing gear were tested.

The "flying wing," as the aviation press insisted on calling it, was finished and flown before most of the aviation world knew of its existence. Colonel Charles A. Lindbergh, Major C. C. Moseley of Transcontinental Air Transport, and Clark Millikan of California Institute of Technology were said to have been allowed sneak previews. A public showing was not made until February 10, 1930.

As might be expected, all the Hearst newspapers featured a lengthy write-up on the new airplane and published the first photographs of the ship. Their writer, aviation publicist A. M. "Rocky" Rochlen, called this first real Northrop airplane "a strange-looking thing of shiny metal," with its "rows of rivets like the sinews of a greyhound."

It might be noted that during the 1920s Jack Northrop's association with the Loughead brothers and Anthony Stadlman had continued. As business and engineering partners, they talked, lived, and breathed airplanes. Pure flying wings were often discussed. Together, Northrop and Stadlman began building a set of wings for a tailless airplane, but they never completed the project.

Jack Northrop had actually built his Avion "flying wing" as of May 1929. Concurrently, Tony Stadlman, who had left his position as shop superintendent at Lockheed, was showing, in model form, his concept of the cargo and passenger airplane of the not-too-distant future. Except for a single empennage at the rear of the twin booms, the model was remarkably similar to Jack Northrop's actual *Experimental No. 1*. It is likely that both airplanes grew out of the lunchtime and off-hours discussions between the two self-taught engineers. Stadlman stayed with wooden construction, while Northrop fabricated his "flying wing" in metal. Unfortunately, the question of the design's origination apparently led to the end of the two men's friendship.

Despite its odd appearance, the Avion/Northrop Aircraft Corporation's little "flying wing" was considered a successful and promising aircraft. United, now the parent company, had plans for a larger version, using the metal skin and multicellular construction now deemed proven. A 200-mph twelve-passenger ship was envisioned, with three rows of four seats in the wing. The passengers would get vision ahead and to the side while "the pilot and assistant would sit in a streamlined cupola in the leading edge of the wing, with vision in all directions." A plane of this type in the future might even have more than one engine, with sleeping accommodations and "fire-proof, noise-proof engine rooms where mechanics might work while the plane is in flight." Publicity releases warned, however, that "the Flying Wing type of plane has not yet been perfected by the Northrop Company."

On September 20, 1930, Northrop informed the Department of Commerce that flights with the experimental "flying wing" would be discontinued, "pending numerous wind tunnel and laboratory tests." Since there is no further record, it is presumed that *No. 1*, a true pioneer airplane in both design and construction, was ignominiously scrapped. Jack Northrop was already producing another innovative but more conventional airplane.

3

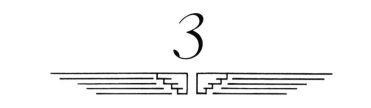

CRASHES AND CATERPILLARS

Jack Northrop's latest vision was a commercial transport airplane. It would follow in the wake of the successful and much-desired Lockheed Vega and would be about the same size, but would have a low wing and be all-metal. Over at Lockheed, Northrop's old protégé Jerry Vultee was developing the Sirius model, built to general specifications outlined in discussions with Charles Lindbergh. Jerry had the fast low-wing wooden two-seater ready for Colonel Lindbergh in December 1929, and its testing continued through the winter. Potential buyer interest ran so high that Lockheed started building eleven Sirius sister ships. Well-heeled buyers put in their orders.

Simultaneously, but quietly, the workers in the little hangar at United Airport put together Jack Northrop's low-wing transport, which he called the Alpha. At first glance it looked like a copy of Lindbergh's much-publicized Sirius. In reality, both air-

planes had their origins in the Lockheed Explorer, the single-float seaplane that Northrop had first designed and started to build in 1927. Vultee carried on using layers of plywood, while Northrop applied multicellular construction and the Alclad skin that had been utilized in his Avion. Static testing of the Alpha was carried out by piling bricks on the thick cantilever wing.

Of all the airplanes that he had a hand in designing, Jack Northrop considered the Alpha his most important contribution to aeronautics:

"I had previously experimented with a wooden monocoque, but now I developed a smooth-skinned metal monocoque. . . . It was the first of its type with the thin skin of the airplane carrying the

---

First Northrop Alpha flies in March 1930.

Short-lived six-passenger Alpha shows speedy lines.

external struts or wires, the Alpha appeared to be good competition for Vultee's Lockheeds.

United Aircraft & Transport Corporation saw to it that the new Northrop airplane received ample publicity, most of which appeared after the prototype was no longer in existence. Licensed experimentally, the first Alpha was test-flown by a number of pilots during March 1930. These included Eddie Bellande, Moye Stephens, and Stephen R. Shore, all on temporary leave from jobs with Transcontinental & Western Air.

With the new ship not a month old, Steve Shore took it up for a test hop on March 27. He was told to make it a short one, as Colonel Lindbergh was waiting to make a flight in the plane. Airborne over Glendale, Shore felt a tremor that became a violent shaking. A pulley bracket had broken, and an aileron tore loose and hit the tail. The Alpha pitched downward in the start of an outside loop, pinning the pilot half out of the cockpit. His goggles flew off. Gasoline streaming from the inverted breather pipe burned and blinded him as he struggled and then dropped free. Unable to distinguish earth from sky, Shore dangled beneath his parachute, which swept him into a patch of cactus. The Alpha came to earth on its back in the brush, caught fire, and burned. The fortunate pilot recovered his sight, but the medics plucked cactus spines out of him for days.

structural load. . . . As far as the structure is concerned, that which was developed on the Alpha was really the pioneer for every airplane in the sky today."

The Alpha had a single cockpit a little back from the trailing edge of the wing. Between pilot and engine was a passenger cabin that would hold six. They sat on bench seats, three to a side, facing each other like subway riders. Provision was made for quick conversion of the seating to cargo bins for mail, express, or freight. With good lines and no

Back at United Airport, Lindbergh waited, got the news, and then shrugged off his chute pack. He was already a four-time member of the Caterpillar Club and was just as glad not to have made it five.

Jack Northrop put the smoldering ruins of the

Aileron trouble with prototype Alpha caused pilot to hit the silk, and plane crashed on its back.

Posing with a Northrop company demonstrator was a Sunday pastime. This plane was briefly fitted with streamlined wheel pants.

airplane out of his mind. A second Alpha was already nearing completion, and this one became the company's principal demonstrator. For nearly two years the plane was wrung out by Northrop and Boeing pilots and others who descended on Burbank in hope of a flight. The Alpha was flown with streamlined teardrop pants and on Edo "K" floats. There was interest from the Army, and the ship was sent to Wright Field in Ohio for testing by the USAAC. Then it went back to Burbank for the installation of extra stiffeners for the wings and hydrostatic fuel gauges. Still later, the number-two Alpha was the guinea pig in the development of a new type of landing gear and in the trials of a 10:1 engine blower for high-altitude performance.

A third Northrop Alpha produced in 1930 went to the top man of government regulation, Assistant Secretary of Commerce for Aeronautics Clarence M. Young. Painted black and orange, the ship was given the lowest of Department of Commerce registration numbers: NS-1. Major Young personally flew the airplane through the winter of 1930–31 and gave it excellent exposure to press and

Number-two Alpha was wrung out by E. T. "Eddie" Allen, the Northrop/United test pilot.

Sold to the U.S. Department of Commerce for the use of Assistant Secretary Clarence M. Young, this orange and black Alpha bore the lowest of American registration numbers.

Publicity for the new Alpha: California's Governor James Rolph and party are flanked by Ken Jay and Jack Northrop.

public. When Young decided that a larger airplane was more in keeping with the needs of the department, the Alpha was traded in on a Ford Trimotor.

With United Aircraft & Transport being the Northrop holding company, it might be supposed that Northrop airplanes would be purchased to fly the transcontinental routes of United's airline divisions: Boeing, Pacific, Varney, and National Air Transport. The four carriers were flying Boeing, Curtiss, Stearman, Douglas, and Ford planes of various types and vintages.

Instead, virtually the entire production of Northrop Alphas went to a United competitor, Transcontinental & Western Air, Inc. This company, predecessor of today's TWA, flew the "central" air route across the country, New York to Los Angeles. It had good mail subsidies as well as the potential of heavy passenger and freight traffic. Young Jack Frye, TWA's vice-president in charge of operations, wanted a new, fast mail plane to shoulder the line's increasing mail loads. Airmail pilots, almost a breed apart, still favored an airplane with an open cockpit, be it biplane or monoplane. Surveying the field, Frye chose Northrop's entry in the scramble for faster intercity transportation.

Transcontinental & Western Air ordered five Alphas, which were built and in the hands of the

First Northrop Alpha on a scheduled airline went to Transcontinental and Western Air, Inc., flying the "Central Route" across the United States.

airline by April 1931, or possibly earlier. Test-flying the Alpha over the routes himself, Jack Frye formulated plans for their effective use. One flight he made with a brand-new Alpha was unexpected.

Flying Kansas City–Los Angeles, a mail-toting Alpha is met by a Richfield oil truck in front of Wichita's Hangar No. 1.

1931 Northrop Alpha. The mail pilot's instruments.

On the morning of March 31, 1931, a Transcontinental & Western Fokker trimotor airliner fell out of the sky south of Bazaar, Kansas. All on board were killed, including the famous Notre Dame University football coach Knute Rockne. Frye, accompanied by Anthony H. G. Fokker, designer-builder of the crashed airplane, immediately flew to the site, a high pasture in the rugged Flint Hills. Those who had rushed to the scene of the accident on foot or in mud-spattered touring cars gaped as Frye and Fokker landed with the Northrop Alpha on dead turf among loose shale. Uncertain of the cause of the accident, the pair remained only a short time. Their subsequent safe takeoff was just as surprising as their arrival—a tribute to Frye's piloting and the rugged Alpha.

TWA put their Alphas into service on April 20, 1931. On that day the carrier inaugurated America's first twenty-four-hour coast-to-coast mail and express service. Westbound passengers on a TWA Ford stayed overnight in Kansas City, but the mail cargo was whisked on to California in an Alpha. Eastbound, a Northrop mail plane left Glendale eight hours *after* the passengers left in a Ford, and another Ford then took over the load for the trip on to Newark.

Another six Alphas were soon purchased by TWA and put on the eastern half of the transcontinental route. They flew the night mail run each way between Newark and Kansas City, where connections were made with the passenger Fords.

As with any new service, there were teething problems. The daily schedules were continuous and exacting and took their toll on the equipment. During the first six months on the cross-country runs, the eleven TWA Alphas suffered no less than eleven accidents. They were ground-looped, they landed short, and they hit other airplanes. The mishaps ranged from "taxiing into an obstruction" (repair: $22.68) to a forced landing at Antrim, Ohio (repair: $4,829.53). Jack Frye's management was strict. Pilots were chastised, suspended without pay, reduced to copilot, and requested to resign. In every case of damage the Alphas were transported to Kansas City, to be repaired at TWA's top-rated shops.

After their run of eleven repairable "mishaps," the airline added two more Northrop Alphas to its fleet, the total at greatest strength being twelve. From National Air Transport, which had flown it briefly, they obtained the former Department of Commerce ship once piloted by Major Clarence Young. The other was the number-two Alpha, which the Northrop company had retained as a demonstrator.

Above left and right: Padding surrounds spartan cockpit of Northrop mail plane flying for TWA.

Transcontinental & Western Air flew its Alphas for ten months without actually losing one. Then, in January 1932, the combination of radio failure, bad weather, and a diminishing fuel supply put Ted Hereford down in a forced night landing near Mobeetie, Texas. In the glare of a dropped flare the pilot picked out a likely spot and circled to take advantage of it. In landing he hit an unseen railroad embankment, sailed on over it, and crashed in the field beyond. Knocked cold, Hereford revived in time to save sixteen pouches of mail from the burning airplane.

Two months later, TWA suffered the loss of another Alpha. Dr. Carol Skinner Cole of St. Louis got word that her daughter was ill in Newark, New Jersey. The doctor inveigled the airline into letting her fly east on the night mail plane, the first TWA passenger to be allowed to do so. At Columbus, donning a parachute, Dr. Cole stowed herself among the mail bags, with Hal George at the controls in the Alpha's cockpit. About 2:00 A.M. and

Converted to single-place ships, TWA's Alphas had trousered landing gear, radios, and Goodrich De-Icers on wing and fin. This one ended up in China.

Only fatal accident involving a TWA Northrop Alpha occurred in March 1932, when pilot Hal George and a passenger plunged into the storm-swept Ohio River.

100 miles out, George ran into fog and a sleet storm. Groping for an emergency landing, the pilot narrowly missed the stacks of West Virginia's Weirton Steel Company and plunged into the swollen Ohio River. George and Dr. Cole were drowned in the freezing water. During nearly four years with Alphas constantly in the air, it was to be TWA's only loss of an Alpha that involved fatalities.

Not that there weren't some hairy escapes, near misses, and painful crack-ups. The pilots, perched on their seat packs and flying the night mail, were all under orders to jump "if conditions warrant." Four of them did find jumps warranted.

Coming into St. Louis in July 1932, the propeller blade of an Alpha mail plane sheared off and the engine tore itself from its mounting. Lacking glider training, pilot Harry Campbell elected to leave via parachute and became member 485 of the Caterpillar Club.

Six months later, Walter Seyerle was high over the Alleghenies en route to Columbus, icing up in gale-force headwinds, radio out, and visibility nil. Seyerle bailed out, to land safely in the crotch of a tree. His Caterpillar Club Certificate 538 dates from February 26, 1933, at Cross Forks, Pennsylvania.

Later the same year, two of TWA's Northrop Alphas were abandoned in the air on the same night in December. A fierce snowstorm was raging as two mail planes approached each other over central Pennsylvania. *Time* laconically reported what Transcontinental & Western Air's Newark radio operator heard in his earphones at 2:26 A.M.:

"Burford calling Newark. Weather is getting bad. Heavy snowstorm at three thousand feet. Will try to climb above it." That was pilot Dean Burford, eastbound. A minute later:

"Andrews calling Newark. Weather thick but I'm going upstairs." That was pilot Harold G. Andrews. In the next fifteen minutes each spoke in turn:

Burford: "Don't look so good. Ice on wings. Maybe I can get above it."

Andrews: "I've got ice, too."

Burford: "Losing altitude. She won't stay with me anymore. I'm going over the side now. So long."

Andrews: "The ice is kind of tough on the old plane. I'm falling five hundred feet a minute. Guess I'll go over the side. So long."

Early next morning both pilots phoned in, safe, and only 15 miles from each other. Burford's smashed Alpha contained a consignment of $73,000 worth of diamonds, recovered intact along with the mail. Andrews and Burford became Caterpillar Club members 605 and 606. Oddly, the destroyed airplanes were the first and last Alphas acquired by Transcontinental & Western Air.

Among those who heard the exchange between Burford and Andrews before they joined the snowbirds was H. J. "Jack" Zimmerman, who happened to be on approach to Newark, flying in fine weather.

As an Alpha pilot, Zimmerman recalled his nights on the mail run to Columbus as "fun, real fun, the best time in my whole career." He was strictly on his own; no passengers to be responsible for, only a few instruments, just his own skill and judgment to rely on. The mail pilot was expected to get through despite bad weather, and usually did.

One of the tricks in flying the Alphas across the "Hell Stretch" of the Alleghenies was to know the terrain below like a book. The pilot learned to identify his position by the cluster and position of lights ahead and below. He tried to stay below the clouds and to follow the pattern of auto lights on the roads and locomotive headlamps on the rails that wound between the mountains, often only a few hundred feet below the wheels of his plane. In

Transcontinental & Western's fifth Alpha awaits a mail load at Grand Central Air Terminal in Glendale, California.

Last of seventeen Northrop Alphas built, TWA No. 11 was flown on TWA's transcontinental routes for much of five years.

doing this, it was also a good idea to be certain of the location of tunnels.

Some nights Zimmerman would practice an early version of blind flying. After taking off from Newark, he would get plenty of altitude and set a course for Harrisburg. Then he'd settle down to read a magazine. A casual glance at the instruments told him if he was on or off his intended flight path. Then back to his story. At Columbus the magazine would be handed to another pilot, who repeated the procedure on to Kansas City.

One black night, unknowingly blown off course, Jack looked down to find the lights of a strange town below his wings. Puzzled, he circled, unable to identify the layout. After several circuits, the Alpha's radio suddenly came to life with a report just in: an unidentified airplane was circling Lewistown, far up the Juniata Valley. Lewistown! With that bit of information, the pilot was able to follow the river down to Harrisburg and get back on course.

TWA's Kansas City shops converted, repaired, and rebuilt the
line's Northrop Alphas.

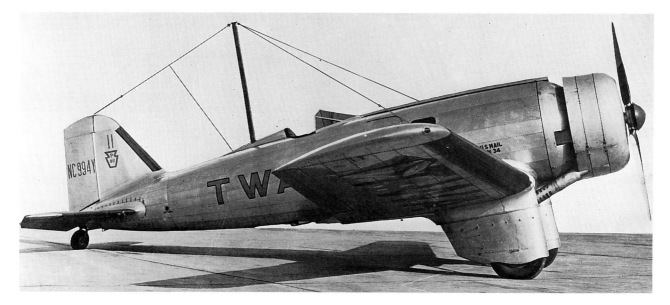

Guyed radio mast and antenna cluttered the late-model Alphas, but were a boon to pilots. Keystone on fin encloses special Pennsylvania State airplane license.

Zimmerman too had a brush with death while piloting the mail for TWA. On the night of January 10, 1933, he was flying a routine run west with 736 pounds of mail in his Alpha. It was a clear night, ceiling unlimited, and the temperature hovering around freezing. At the new $5 million Allegheny County Airport south of Pittsburgh, Jack stopped to refuel. Then, on takeoff, for no accountable reason the engine stopped. Normally the procedure would be to keep on in a glide and come down straight ahead. But on this hilltop airport, Zimmerman elected to bank in a suicidal "dead man's turn." The Alpha stalled and crashed on the end of the runway.

H. A. Duggan, TWA night operations manager, saw the plane hit and dashed for his parked car. Airport weatherman Bob Totten leaped on the running board as Duggan tore down the field. Half-way there, they saw tongues of flame and then an explosion of light as the parachute flares let go. Arrived at the crash, the men ran to the cockpit to find an unconscious Zimmerman, with his head smashed against the instrument panel. In the intense heat of the burning plane they struggled to get the pilot, swaddled in heavy flying clothes, up and out. They groped for the buckle of the safety belt. Pulling, scraping, and yanking, they hauled him to safety just as the Alpha's main fuel tank went up with a whoosh.

Duggan and Totten got a bravery award and a testimonial dinner from the Aero Club of Pittsburgh. Jack Zimmerman survived and went on to become chief pilot of Transcontinental & Western Air.

Jack Northrop himself recalled an incident which confirmed the ruggedness of the Alpha: "One of the early air mail pilots was forced into a restricted field and had to ground loop the airplane very violently in order to keep from going into a hill. . . . He bent the wing up at about 45 degrees. . . . They sent a crew out from Kansas City, bent the wing down with some block and tackle and flew it back for more permanent repairs. . . ."

Though TWA's five original Alpha 2s, plus one additional, were six-passenger jobs, the second batch were Alpha 3s. In this model only one or two passengers were accommodated. A radio altimeter was installed as well as landing lights and a bigger battery. A large red hazard light was attached to the leading edge of the left wingtip. TWA supplied its own Pratt & Whitney Wasp engines and paid $14,200 for each airplane. As they flew into California, the other six Alphas were converted in turn at the Northrop factory into two-place Model 3s, under Approved Type Certificate Group 2-335.

The changeover to two-passenger configuration was scarcely complete before the plant was busy with another conversion, this time to Alpha 4s, a pilot-only model. The Alpha 4 entailed factory installation of big trousered wheel coverings, NACA cowl, battery, electric starter, low-pressure tires and wheels, flares, and new baggage compartments

GOODRICH DE-ICERS PERFECTED
on TWA planes....!

Wayne Williams, TWA mail pilot, with Goodrich De-Icer equipped Northrop No. 1. Note specially treated rubber spinner cap and covering that keeps propeller units in balance under icy conditions.

"We are happy to have worked with Goodrich," says Jack Frye, Vice-President in charge of operations, Transcontinental & Western Air, Inc., general offices, Kansas City, Mo.

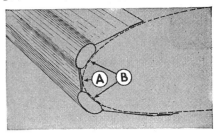

ACTION OF THE DE-ICER: Tubes marked "B" inflate, then deflate. Tube "A" inflates while "B" is deflating, then deflates. Pulsation rate is about 1 per minute.

Outside tubes inflated (*cross section shown*)

De-Icers on tail surfaces

Combined experience of "The Lindbergh Line" and Goodrich Laboratories solves ice problem

WORKING together in the interests of aviation, Transcontinental & Western Air, Inc., Eclipse Aviation Corp., and Goodrich have solved the problem of ice formation. Through the Goodrich DE-ICERS, mail planes can now maintain uninterrupted schedules . . . transport planes can carry their passengers with every assurance of safety . . . in the worst kind of icy weather.

Mr. Jack Frye, Vice-President in charge of operations, Transcontinental & Western Air, Inc., says: "The Goodrich De-Icers installed on all Transcontinental & Western Air, Inc., Northrop mail planes have enabled completion of mail schedules under icing conditions which would have prevented operation of planes not so equipped.

"We are convinced that De-Icers are a practical means of eliminating ice from transports," Mr. Frye continues.

What are De-Icers? . . . Thin sheets of rubber containing long inner tubes cemented to the leading edges of wings and tail surfaces. A valve, operated by the pilot, releases compressed air into these tubes and causes them to expand and contract automatically. The ice, which is cracked loose by this "breathing" action, is ripped off by the air stream as fast as it is formed.

For further information on Goodrich De-Icers or Airplane Tires, write the Aeronautical Sales Department, The B. F. Goodrich Rubber Company, Akron, Ohio.

Goodrich DE-ICERS

Made by the Makers of Goodrich Airplane Silvertowns

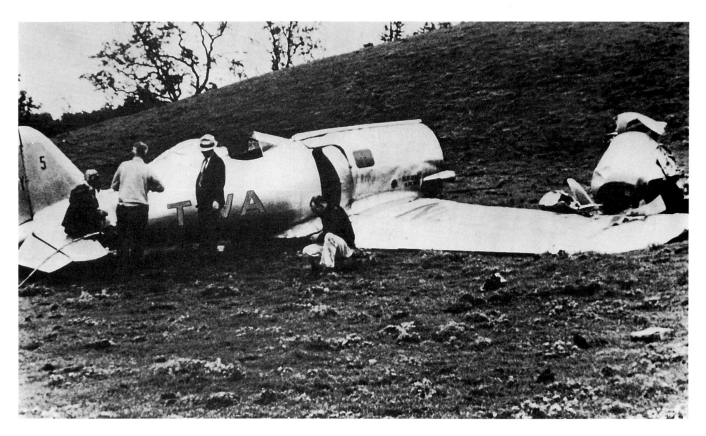

for mail and express. All eleven airplanes, plus two acquired later, were made into this model under ATC 451 of September 10, 1931. Except in the case of the unfortunate Dr. Cole, passenger-carrying was not done.

Still another important improvement was the addition of Goodrich De-Icers, installed on the leading edges of the wings, radio mast, stabilizer, and vertical fin. These were inflatable rubber air bags attached to the vulnerable spots where ice was apt to form. Compressed air set the de-icers to pulsating regularly, and any accumulated ice broke off to disappear in the slipstream.

Ten Alphas got the Goodrich De-Icers under ATC 461 (February 25, 1932). For installation the planes did not go back to Burbank this time, as the conversion was completed right in TWA's own Kansas City service shops. They continued to fly as pilot-only all-weather day-and-night mail planes.

Three more accidents reduced the airline's Alpha fleet to three by 1935. R. S. Le Roy washed one out

Opposite: Goodrich advertises de-icer action, together with an endorsement from Jack Frye, TWA's pilot and vice-president.

After forced landing number five on a hillside near Newhall, California, in 1934, pilot George Rice walked away.

in a forced landing near St. Clairsville, Ohio. George Rice, coming into Glendale, cracked up on a remote mountain ranch near Newhall, California, losing the landing gear and a wing. He was not found until the next morning when Jack Frye, by then president of TWA and always solicitous of his pilots, flew out to look for the overdue ship. It took most of a day to get Rice and the mail down off Oak Mountain with a horse-drawn wagon.

The last crash involved Ernest L. Smith, best known for his pioneer ocean flight to Hawaii in 1927. Ernie, at the controls of the last Alpha built, suffered partial engine failure on approach to Grand Central Air Terminal. He tried to glide to the nearby National Guard field but was too low. The plane struck high-tension wires in a blinding flash, spun around, and pancaked in the muddy Los Angeles River. Shaken, dazed, but only slightly injured, Smith was found guarding the wreck with a drawn revolver in true mail-pilot tradition.

The Northrop Alpha was the first TWA airplane used exclusively for mail, but it was flown in conjunction with other single-engined airplanes that

The Alpha was flown concurrently with the wooden Lockheed Orion, which was roughly the same size and had retractable landing gear.

also carried mail, express, and freight cargos. At major TWA terminals, Alphas would be found parked next to others of the airline's mixed fleet: four Lockheed Vegas, three Orions, and an Altair. As the Alpha mail carriers, one by one, were lost, they were replaced by seven Consolidated Fleet-

Only existing Northrop Alpha began as government's NS 1, with the Department of Commerce.

ster 20As, all built expressly to the order of Transcontinental & Western Air.

TWA's Jack Frye realized that standardization of equipment was the future course that a practical, economical airline should take. In 1932 he laid down requirements for a transport aircraft that could speedily carry both passengers and mail. Distributed to manufacturers, the prospective specifications got an affirmative response from Donald Douglas. Anxious to reenter the commercial aircraft market, Douglas engineers devised the one and only DC-1.

TWA's search for the "standard" airliner lasted many months. Colonel Charles A. Lindbergh, the airline's technical adviser, was not sure that the twin-engined ship Douglas had under construction

was the right plane for the job. He wanted to explore all the options.

In the aftermath of his son's kidnapping, Lindbergh had not flown in several months when on February 21, 1933, he decided to make a quick round trip to Baltimore. He wanted a look-see at the metal transports that General Aviation Manufacturing Corporation was building. For the trip, the colonel borrowed one of TWA's Northrop Alphas. After taking off from Newark, Lindbergh flew across Manhattan to North Beach Airport.

Added to the TWA mail-plane fleet in 1931, NS 1 became TWA No. 12.

Climbing aboard at Newark on February 21, 1933, Colonel Charles A. Lindbergh flies No. 12.

There he picked up Ernest R. Breech, an executive of General Motors and a director of both TWA and General Aviation. Ernie Breech made the journey in the rear mail compartment, sitting on the floor ahead of Lindbergh's feet. There was no heat, no seat belt, and, in fact, no seat. Pilot and passenger were unable to talk above the heavy drone of the Wasp engine up ahead, but did exchange a few written notes over New Jersey.

At the Dundalk factory outside Baltimore, the visitors looked over General Aviation's contenders for the airline jackpot, a single-engined all-metal transport (the General or Clark GA-43) that could carry ten passengers, and a trimotor (GA-38), a low-wing job that had sixteen seats.

This chilly winter inspection trip in the borrowed Alpha mail plane convinced Ernie Breech that General Motors' airplanes would be unable to compete with Douglas's DC-1. Later, when he became head of North American Aviation, Inc., General Aviation's successor, Breech scrapped the GA-38 project. The Douglas plane proved itself, even to Lindbergh. It and its later models, the DC-2 and DC-3, were all built with the multicellular construction and stressed metal skin first used by Jack Northrop. They became TWA's chosen airplanes and went on to be acknowledged as the world's most successful transport aircraft. Donald Douglas went even further. Speaking in the 1940s, he said: "Every major airplane in the skies today has some Jack Northrop in it."

TWA No. 12, the Alpha flown on the Lindbergh-Breech junket, continued to carry the transcontinental mails for another two years. The airline's two other Alphas were sold overseas and found oblivion in China. Altogether, Northrop Alphas were flown 5,413,736 miles in the service of Transcontinental & Western Air.

No. 12 was sold to Frederick B. Lee. A New Yorker, Lee had the ship mounted on Edo floats and planned a special long-distance world flight that never came off. Subsequent owners included Murray B. Dilley of Kansas City, who also thought to make a special record flight. By 1940, however, both interest in and backing for any individual ocean-flying had diminished to next to nothing.

Foster Hannaford, Jr., of Minneapolis acquired No. 12 in 1945. He already had the remains of an Alpha, salvaged from TWA pilot Le Roy's Ohio accident ten years before. Up until his death in 1971, Hannaford had plans to make a flyable antique Northrop mail plane from the two Alphas.

TWA No. 12—in reality the third of its type to be built—was donated by the Hannaford family to Wisconsin's Experimental Aircraft Association and stored with the extra parts in anticipation of eventual restoration. Then it was passed on to the Smithsonian Institution in Washington, D.C., as a key airplane for the new National Air and Space Museum then being built on the Mall of the nation's capital. It was to be placed with other early airplanes used by the airlines: a Pitcairn Mailwing, a Ford Trimotor, a Boeing 247D, and a Douglas DC-3.

TWA's Technical Services Center in Kansas City learned of the plans and undertook to restore the airplane. The components were trucked from a barn in Burlington, Wisconsin, to the Trans-World Kansas City facility in March 1975. The project was coordinated by Daniel W. McGrogan, a TWA flight operations instructor. Fifty-seven volunteers, some of them retired employees who had converted and repaired the originals in the 1930s, restored the Alpha to pristine newness in eight months. Described as "a near miracle in terms of quality and attention to historical detail," the burnished natural-finish Alpha was delivered to the Smithsonian in time for the 1976 opening of the National Air and Space Museum.

Suspended in flight position from the lofty ceiling, the gleaming mail plane, the last and only existing Northrop Alpha, is there for future air-minded generations to admire.

Above: *TWA No. 12 next appeared in 1935, on floats for an aborted world flight.*

Below: *After long storage, the last existing Alpha emerges from a Wisconsin barn, en route to restoration by TWA and honored display in the National Air and Space Museum in Washington, D.C.*

4

CLOUD LANDINGS

The next design of the Northrop Aircraft Corporation was a trim low-wing all-metal two-seater. With private and personal aviation slowed by the onset of economic depression, it appears to have been a poor time to introduce a new plane "for the sportsman pilot." Still, there were some who had survived the stock-market crash and were willing and financially able to obtain the latest in airplanes just to fly for fun.

The new small tandem-seat Northrop plane continued the Greek-letter sequence and was called the Beta. In another collaboration with Northrop, Al Menasco supplied one of his C-6 Buccaneer engines to power "the sportsman's version of the Northrop Alpha." The plane's monocoque fuselage faired neatly with the six-cylinder in-line engine. A special cowl, incorporating an air scoop, completely enclosed the 160-hp Menasco. The Beta's clean lines and Alclad natural-metal skin, left unpainted, was enough to attract potential buyers at any airport. The shiny ship resembled a racer.

Quiet, prudent Edmund T. Allen, long associated with Boeing airplanes and the United Aircraft holding company, took the Beta up on her tests and evaluation trials. Eddie made a fast run from Los Angeles to Salt Lake City and then on to Detroit in only fifteen hours and forty-three minutes flying time. Bundled in the open-cockpit ship, he cruised "the high altitude route" over the Rockies at 145 mph, and "with no effort." This performance and the subsequent exhibit of the plane at the Detroit Air Show caused a minor sensation.

Back in California, Allen ran some final testing that would lead to Department of Commerce certification. Over the Verdugo Hills, he inadvertently pushed the controls too hard, and the Beta's ailerons went beyond their stops and locked. The result was to put the ship into a series of continuous barrel rolls. Eddie seriously considered bailing out, but the Beta was "such a nice little ship" that he hated to lose it. With some ex-

---

The Beta two-place sport plane was abandoned in midair by a Department of Commerce inspector.

Trim, first-built Northrop Beta had in-line Menasco engine.

perimentation, the test pilot found that for short periods he could maintain normal flight with full opposite rudder. The problem was how to land with a plane doing a continuous horizontal spiral at 100 mph.

Allen, one of the best at his profession, set his keen analytical mind to work. Gaining altitude, he spotted some fluffy white cumulus clouds. Barrel-rolling above them, he selected a big flat cloud on which to practice landing. Straining on stick and rudder, he tussled the gyrating airplane and came out level for a "landing" on the cloud.

After eight or ten simulated approaches of this sort, Eddie felt enough confidence to try for the ground. Then he realized he had too much gasoline aboard to risk it, and spent another hour barrel-rolling across the southern California landscape. Had he thought to count them, the Beta might well have set a record for continuous rolls. With fuel near exhaustion, Allen came literally barreling into United Airport. As he told it:

"I maneuvered just as I had done so many times for the cloud, and came rolling in. At a hundred feet, the big test had to come and I straightened her out, holding that stick over to the left with both my hands and my knees to keep level until the Beta set down.

"It seemed I would never get near enough to that ground and my strength was about all gone. I would have to let loose in a minute. Then I cut the motor and gave one final tug to hold her a wee bit longer. . . . I was exhausted. As I was beginning to

let go and as she began to roll, she set down. Naturally the ship hit fast on one wheel and then the other, oscillating back and forth and in addition bouncing up and down. For a minute I thought I

Eddie Allen, who landed on clouds.

would go over on my back. I cut the switch and braced myself. But . . . she didn't."

The fast and bouncy landing took up all the field and threatened to go right on into Burbank, but everything turned out all right.

Northrop and Menasco advertised the Beta extensively. It was flown to air shows and demonstrated before the eyes of the public for four months. The price for a Menasco-engined job, just like the prototype, was quoted as $8,500, flyaway Burbank: "a high speed utility plane and advanced trainer." Had it not been for the worsening hard times, the Northrop Beta, on the basis of appearance alone, should have sold by the dozens.

Though plans for production were proceeding, the Beta had still not received its Department of Commerce certification. Lester J. Holoubek, the department's resident inspector, took the shiny little Northrop through a new series of tests. Like Eddie Allen, the inspector had trouble with the ailerons and found the ship unmanageable. Unlike Eddie, he had no great affection for the airplane. Already a member of the Caterpillar Club because of a forced jump at Dallas two years before, Holoubek elected to leave by parachute. The Beta augered itself into a Glendale hillside.

Second Beta had a single cockpit, all-metal construction, and typical Northrop streamlining.

The first Northrop Alpha had been destroyed in initial testing, and now the Beta had met a similar end. For many Depression-hit airplane manufacturers, the loss of the precious prototype meant failure and bankruptcy. But at Northrop, the setback had been overcome and seventeen Alphas had been built. It was the intention to go ahead with the promising Beta.

An Army fighter? Northrop's little "sport" Beta of 1931 was the shape of things to come.

Test pilot Allen brings the Beta in to a neat landing at United Airport.

Jack Northrop's chief engineer, Donovan R. "Don" Berlin, already had a new version ready, with an engine of about twice the horsepower, a big Pratt & Whitney Wasp, Jr. This plane had only a single cockpit.

Shortly after the second Beta was completed at Burbank, the Northrop facility was consolidated with another United Aircraft division, the Stearman Aircraft Corporation of Wichita, Kansas. At this juncture, preferring to stay in California, Jack Northrop resigned. He commented: ". . . it was a perfectly logical move, but . . . my family came from Nebraska to California, and I wasn't about to move to Kansas."

Plans to continue Alpha and Beta aircraft manufacture were begun by the transfer to Wichita of Northrop assets, machinery, and materials. The second Beta went along with the move.

The Stearman Corporation ran further tests of the Beta, now called a Model 3D. The evaluation proceeded, again with Eddie Allen, but with no desperate cloud landings this time. Eddie had the satisfaction of seeing the Beta given a Group 2 Approved Type Certificate on February 2, 1932.

The little single-place job was sold to Kenyon Boocock, a New York City sportsman pilot. Undertaking the delivery flight from Wichita, Eddie Allen got a stiff tail wind and said he averaged better than 200 mph on cross-country. At a stop at Wright Field in Ohio, Army Air Corps engineers spent a cold February day going over the Beta, "with a view to its possible usefulness for military work." Their cameras, slide rules, and calipers recorded the shape of things to come. Here were all the makings of the all-metal fighter monoplane of the next decade. But in 1932, the Army was still oriented toward frame-and-fabric biplanes.

By the time Mr. Boocock bought the airplane, it had a new raised fairing from cockpit to tail fin and was called a Stearman Beta. The New Yorker enclosed the cockpit and coaxed the top speed up to 212 mph, but he didn't fly the ship very often. The Beta was up for sale in December 1932 with a total time of only 129 hours. At a price of $5,000, Boocock found a buyer in George W. Hard, the twenty-year-old son of a Manhattan broker.

Hard took delivery of the Beta at Roosevelt Field and the same day hopped it over to the Long Island Aviation Country Club field at Hicksville. In landing, plane and pilot went through a fence and ended up in an inverted position on the Long Island Parkway. Young Hard crawled out unhurt.

With wing and other damage, the "Northrop-Stearman" was stored and then sold back to United Aircraft. The Stearman shop rebuilt it in Wichita, intending to experiment with Zap, Fowler and Wright flaps. An accident the day after relicensing, however, completely destroyed the airplane.

Today, of the Northrop Greek-letter series one Alpha, one Gamma, and one Delta exist. But there are no Betas, unless some ambitious home builder decides to construct a replica.

Further production of Northrop Alphas and Betas was never undertaken by United Aircraft & Transport's Stearman Division in Wichita. Jack Northrop, Don Berlin, and many of the old employees of the United subsidiary at Burbank never left California.

Northrop's former benefactor, Donald W. Douglas, had "more than he could handle" in military orders at the Douglas plant in Santa Monica. The two friends arranged the organization of yet another firm, The Northrop Corporation, founded January 1, 1932, as a subsidiary of Douglas Aircraft Company, Inc. John K. Northrop was named president and Ken Jay vice-president, and Don R. Berlin continued as chief engineer. Berlin had able assistance from John Clifford Garrett as purchasing agent, Arthur Mankey as chief draftsman, and Gage H. Irving as pilot-salesman. A new manufacturing site was found, a small factory formerly occupied by the White Truck and the Moreland Aircraft companies, situated on Mines Field in Inglewood, California. Plans for the Northrop subsidiary of Douglas called for the building of "innovative, experimental aircraft."

5

RECORDS AND RACING

P erhaps the personification of "speed" in aviation circles during the early 1930s was Frank
Monroe Hawks. A sometime swimmer, Hollywood bit player, and bank clerk, Frank was a
friendly fellow who enjoyed life but didn't
hesitate to attempt something new and untried
when it came to flying. After leaving the Army Air
Corps in 1919 he flew fish and mining company
payrolls in Mexico and barnstormed the South and
West in decrepit crates that lumbered from town to
town, coaxed along only by curses and prayers.

When aviation went respectable, so did Hawks.
Eager and enthusiastic to share his love of flying,
he sweet-talked the Maxwell House people into

*Frank Hawks and Jack Northrop confer on Gamma nearing
completion. Big twin-row Wright Whirlwind engine was first
to be installed on a commercial airplane.*

*Frank Monroe Hawks (1897–1938). The "Meteor Man"
brought the Northrop Gamma fame, and new orders.*

buying an airplane "just like Lindbergh's" (it was Hawks's own Ryan B-1) and sending him on a tour of the country to advertise coffee. Then he hit the big time, persuading the officials of an oil company to buy an airplane.

The firm was the giant Texas Company, which formed an Aviation Department in December 1927. The company's products were sold in every state of the union. Frank flew its *Texaco 1*, a big Ford Trimotor, some 56,000 miles, advertising, giving joy rides to some 7,000 passengers in 175 cities, and in the long run selling both aviation and Texaco gas and oil to a public rapidly growing "air-minded."

In his travels, the genial flyer soon formed a general opinion. What the airplane offered, he reasoned, was an opportunity to get people safely from one place to another far faster than had ever been possible, and then improve on the elapsed time required. With a Lockheed Air Express, a design originally roughed out by Jack Northrop, Hawks set a new nonstop record for Los Angeles–New York travel. After inducing The Texas Company to buy the airplane, he established himself as the first man to fly coast to coast nonstop in both directions. He did it alone, and in two days.

A captain in the Army Reserve, Hawks next acquired a wire-braced Travel Air R, a racer dubbed the "mystery ship" by reporters. With this plane he plugged Texaco products to new lengths, and heights. The speedy little racer set new transcontinental and intercity records. On a whirlwind European tour the captain covered 20,000 miles and racked up fifty more speed marks. With seeming ease, he'd have his breakfast in London, lunch in Berlin, and dinner in Paris. The press, not without good reason, called Frank Hawks "the Meteor Man," and his friends often quoted a tongue-in-cheek admonition: "Don't telegraph—send it by Hawks!"

During a hectic two-year period, 1930–32, the red-and-white Travel Air and Frank's infectious grin might turn up at any major American airport, usually establishing a new speed mark. At one time Hawks held some 214 of them. This spate of record-setting only came to an end in April 1932 when the captain wrecked the "mystery ship" in taking off at North Grafton, Massachusetts. Hawks's face was badly smashed and required plastic surgery.

During weeks of recuperation, the speed pilot switched services and became a Navy lieutenant commander. By midsummer he was ready to fly again. Back in February his company had ordered a new mount for the head of its Aviation Department, the first of the Northrop Gammas.

This had come about when Hawks scribbled his specifications on the back of an envelope: "Super mail express . . . radial or in line [engine] . . . fuel for 2,000 miles, cruising speed at 85% of power, 220 mph minimum. Landing speed with one hour fuel, using dump valves, 70 mph or less, maximum. Designer's choice on engine. Single-seater. Ceiling 15,000 to 20,000 feet. . . ."

With these criteria, Jack Northrop, now in the factory on Mines Field, went to work. Actual design work was begun in May, and a semiconvalescent Hawks watched the new ship take shape during the summer. Designer-builder Northrop and practical flyer Hawks conferred on such things as the supercharged fourteen-cylinder double-row Wright Cyclone engine to which the fuselage was tailor-matched, the experimental "park-bench" ailerons, and the new robot pilot.

After reorganization under the wing of Douglas, Northrop had begun building two special orders, the single-place Gamma for Texaco and Hawks and one with two cockpits for explorer Lincoln Ellsworth. Essentially an enlarged Alpha, with 363 square feet of wing and a souped-up 700-hp engine, the first Gamma was equipped with two-way voice radio and special instruments by Pioneer for both day and night navigation. The detached ailerons, mounted on pylons at the outer ends of the wings, allowed the entire trailing edge to be fitted with new split-type flaps. It was claimed that the ship could be landed at 40 mph and that the use of flaps decreased the takeoff run by almost a third.

With gleaming natural aluminum alloy finish and fully streamlined right down to a teardrop tail wheel, the new Gamma was a beauty, a plane to capture the imagination. First flown on December 3, 1932, the big Northrop was prosaically named *Texaco 11*. Under Commander Hawks, she became known as the *Texaco Sky Chief*, named for a brand of premium gasoline that the oil company was introducing. Hawks carefully tested the capabilities of the glistening Gamma through the winter and spring of 1933. Then he was ready to resume record-setting. His first objective was a new nonstop transcontinental speed mark.

Above: *Northrop and Hawks pose with Gamma's instrument panel. Autographed inscription by Hawks calls the plane "our dream ship."*

Below: *Completed Northrop Gamma set coast-to-coast and intercity records, brought attention to Texaco's petroleum products.*

Red fire hat embellished the shiny aluminum finish of the Sky
Chief. "Park-bench" ailerons are a prominent feature.

On June 3, 1933, Frank Hawks left Los Angeles
with the *Texaco Sky Chief*. Fog in Cajon Pass de-
layed him and he jockeyed the ship along until he
approached the Rockies. Then he turned the controls over to "a-little-thing-in-a-box," the DeBeeson
automatic pilot that could guide the plane and keep
it level. Occupying only a cubic foot of space in the
baggage compartment, the robot performed beauti-
fully for its human pilot and allowed him to concentrate on his cross-country navigation. Not until
it began to get dark over the Alleghenies did Frank
again take the stick. Buffeted by headwinds, he
touched down at Floyd Bennett Field a little under
thirteen and a half hours from the West Coast. Well
pleased with a new nonstop record crossing of the
continent, Hawks patted the little 25-pound robot
affectionately and called it "my brainless assistant."

Hawks's title was now aeronautical adviser to
The Texas Company. With the *Sky Chief* he
chalked up half a dozen more speed records. In
July, Frank flew the Gamma 1,620 miles from New
York to open the World's Grain Fair at Regina,
Saskatchewan. After setting a few new Canadian

intercity speed marks, he urged the big shiny plane
back to Bridgeport, Connecticut. This was to pay a
hospital visit to the English flying couple Jim and
Amy Mollison, who had cracked up there after a
transatlantic flight.

In late August, the Meteor Man and his brainless
assistant were back in Canada, plotting a new coast-
to-coast flight. Leaving Vancouver late in the afternoon, the *Sky Chief* flew eastward through the
night, high over Crowsnest Pass in the Canadian
Rockies. Then fog and radio interference, which
Hawks blamed on the northern lights, forced him
to land at Kingston, Ontario. Getting his bearings,
he pushed on to Quebec City and a new one-stop
trans-Canada speed mark.

All the record-setting was excellent publicity for
Texaco, but soon regular commercial airline
planes—Northrops, Vultees, and Douglas DC
transports—were flying between America's major
cities with time schedules that equaled or bettered
the existing speed times set by individuals only a
few short years before.

Having helped sell aviation to the general public,
as well as creating a new market for fuel, oil, and
lubricants, Commander Hawks left The Texas
Company. He took on a variety of demonstration
work, selling airplanes in South America and the
Orient.

Jacqueline Cochran, beautician turned flyer, who was to best her male contemporaries in air racing.

Texaco's Northrop Gamma had served its primary purpose—gaining publicity for Sky Chief gasoline. Along with the red fire hat, the name would be familiar to motorists on gas-pump decals for years to come. The Gamma was sold in 1934 to a man who could afford to have it flown as a showpiece—Gar Wood, the Detroit industrialist who engaged in making and breaking speed records on land, on the water, and in the air.

Among the records set by Commander Hawks and his famous Gamma may be an odd one that still stands. Has anyone since 1933 flown a piston-engined airplane nonstop from Regina, Saskatchewan, to Bridgeport, Connecticut, in less than seven hours and fifty minutes?

While Jack Northrop was beginning to put two Northrop Gammas into production, a twenty-six-year-old beautician was shunting back and forth between work at the Saks Fifth Avenue stores in New York and Miami. Small, blond, and pretty, she was self-educated, self-assured, and self-oriented. Originating in the swamplands of Florida, she had virtually no childhood, but was driven by a determination to *be* somebody. Choosing a name at random from the telephone book, she became Jacqueline Cochran. Things that Jackie Cochran didn't know she set herself to learn. Her drive and willpower gradually brought success in her chosen profession, plus money and influential friends.

Among the friends was Floyd Bostwick Odlum, a lawyer-financier from Colorado and a millionaire, who would later become Jackie's husband. Adept at the business of permanent waves, makeup, and lotions, Miss Cochran was thinking of going on the road for a cosmetics company. It was jokingly suggested that to cover the territory she'd probably need wings. Floyd bet her the $475 tuition that she couldn't learn to fly during an upcoming six-week vacation from Saks. Jackie got her pilot's license in three.

So it was in the summer of 1932 that Jackie Cochran acquired a new passion: to succeed in aviation; to be the best. She proceeded to do just that, but not without failures and disappointments. On transferring her work to the West Coast, Jackie took additional flight instruction. She hobnobbed with naval aviators and airmail pilots to absorb their know-how, and bought a battered old Travel Air to get in air time and experience during any possible spare moment.

One day, taking off from Grand Central Airport in Glendale, the tired Travel Air's engine quit. As she'd been instructed, Jackie kept going—straight through a metal fence to end up against a parked car on an adjacent highway. When the dust settled and the crowd, seeing no blood, began to drift away, two strangers from the airport sauntered over and offered their advice and services in fixing up the airplane. One man was Al Menasco and the other was Jack Northrop. As Jack studied the damage, Jackie gushed confidently: "Someday I'll be flying one of your planes!" Preoccupied, the designer replied with a thoughtful nod: "Of course you will!"

Tactfully, he suggested that perhaps Miss Cochran could profit from a bit more instruction, little thinking that within a year she would indeed be flying one of his airplanes.

Once airborne, Jacqueline Cochran's imagination was fired by a 1933 announcement from Sir MacPherson Robertson, an Australian whose money had been made in the confectionery industry:

"My objects in sponsoring the MacRobertson International Air Race from London to Australia are:

To deliver Australia from its isolation, which can only be effected by airplanes; to prove that fast communication between Australia and England is possible; and to get people to dig up their atlases in order to find out where Melbourne is situated on our planet." Jackie consulted her atlas. She'd always enjoyed travel.

The Great Air Race, as it came to be called, was scheduled for October 1934. It drew the attention of flyers from all over the world. In addition to the $50,000 first-prize money, there was the prestige and glamour of being involved in this once-in-a-lifetime event. Top-rated aviators from four continents prepared to compete.

Jacqueline Cochran, who had only been flying a year, set her sights on winning the MacRobertson Race to Australia. "That beauty operator from New York" set herself a rigorous program of training: celestial navigation, blind flying, mechanics, radio. She learned it all from scratch, hiring the best of instructors. Then it was practice, practice, and more practice.

Money? Jackie put all her own resources into the project and borrowed more, notably from a lawyer and fellow pilot, Mabel Willebrandt. Then there was Floyd Odlum and his Atlas Corporation to help, with infusions of cash, credit, and worldwide connections.

Despite her growing proficiency and knowledge of the flying game, Miss Cochran needed a copilot. With typical thoroughness, she hired two: Wesley

Long and lethal-looking—the Cochran Gamma, 1934 version.

Smith and Royal Leonard. She confidently posted her application to the race authorities in London and received the number 30 in a field of sixty-four entries.

Temporarily on leave from the passenger and mail routes of Transcontinental & Western Air, tough-talking Smith and soft-spoken little Leonard, both with thousands of hours in the air, were an ideal pair to complement the beauty-parlor fugitive who had turned to the skies.

Back and forth across the continent Cochran rode with Smith, who patiently taught her to interpret maps and fly the beam, coaxing, cussing, and cajoling. Leonard got $750 a month and expenses. His first job was a sixty-day world tour to establish service depots, complete with spare parts, fuel, supplies, and manpower, along the 12,000-mile route. He set these up at places where the Mac-Robertson Race participants would touch down: Baghdad, Allahabad, Singapore, and Charleville, in Australia.

Leonard got back to the United States with just five days left to test the airplane that Jacqueline Cochran had agreed to buy. The "someday" to be flying a Northrop plane had arrived, and Jackie had a very special brute of a big racer.

The Cochran ship for the MacRobertson Race was a Gamma, a 2G, the only one of its kind. It was a two-place job, with tandem cockpits covered by a sliding canopy. On the nose was a new Curtiss Conqueror water-cooled twelve-cylinder engine, quite a departure for Northrop, whose planes were for the most part equipped with air-cooled radial engines. With a nose spinner, the plane had a

lethal, sharklike appearance. A new General Electric supercharger had been installed, which was supposed to deliver a 20-mph increase in speed. Crammed with fuel, the Gamma had a range of 3,000 miles.

Around the hangars, the talk was that Jackie Cochran had a sure winner. With that super Gamma, copilots to spell her, and the service depots set up and ready, she ought to beat the pants off both the other American entries and the European competition.

Entrants in the race had now dwindled to twenty, but some were formidable. In England, De Havilland had built three Comet racers especially for the event. KLM, the Dutch airline, had entered an American Douglas DC-2, and there was Roscoe Turner's Boeing 247, plus various Faireys, Airspeeds, and other entries.

In California, Jackie Cochran loaded her Gamma with "all the latest and best" in engine and radio equipment and instrumentation. One piece of machinery proved to be a stumbling block to her race-winning ambitions.

The culprit was the new turbo-supercharger. As a warm-up for the Australian jaunt, Jackie had planned to enter and fly her plane in the Bendix transcontinental race to Cleveland, a major annual event of the National Air Races. Two days before the Bendix was due to start, the GE charger blew up on the test stand at the Northrop factory. Curtiss-Wright hurriedly offered another Conqueror engine, complete with an experimental charger of its own. By the time the new engine got to Northrop for test and installation it was too late for the Bendix. Then the all-Curtiss power plant also proceeded to blow up. It was apparent the engine couldn't take the extreme speed.

Desperate, the Northrop people readied a third engine, minus the supercharger, all in forty-eight hours of agonized labor. The Gamma was approved by a Department of Commerce inspector on September 29, 1934, and Jacqueline Cochran took it over the next day.

With Roy Leonard, she took off for New York at 2:00 A.M. They had a date with a boat for Europe. A couple of hours out, while they were cruising at 15,000 feet, the heater malfunctioned. Then the engine sputtered and slowed. Something let go and oil came splattering back on the greenhouse. Roy was ready to hit the silk, but Jackie was immobilized by leaking carbon monoxide. When he

slid back the canopy the rush of cold air cleared her head, but she could hardly lift a finger. Her major thought was thankfulness that she'd had the plane insured. Leonard somehow got the heavy Gamma safely down on an Arizona emergency field.

With spare parts on their way from Inglewood, Jackie took the next TWA flight east to New York. After repairs, there was one more valiant try to make the boat in time for the race. And once more the "stupid engine" conked out.

Reports are contradictory as to whether Leonard or Wes Smith was at the controls and as to a possible passenger. The airplane was landed "via barbed wire and arroyos" near Tucumcari, New Mexico, with no injuries to the occupants.

The Gamma and its balky power plant were ignominiously trucked back to California, "for repair of wing section and the lower half of the fuselage." Miss Cochran, frustrated but not yet defeated, quickly contracted for another airplane, an untried and insufficiently tested Granville Brothers racer, the *Q.E.D.* (She and Wesley Smith ultimately entered the MacRobertson Race, but were forced to withdraw in Rumania.)

In England, the race committee had two other Northrop airplanes to consider as entries, one stillborn and one real.

An outspoken advocate of American aircraft had been well-to-do Lieutenant Commander Glen Kidston. In 1931, Kidston had set new London-to-Paris and London-to-Capetown speed records, using his imported late-model Lockheed Vega, which had a metal fuselage.

After Kidston's untimely death in South Africa, his pilot, Owen Cathcart-Jones, continued using the Vega on free-lance charter flights. In this he was joined by a talented flyer, Marsinah Neison, who at nineteen had become the youngest woman to receive Britain's coveted commercial pilot's license.

When the MacRobertson Race was announced, Cathcart and Neison determined to enter. The Kidston Lockheed was already spoken for, so the pair proposed to buy a Northrop Delta. To them it appeared to be "the best possible aircraft . . . to meet all the conditions of the race."

Beginning in August 1933, Miss Neison and "Seajay," as she called Cathcart-Jones, spent over a year endeavoring to find backing and raise money to purchase a Northrop. The price tag of $36,000, an import duty of 33⅓ percent, and costs of race

Jackie's big Gamma with radial Wasp, Jr., engine installed for 1935 Bendix race. She used a "running hare" insignia.

preparation, fuel, and other expenses made the task a nearly unsurmountable proposition. In an effort to overcome apathy, the effect of Depression times, and a stout "Buy British" attitude, the two pilots made innumerable phone calls, circulated some 2,000 letters, and traveled 40,000 road miles in search of financial backing. Their dedication and strength of purpose nearly equaled that of Jackie Cochran, but it was not to be. On the eve of the race, in October 1934, Miss Neison sportingly suggested that her partner seek another mount. (Cathcart ultimately placed fourth in the speed division of the Great Race, flying with Ken Waller in a De Havilland Comet.)

Entry 22 was the A. B. Aerotransport (Swedish Air Lines) Northrop Delta, which was to be flown by company pilots Marshall Lindholm and newlywed George Linlow. Despite great expectations, the entry was scratched. No Northrop airplanes participated. British aeronautical prestige was maintained by the triumphant arrival in Melbourne of C. W. A. Scott and Tom Campbell-Black, flying the winning wooden DeHavilland Comet. The second- and third-place American aircraft, KLM's Douglas DC-2 and the Boeing 247 piloted by Roscoe Turner and Clyde Pangborn, quietly projected all-metal transport aircraft as the couriers of the immediate future.

Though thwarted in her attempt to win the Mac-Robertson Race, Jackie Cochran still had her powerful Gamma. There was always next year's

Bendix transcontinental race to think about, and she set her sights on that.

At the Inglewood factory, Northrop workers repaired the damaged Gamma. The questionable Curtiss Conqueror V-12 engine was finally given up as a bad job and a twin-row 700-hp Pratt & Whitney Wasp, Jr., radial was installed. This engine was fitted with a controllable-pitch propeller, a boon in heavily laden takeoffs. Almost a year after the Mac-Robertson fiasco, Miss Cochran got the Gamma approved, with a restricted license, for racing only. One cockpit had been closed off and Jackie now rode alone, far back toward the tail.

Also entered in the 1935 Bendix competition was another Northrop Gamma, four months younger than Jackie's, very similar, and just as powerful, with a 710-hp Wright Cyclone engine up front. This ship had been bought on the order of Mrs. Marron Price Guggenheim of the philanthropic Guggenheims, a family notably active in promoting the many facets of aviation, particularly those that promoted safety in air travel.

Based at Roosevelt Field on Long Island, the Guggenheim Gamma was registered in the name of Russell W. Thaw. A good-looking young man who could have spent an idle life in moneyed social circles, Thaw chose instead to earn his way as a hardworking personal pilot for others. The Guggenheim Northrop he piloted was used for flying Mrs. Guggenheim and testing the new Sperry automatic pilot. Russ Thaw flew it to California to enter the 1935 Bendix Race.

The Bendix was an elapsed-time affair. Flying from Los Angeles to Cleveland within a given period, the contestants could take off when they wished. That September, the weather in California and all across the nation was atrocious. Fog from the Pacific rolled in, so thick that one side of Union Air Terminal was invisible from the other. Jackie Cochran had badgered the race committee to get a slot in the starting lineup; she was the first woman to be allowed to fly solo in the Bendix. The competition was top-drawer: Roscoe Turner with a Wedell-Williams racer; Benny Howard with *Mr. Mulligan*, his self-built cabin monoplane; Roy Hunt and Amelia Earhart with Lockheeds; and even Royal Leonard, flying Jackie's old jinxed Granville *Q.E.D.*, left over from the MacRobertson Race. Russ Thaw, in the Guggenheim Gamma, with Northrop plant engineer E. H. Moore, roared off into the fog at 4:01 A.M.

At intervals, more planes got away into the wet, swirling mists. Jackie Cochran waited her turn, sipping soda pop. She panicked momentarily when she lost the good-luck yellow rosebud that Floyd

Above: *Russ Thaw, Guggenheim family's pilot, was top competition in the Bendix.*

Below: *Hot after the Bendix trophy in 1935 were, front, Roy O. Hunt, Russell W. Thaw, Jacqueline Cochran, and Earl Ortman; rear, Royal Leonard, Roscoe Turner, Benny Howard, and Cecil Allen.*

Odlum, now her fiancé, had given her. Auto headlights and popping flashbulbs revealed the nosegay as a spot of color 100 feet down the runway.

One after another, field reps from Northrop, Pratt & Whitney, and the DOC pleaded with Jackie not to take off. She told them to "go away and hush," or words to that effect. She called Floyd for advice, and he reminded her that only a fine line existed between logic and emotional urge. Jackie made her decision.

Fueled to the tank brims, the Gamma had been rolled out on the wet apron, and the first lone woman to enter the Bendix climbed up and dropped into the cockpit. Headed down the flare-lit runway, followed by a speeding ambulance and a fire truck, Jackie let power build up in the whining Wasp. Only a third of the field remained when her strong hands pulled back on the stick and the Gamma unstuck. The trailing radio antenna caught on the boundary fence and was left behind, and the trousered wheels just cleared the telephone wires beyond. Back at the hangars, the race officials, ground crews, and press could see nothing and could only hear the fog-muffled barking of the exhaust as Jackie and the Gamma clawed for altitude.

Her takeoff had been to the west. Slowly, Jackie made shallow turns, circling to gain the height required to get over the San Gabriels and then go

Thaw took third place in 1935 Bendix, racing with Northrop Gamma.

all-out for Cleveland. At 9,000 feet she broke into starlight, and before long the Grand Canyon appeared in the dawn.

Then came the all-too-familiar engine splutter, followed by a slowing of speed and a jarring vibration. There was nothing for it but to turn back to Kingman and get the plane on the ground. En route, Jackie dumped some 400 gallons of high-octane fuel, some of which was sucked into her cockpit. Saturated and reeking, she landed and taxied up to the hangar. For her another air race had gone by the board.

Russ Thaw flew the Guggenheim family's Gamma over the weather, nonstop to Cleveland, and took third place in that fifth annual Bendix Race. Benny Howard and *Mister Mulligan* beat Roscoe Turner to win the trophy—by just twenty-three seconds!

Back in Los Angeles, Jacqueline Cochran felt discouraged with her Northrop Gamma. She wasn't Mrs. Floyd B. Odlum yet; all the funding he would make available to her was still in the future. Late one night she was sitting dog-tired in her hotel room when the phone rang.

"Jackie?" inquired a male voice. "This is Howard."

The caller was Howard Robard Hughes, and he wanted to buy her airplane. Hughes was already a legendary character in 1935. Heir to a Texas fortune made in oil-drilling tools and producer-director of the aviation film epic *Hell's Angels*, he'd soloed at sixteen and had long been an experimenter with aircraft.

At the time, Hughes was obsessed with speed. With the aid of Dick Palmer, Glen Odekirk, and some engineers from the California Institute of Technology, he had just built a racing monoplane, which he kept in a guarded hangar at Mines Field.

A few days after Jackie Cochran returned from her aborted try for the Bendix Trophy, Hughes summoned the local Fédération Aéronautique Internationale's official timers and observers and climbed into the single-seat racer. Flying this "Model A," over a 3-kilometer course at Eddie Martin's airport near Santa Ana, he tried for the world's speed record. It became too late and too dark for the FAI's sensitive instruments to register, so the next day, which was Friday the 13th, the millionaire pilot flew the course again. This time, at 232.388 mph, Howard Hughes set a world Class C maximum speed record.

Jackie Cochran had seen and admired the powerful, streamlined little ship at Mines, and Hughes had apparently sized up her Northrop. He'd determined to set a new transcontinental speed record, and his Model A racer would not be ready for cross-country work for some time. Meanwhile Howard was itchy. The current mark was ten hours, two minutes, and fifty-seven seconds, set on September 1, 1934, by Roscoe Turner, who'd flown on to New York after winning the Bendix Race in a

Howard Hughes leased Cochran's Gamma, installed an 800-hp Wright Cyclone engine, and went after speed records.

Wedell-Williams racer. Hughes thought the record could readily be beaten, and this led to his nocturnal request for Jackie Cochran's Northrop Gamma.

Even though she'd not done well with it so far, Jackie didn't want to sell the Gamma outright, and she didn't even have a bill of sale that gave her outright possession. Listening to Hughes's financial propositions, she decided that she couldn't afford not to at least lease the airplane to him. She got clear title and did that.

In November 1935, the Gamma was trundled into the closely watched "secret" hangar that housed the Model A, and Hughes, Palmer, and the Cal Tech boys went to work on souping it up for a transcontinental try. The Hughes Development Company, as the group was called, yanked the Wasp engine out of the Gamma and installed a new 800-hp Wright Cyclone with a three-bladed constant-speed propeller. Three new gas tanks went in, and the crew tinkered with the big engine, hoping to get nearly 1,000 hp out of it.

Just after noon on January 13, 1936, Howard Hughes lifted off from Union Air Terminal, the leased Gamma straining to get airborne. Again, the radio antenna was snapped off and left behind. Hughes flew on instruments high above the wintry weather, "smoking" oxygen at 18,000 feet. Emerging in the clear over New Mexico, he sped on until an air pocket jarred his compass off the pin. After that it was getting dark and the pilot checked off cities by the light masses. Indianapolis-Columbus, thirty-five minutes; Columbus-Pittsburgh, thirty-two minutes. A tail wind slewed around to help.

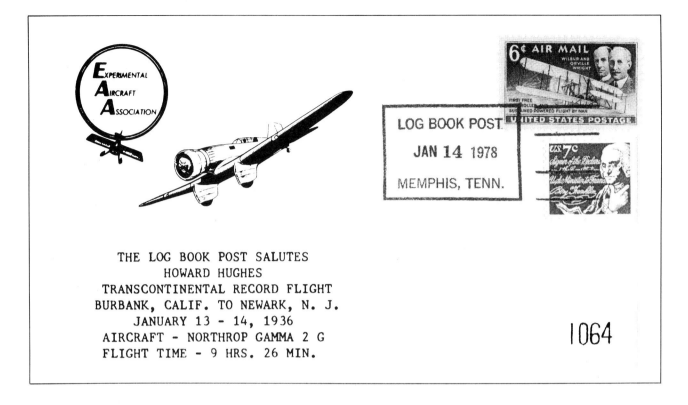

THE LOG BOOK POST SALUTES
HOWARD HUGHES
TRANSCONTINENTAL RECORD FLIGHT
BURBANK, CALIF. TO NEWARK, N. J.
JANUARY 13 - 14, 1936
AIRCRAFT - NORTHROP GAMMA 2 G
FLIGHT TIME - 9 HRS. 26 MIN.

Forty years later, the Hughes transcontinental record flight is still commemorated by philatelists.

Half an hour after midnight the glow of Manhattan lit the horizon, and an elated Hughes let the Gamma down to land at Newark Airport. Chopping thirty-five minutes off the Turner record, he'd been in the air only nine hours, twenty-six minutes, and ten seconds. John P. V. Heinmuller, official timer for the National Aeronautic Association, wearing his six-watch timing vest, confirmed that once again a Northrop airplane held the coast-to-coast speed record.

Hughes made several additional jaunts in the rented airplane. In April 1936 he set a new inter-city record between Miami and New York, and another one in May. Bringing the Gamma back to Glendale from Chicago put Hughes though a series of aerial crises. The wrong maps were given him. The radio soon went dead. He took on ice over the mountains, and his oxygen system failed. Finally, as he approached the Colorado River, the fuel pump quit, leaving Howard to furiously hand-pump gas all the way into Los Angeles. Weary and bleary-eyed, Hughes had himself another record (eight hours, ten minutes, and twenty-five sec-

Howard R. Hughes, dressed for his mid-winter, record-breaking, transcontinental dash of 1936.

Jackie Cochran's Gamma in final guise, with still another Wasp engine, 1936.

onds), but felt he'd hand-carried the Gamma all the way.

Jackie Cochran's fortunes improved when she married Floyd Odlum in May 1936. By this time Hughes was preoccupied with modifications to his own Model A, grooming the racer to beat his own transcontinental record. He apparently had an option to buy the Cochran Gamma. Jackie always claimed that the rental from "poor Howard" was more than she had put into the ship all told, and if she'd accepted his check for the plane she'd have been well ahead financially. But, stubbornly, she wanted the plane back, particularly now that it was a real record-holder. In the end, she made a deal. No bills of sale were ever recorded.

In June, Jackie had a new Pratt & Whitney twin-row Wasp, Jr., engine put in the plane. Though she always suspected that the power plant put the center of gravity too far forward, she got it reapproved for a restricted license. Surprisingly, in two years, the hard-luck Gamma that finally broke a record had a total air time of only ninety-six hours and thirteen minutes.

Mrs. Floyd B. Odlum still had the yen to win a Bendix Race, a goal toward which her husband continued to encourage her. The summer saw her flying her Gamma along the airline route to Cleveland, testing, always building up more experience.

On one of these flights, approaching Indianapolis at 5,000 feet, Jackie was startled to see flames licking back out of the cowl of her new Wasp engine, followed by clouds of black smoke. She'd always thought that in the event of fire in the air she'd take to her chute. Instead, she found herself radioing to clear the airport, sideslipping to avoid smoke, and miraculously guiding the burning airplane for ten miles, down to a no-flaps landing. The Gamma rolled off the end of the short runway, and the dry grass around it began to burn. Jackie had no time to powder her nose and even left her precious cosmetics case behind when she piled out of the cockpit. In the 8-foot jump she broke a toe. Fire trucks sped to the scene to blanket the flames with foam.

A week later, July 10, 1936, the scorched airplane had undergone repairs. On takeoff from Indianapolis for New York, the Gamma once more suffered motor failure. Jackie hit the runway so hard that the offending engine was torn off and cast aside. She ended up in a nose-over, covered with high-octane fuel and motor oil, but unhurt. Twenty minutes after one of her closest brushes with death,

Rebuilt for Cochran, the former Thaw racing Gamma gets a
California tryout in 1937.

Jackie was on a TWA flight to New York and a
promised dinner with Floyd.

Tenacious Cochran, still considering herself a
contender for the Bendix Trophy, insisted on another rebuild. The stricken Gamma was gathered
up and shipped back to the Northrop factory in
California. To aid the work, Jackie bought a dupli-
cate ship, the Thaw/Guggenheim Gamma, which
had been in an accident and stored for a year.

Later owner of Thaw-Cochran racer was publisher Bernarr
Macfadden, who enjoyed seeing his name in large print.

It was expected that parts from the Thaw plane
would be used to fix up the Cochran Gamma, but
it turned out the other way around. The rebuild
was licensed to Jacqueline Cochran in April 1937.
(Jackie chose a staggerwing Beechcraft 17 to race in
the Bendix that year, and finally *did* win the race in
1938, flying an experimental Seversky racing
monoplane.)

The former Guggenheim and Cochran Gamma
was sold to sixty-nine-year-old publisher, physical
culturist, and aviator Bernarr Macfadden. The
flamboyant Macfadden, always mindful of publicity
for himself and his magazines, had his signature
emblazoned in huge letters on each side of the
fuselage. He announced his intention of entering
the ship in the 1938 Bendix, but an accident a few
months before the race put him out of the running.

One more Northrop airplane took part in a Ben-

dix Race. This was the first Gamma built, which had flown to fame with Frank Hawks as *Texaco Sky Chief*. The oil company had sold it in August 1934 to Garfield Arthur "Gar" Wood of Detroit. Inventor of the hydraulic dump-truck lift and builder of truck bodies and speedboats, Wood had owned and used a number of airplanes, both for business and for pleasure. Being a single-place ship, the former *Sky Chief* apparently had little use during the two years of Gar Wood's ownership. Roscoe Turner flew it in one race at Detroit. However, in 1936, Wood made arrangements to enter the Gamma in the transcontinental Bendix Race, being flown that year from New York to Los Angeles.

The industrialist hired a young aspiring race pilot, Joseph P. Jacobson, to fly the big Northrop nonstop to L.A. An aerial billboard now, the Gamma advertised "Gar Wood Industries" on its fuselage, and by a whim of the owner, the name *Kinjockety II*.

Flying in from the West Coast to pick up the plane, Joe Jacobson arrived at Brooklyn's Floyd Bennett Field after midnight, with less than three hours to takeoff time. He found no parachute in the airplane and at first intended to fly without one.

But prudence prevailed and he donned a borrowed Navy chute just before climbing into the gleaming Gamma.

With the sun coming up behind him, Jacobson cruised contentedly over the Alleghenies, but beyond the Mississippi the skies were murky with dust storms. Skirting line squalls, Joe was flying at 5,000 feet some 60 miles west of Wichita when it happened. There was no warning, no explanation, but "like a blow in the face" the airplane suddenly exploded. Jacobson found himself thrown clear in midair and pulled the rip cord of his providentially borrowed parachute. Pieces of *Kinjockety II* rained down on the Kansas plains of Stafford County. Landing unhurt, lucky Joe got a ride to Wichita and continued on to California by commercial airliner.

Flying a standard Beechcraft 17, Louise Thaden and Blanche Noyes carried off the 1936 Bendix Trophy. Though Northrop airplanes were formidable contenders, none was destined to win a major air race.

Day of reckoning. Joe Jacobson leaves New York on the old Texaco Sky Chief's last flight.

6

ASSAULT ON THE ANTARCTIC

incoln Ellsworth was a Chicago-born railroad and mining engineer and a man of many interests. He enjoyed hunting, geography, and delving into history. He liked learning new skills, travel, and, most of all, exploration. Happily, he had the money to indulge his enthusiasms; his father had amassed a fortune in exploiting coal mines. Though he maintained property in the United States, a villa in Italy, and a castle in Switzerland, Ellsworth was more apt to be found navigating a small boat, climbing mountains, collecting fossils, or hunting jaguars. His greatest passion became polar exploration, which he began at the age of forty-four. He made two Arctic flying expeditions with Roald Amundsen, the great Norwegian explorer, and then set a goal of his own, down at the bottom of the world.

In 1932, some 5 million square miles of Antarctica lay unknown, never seen by man. Laying out his sketchy charts, a would-be explorer could contemplate great blank spaces where there might be ice-strewn plain, lofty mountains, or perhaps even frozen water dividing the land into two continents. Here and there around this great frozen landmass were spots touched by previous explorers, nibbling at the edges. Only one area might be called a geographical bite of the continent, a triangular wedge where the Amundsen, Scott, and Byrd expeditions had made their dashes to the South Pole and fame.

Lincoln Ellsworth proposed to make the first transcontinental flight across Antarctica, from the Ross Sea south of New Zealand, around under and

Especially built for the Ellsworth Antarctic expeditions, new Gamma basks in California sunshine.

up to the mountainous Palmer Peninsula, now known to be an extension of the Andes mountain chain of South America. The distance was some 2,700 miles, something like flying from New Orleans to Seattle.

A grandstanding record nonstop flight was appealing, but Ellsworth intended to make a more leisurely crossing. The atrocious Antarctic weather might prevent a long-distance flight. Should a plane be forced down, the explorer believed that landings and takeoffs from the great snow-covered plateau were entirely feasible. The terrain was unknown, yes, but landing en route to camp and make scientific observations seemed to Ellsworth more useful than a high-altitude dash from one Antarctic coast to another.

Lincoln Ellsworth hired top talent for his polar venture. His scientific adviser and chief organizer was Sir Hubert Wilkins, the Australian explorer who had already studied, mapped, and flown in both the Arctic and Antarctic regions. As pilot, Ellsworth chose Bernt Balchen. An experienced naval, aeronautical, and polar expert, Balchen had flown Commander Byrd over the South Pole in 1929.

Next on the agenda was the acquisition of a suitable airplane. Wilkins had been more than satisfied with the early Lockheed Vegas with which he had carried out exploration at both ends of the earth. These had been designed by Jack Northrop, who had just been set up by Douglas in his Northrop Corporation plant on the south side of Mines Field in southern California.

With concurrence from both Wilkins and Bernt Balchen, Ellsworth ordered, sight unseen, a special built-to-order Northrop Gamma. It was constructed in the Inglewood factory at the same time that Texaco's *Sky Chief* was being put together for Frank Hawks. Both had the inovative feature of "park-bench" ailerons, mounted above the wings, and both were completed in August 1932.

Ellsworth reasoned that a low-wing configuration was "especially adapted to Antarctic flying, since two men could quickly scoop out trenches for the skis, allowing the wing to rest flat on the snow where the winds couldn't get under it." Sir Hubert's enthusiastic comment was that the new Northrop Gamma was "the Rolls-Royce of airplanes."

It was left to Bernt Balchen to watch over construction of the Gamma taking shape in the factory. Wearing his customary visored cap, he had many conferences with Jack Northrop and Don Berlin, as well as with his friend the test pilot Eddie Allen. Balchen usually expressed approval by saying; "Yah, ve do it!"

Balchen, Allen, and Frank Hawks all test-hopped the Ellsworth ship in California. During the winter of 1932–33, Balchen, accompanied by his friend and mechanic Chris Braathen, took the

---

Given conventional ailerons, the Ellsworth Gamma was soon named Polar Star. *She was shipped some 65,000 miles in order to achieve a single epic flight.*

plane to Canada. Joined by Wilkins, they tried out the ski installation, flying in the bush country north of Winnipeg. Satisfied, Bernt flew the new Gamma, now named the *Polar Star*, to New York and put it aboard a Norwegian ship bound for Oslo. Arrived in Norway, the *Star* was stored at the Horten Naval Station while Balchen and Wilkins selected a proper ship to take them to Antarctica.

They bought a 135-foot, 400-ton semi-diesel fishing trawler, the *Fanefjord*. Bernt made sure she had room for the dismantled Northrop plane, either stowed in the hold or lashed on deck ready to be swung ashore. Fitted with ¾-inch armor plate for ice-bashing, the ship left Norway in late July for the 18,000-mile trip, rounding the Cape of Good Hope en route to "down under."

Lincoln Ellsworth insisted on honoring a long-time personal hero, a legendary frontier marshal of the American West. *Fanefjord* became the *Wyatt Earp*. The owner first saw his new vessel and his airplane in November 1933, when he joined the eighteen-man crew at Dunedin, New Zealand.

Wyatt Earp rode through a typhoon en route to Antarctica, and soon after the first of the year she arrived at the Bay of Whales in the Ross Sea, only 12 miles from Admiral Byrd's old abandoned camp at Little America. The Gamma was slung out on the ice for assembly. Flocks of curious penguins watched as the wings were attached and skis fitted to the undercarriage. Balchen and Braathen made two short flights on January 12, 1934. Then Ellsworth was taken on a hop in the beautiful Northrop Gamma he'd bought, on trust, and paid $37,000 for. Everything appeared to be working perfectly.

Later in the day the crew noticed the ice of the bay was being pounded by sea swells and was beginning to break off here and there. Balchen moved the *Polar Star* back about a mile from the water. During the night there was an unprecedented and vast underwater disturbance. The men aboard ship awoke to find the entire thick ice surface of the Bay of Whales breaking up. Balchen and Braathen started on skis to reach the airplane and taxi it to a safe spot, but it was too late. Cracks began appearing beneath their skis. Looking ahead, Balchen saw a wing of the *Star* dip and shouted for help from the ship. The Gamma slowly settled into a crevasse over open water, crushing a wing and the ski-shod landing gear. The men from the *Wyatt Earp* rigged a block and tackle and hauled the damaged plane to

a larger floe. There it floated, swinging with the currents in the jam of broken ice.

After a night speculating that their airplane was as good as lost, the members of the expedition spotted it in the morning still intact and being slowly drawn around the edge of the ice pack. Captain Holth of the *Earp* maneuvered close in and attached ice anchors to the floe. Balchen, Braathen, and the assistant engineer jumped down on the ice and hooked onto the *Star*. In half an hour she was saved, safely on deck.

Whatever caused the Bay of Whales to break up so swiftly was never determined. On examination, the Gamma was found to have both spars of the left wing broken, and her ski undercarriage was damaged beyond repair. The freak catastrophe brought an end to the Ellsworth trans-Antarctic flight's first attempt. The *Wyatt Earp* and her dejected crew set course back to New Zealand. Only the Northrop factory in California could put the *Polar Star* back into flying condition.

The Texas Company, makers of the petroleum products that Ellsworth was using, now helped materially. Balchen, Braathen, and the airplane were transported without charge from New Zealand to California aboard the tanker *Texaco South Africa*, completing a sea voyage around the world.

At Inglewood, Northrop workers straightened out the broken Gamma and gave it a complete overhaul. In addition to a left wing, a taller tail fin and rudder were installed. The novel "park-bench" ailerons were discarded in favor of conventional ones, set into the wings on the outer edges of the split flaps. The plane's name, *Polar Star*, now appeared prominently on the fuselage.

Again, Bernt Balchen stayed with the airplane and did the test-flying. This included shuttling across the continent to New York and picking up Mr. and Mrs. Ellsworth in Chicago, plus temporary installation of floats at the Edo Aircraft Corporation on Long Island. A change in plan brought about the trials of the *Star* on pontoons. Ellsworth had now decided to attempt his trans-Antarctic flight the other way around. He would leave from one of the islands of the Palmer Coast Archipelago and fly across to Byrd's Little America. A new Byrd expedition had reestablished this camp in 1934, complete with radio communication and continuous weather reporting. It would make a welcome goal. Since there might be a need for flying over water during reconnaissance of the is-

lands, the Edo floats went along for quick installation on the Gamma.

In July, the crated *Polar Star* was on board the Matson liner *Monterey*, headed for the South Seas and a rendezvous with the *Wyatt Earp*.

This time the expedition proceeded to Deception Island, the top of a sunken volcano from which Wilkins had successfully flown his pair of Lockheed Vegas for two successive Antarctic summers. This year the central bay was ice-free, but after a blizzard there appeared to be sufficient snow for a takeoff from the beach. Accordingly, the Gamma was put ashore on October 29, 1934, and Balchen prepared for a test hop. After priming and warm-up, and being turned over several times by hand, the Wasp engine made two starts, stalled, back-fired, and then froze with an ominous knocking. A connecting rod had bent, broken, and scored a cylinder of the big radial power plant.

A hasty and then a more thorough search through the extra parts from Pratt & Whitney revealed everything but a spare connecting rod. A radio message went off to the manufacturers in East Hartford, Connecticut, and Pan American–Grace flew new rods to Cape Horn. It took a three-week voyage by the *Earp* to go to Chile to get them. When the ship returned in November, the proposed takeoff site had been blown free of snow by gales. Wilkins's old doglegged dirt strip, now bare

Testing took place using floats, but trans-Antarctic flight was accomplished on skis.

and muddy, was far too inadequate to attempt a wheeled takeoff with a loaded Northrop. With the *Polar Star* on deck, the expedition sailed off in search of a new flying field.

Days of scouting brought the *Earp* to Snow Hill Island, on the coast of the Weddell Sea. Twenty-five miles long, the island was capped by a smooth glacier from which an airplane could readily take off. Again, the tools, supplies, and twelve drums of Texaco aviation gasoline were put ashore and hauled up the steep slope to the plateau. Balchen taxied the *Polar Star* up under its own power, the repaired Wasp ticking over to perfection. Haste was essential, as little remained of the flying season, and Byrd's radio operator in Little America was sending out reports of continuous bad weather on the other side of the continent.

Balchen and Braathen made a test flight on December 18, but not until January were the meteorological reports bright enough to even consider flying. Meanwhile, contention had arisen between the expedition's leader and his pilot. Balchen, his own meteorologist, found it difficult to believe even the rare good reports of the group's own weather forecaster. Brooding, he began to insist that a third man be taken along on any trans-Antarctic flight attempt, believing that in the event of a forced landing it would take three to get the airplane airborne again. Ellsworth reasoned that a third man could be taken only at the sacrifice of gasoline and survival equipment, and less gas would mean less range.

At almost the last possible date left for flying, the weather conditions at both Snow Hill Island and Little America were reported clear. Balchen and Ellsworth agreed to make a try and bundled into their bulky flying clothes. New snow blanketed the glacier on Snow Hill, blown into bumpy ridges called *sastrugi* (meaning "snow waves").

After an hour of fruitless taxiing, Balchen set the propeller pitch, opened the throttle, and let nearly 4 tons of airplane, men, and material go thundering down the south side of the glacier in a crosswind, off into the air. Watchers on the *Wyatt Earp* kept their fingers crossed.

Cruising south along the coast of Graham Land, Ellsworth settled down to making observations and taking notes. An hour and a half passed before he suddenly realized that his pilot had made a gradual turn and was going back.

"Bad weather!" shouted Balchen.

All Ellsworth could see was a small squall off to the rear. He thought it had been agreed that the Gamma would be landed if a really sizable storm should threaten. The explorer was, naturally, terribly disappointed. On arrival back at Snow Hill after this 400-mile flight to nowhere, Balchen remarked to Wilkins: "Ellsworth can commit suicide if he likes, but he can't take me with him."

On this note the Ellsworth Expedition's second season in the Antarctic ended. It was just in time, for the *Wyatt Earp*, in breaking out before winter, was nearly caught in the ice. Pausing only briefly at Deception Island to pack the airplane away in the hold, the unhappy explorers proceeded to Montevideo, Uruguay. Here the ship and plane would be laid up until their owner decided what, if anything, he was going to do next.

At this point Lincoln Ellsworth almost gave up his dreams of a trans-Antarctic flight, but cynical remarks from the press stiffened his resolve to return for another attempt. While still in the polar seas, Balchen had announced his intention of returning to Norway, where he had an offer to go into commercial aviation. Wilkins, ready to go

again, readied the *Earp* and the *Star* in Montevideo. Ellsworth advertised for a new pilot.

Response came from all over, as these were lean times for flying jobs. Ellsworth leaned to Canadian bush pilots who had had experience in the Far North. The choice was narrowed down to two: Herbert Hollick-Kenyon and James Harold "Red" Lymburner, both in their thirties, married, and pilots for Canadian Airways, Ltd.

British-born Hollick-Kenyon, who operated out of Winnipeg, was solid and laconic, a fastidious dresser, and "a wizard at the conrols." Red Lymburner, flying out of Montreal, had grown up on an Ontario farm and "had a genius for engines." Ellsworth hired both men.

For the third time, the *Wyatt Earp* entered Antarctic waters. Expedition members hoped that the 1935 season might bring success at last. In November they established a new base at the northwestern end of Dundee Island, which, like Snow Hill, offered long, sweeping slopes of hard snow. This time there would be no weather reports from Little America. Admiral Byrd's party had left, abandoning the camp once again. Ellsworth's inquiries about food left there went unanswered,

Both Kenyon and Lymburner took the *Polar Star* up on test flights, accompanied by the expedition's leader. By November 18 the much-traveled Gamma stood in a warming tent, loaded, gassed, and ready. Her fuselage was packed with clothing, food, radio equipment, tools, heating stoves, tents, engine covers, and a sledge that had been handfashioned by Bernt Balchen.

Hollick-Kenyon and Ellsworth made a short trip on November 21, but turned back when a broken fuel-flow gauge threatened to flood the cockpits with gasoline. The next day they tried again, passing down the coast and Cape Northrop, on which Sir Hubert Wilkins had bestowed the aircraft designer's name in 1928. Reaching the bulk of the continent, the flyers could see new, uncharted mountains ahead, but ran into a terrific headwind and again returned to Dundee Island.

Wilkins, noting the scarcity of seals and penguins in the Weddell Sea this year, was still worried about the availability of food at Little America. He insisted on packing aboard another 100 pounds of pemmican, oatmeal, sugar, butter, biscuits, nuts, and tea. To partially offset this, the men's heavy skis were left behind on the morning of the final takeoff, November 23, 1935.

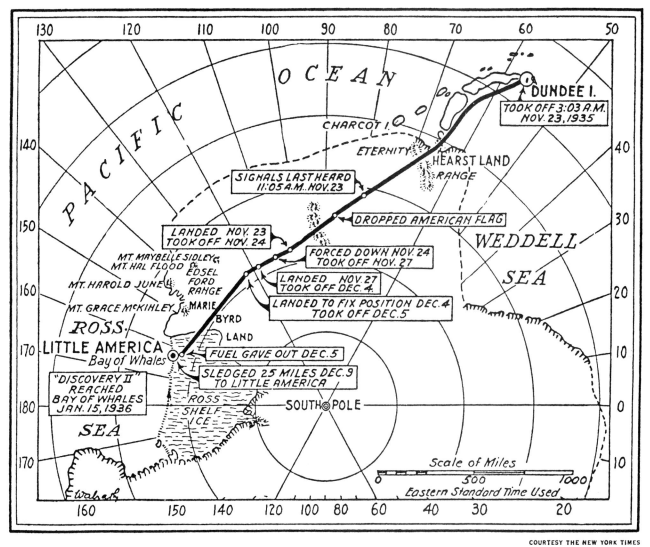

Lincoln Ellsworth's route across the icy wastes of the Antarctic Continent

Once more goodbyes were said. Lymburner had been fine-tuning the Wasp since 1:00 A.M. by the light of the midnight sun. In furry flying clothes, Kenyon and Ellsworth climbed aboard and closed the canopies. Again, with a maximum load and more, the *Polar Star* charged down the snowfield until the tail lifted and the skis unstuck. All that Lincoln Ellsworth could think was: "This time we *must* succeed!" Following the route of two days before, the explorers flew down the coast of the Weddell Sea for 300 miles, approaching the headlands of the continent. They climbed to 13,000 feet in smooth air, with the temperature +10° and visibility some 150 miles in all directions. After three more hours of flying, the mountains gave way to a polar ice plateau.

Back on the *Wyatt Earp*, radio officer Lanz was getting imperfect reception, and signals fron the *Star* came to him in a jumble. After nearly eight hours of monitoring the airplane, he picked up a garbled message which estimated the flyers' position as 71° west longitude. Then: ". . . still clear . . . little no wind . . ." An indistinct contact followed fifteen minutes later. Then nothing.

On Dundee Island, Wilkins at first thought little of the break in communication, since no trouble had been indicated. He assumed it would be restored when Kenyon and Ellsworth reached Little America. Other old Antarctic hands were of the same opinion, and cited the vagaries of radio over mountains and unknown terrain. But whatever his private convictions, Sir Hubert had no recourse but to put contingency plans into action.

It had been decided that if he was forced down,

Ellsworth would allow five weeks to cross Antarctica or get to the coast. It was arranged that in any event, the *Wyatt Earp* would pick up the flyers at Little America on or about January 22, 1936. Should the *Polar Star* be thought to be down and disabled, an amphibian, fitted with skis, was to be secured in the United States and flown to a rendezvous with the *Earp* in Chile. The ship's duty in the Antarctic would not be to search, but to lay food caches at three predetermined spots of which Ellsworth and Kenyon had record and toward which they might travel.

Two days after the explorers had left and their radio calls had ceased, a former member of the Second Byrd Expedition belatedly radioed Wilkins that, yes, there was "ample" food in deep freeze at the abandoned Little America camp, plus caches of trail rations at other spots in the vicinity. Radioman Lanz broadcast this news repeatedly in hopes that it would be picked up by the "missing" flyers. Wilkins now radioed the States to ask for the relief plane.

In New York, a hastily assembled group of Ellsworth relatives and friends formed a committee to activate his emergency plan. No suitable amphibian could be found on such short notice. Casting about, the committee chartered another Northrop Gamma, the Guggenheim family's ship, in charge of their pilot, Russell Thaw. Thaw had the Gamma's Cyclone engine checked out by Curtiss-Wright at Caldwell, New Jersey, and took mechanic William H. Klenke on board for the long flight to Cape Horn.

Left: *Postage stamp of British Antarctic Territory pictures Lincoln Ellsworth and his Northrop Gamma.*

Right: *A 1988 U.S. postage stamp commemorates Lincoln Ellsworth and the Northrop Gamma, Polar Star.*

Unfortunately, the pair got only as far as Atlanta, Georgia. There, on December 9, the engine cut out on takeoff. The Guggenheim Gamma grazed trees and then skidded 200 feet into a ditch; it was a near write-off. Russ Thaw and Bill Klenke got out unhurt.

Again, The Texas Company stepped in to help. It no longer had its famous *Sky Chief* in which Frank Hawks had set so many records, but it was dickering for a similar later-built Gamma. Transcontinental & Western Air had been flying mail and cargo with it.

The day after Thaw's accident, the company took title to the ship and offered it to the Ellsworth relief committee. Workmen at the TWA shops in Kansas City attached ski and float fittings and put an observer's seat in the mail compartment.

Frank Hawks was not free to fly this Northrop Gamma, now called "Texaco 20."

Veteran Eastern Airlines transport pilot Henry T. "Dick" Merrill had just landed after an overnight flight on instruments from Miami when Hawks, accompanied by Mrs. Ellsworth, met him at Newark Airport. It was five-thirty in the morning, but Merrill readily agreed to the assignment.

"Frank, I'll be glad to," he said. "When do I get started?"

Dick got leave from his boss, Captain Eddie Rickenbacker of Eastern, and was bundled onto the next flight to Kansas City, together with passport, visas, and a thick packet of Latin American aerial charts to study. Bill Klenke was still game to try the flight and was crowded into the Northrop's cramped cabin ahead of Merrill.

Dick had been flying Douglas DC-2's on his airline runs and had time only to taxi the ship around a bit to get the feel of flying from the rear again. Finally he got up enough nerve to take off—right into a blinding snowstorm. But once airborne, his first thought was, "Boy oh boy, what a great machine!"

Merrill, a complete stranger to the route, used careful navigation, dead reckoning, seat-of-the-pants instincts and just plain good luck to fly the Gamma down the west coast of South America and over the Andes to Argentina. The trip took six days and covered some 8,000 miles in forty hours of bad weather flying.

Despite his later, well-publicized pioneer flights across the Atlantic Ocean, Dick Merrill always thought of this journey with the Ellsworth relief

Above: *Russ Thaw and Bill Klenke started for Cape Horn, cracked up at Atlanta.*

Texaco 20 was flown 8,000 miles in forty hours to aid in locating Ellsworth and Hollick-Kenyon. Both Gammas rest on Antarctic ice shelf after Polar Star was found at Little America.

plane as his most spectacular. As for compensation: "I got my expenses down and back."

While the Ellsworth relief airplane was being procured in the States, Hubert Wilkins was in daily contact with New York by radio, and the *Wyatt Earp* proceeded to Cape Horn. Reserve pilot Red Lymburner met Merrill and flew *Texaco 20* another 1,000 miles to Rio Gallegos for installation of the *Polar Star's* floats, which had been trucked up from Magallanes. By the evening of December 22, the airplane, ready to fly off and lay food caches, was on the deck of the *Earp*, which was headed through the Strait of Magellan, back to the Antarctic.

Though not requested, the Australian government dispatched its Antarctic research vessel *Discovery II* from Melbourne two days before Christmas. She carried a pair of De Havilland D.H.80 seaplanes, pilots of the RAAF, sledges, and enough rations for long forced marches over snow and ice. There had been no word or clue as to what had become of Ellsworth, Hollick-Kenyon, and their Northrop Gamma. It had now been nearly a month.

Where *was* the *Polar Star*?

Back in November, the flying explorers had been 1,000 miles out when radio contact broke down and they could no longer send or receive. (The trouble was later found to be a defective switch leading to the trailing antenna.) Their next log entry read: ". . . only thing is to go on."

Continuing in high flight, the *Polar Star* passed isolated peaks that poked up from the limitless snow plain, one of which, a 2,500-footer, Ellsworth named for his wife. After 1,550 miles and nearly fourteen hours in the air, making every effort to keep on their predetermined course, the flyers found the visibility growing poor, and Kenyon set the plane down on the misty, hard-packed snow of the high plateau. The Gamma's fuselage was "crumpled" in landing, but the damage did not seem serious enough to prevent flying. The men pulled out the tent, had a meal of oatmeal and bacon, slept, and tried to establish their position with their sextant. Attempts to transmit radio messages with a hand-cranked generator proved unsuccessful.

This was the first of four landings made by the Ellsworth Expedition, an odyssey unprecedented in the annals of polar travel. Hollick-Kenyon and Ellsworth showed that a downed airplane in a deso-

late, hostile climate was not necessarily down for good. Four times they warmed up their Pratt & Whitney Wasp engine with a fire pot in its nose tent, and four times they made swift 50-yard takeoffs.

For some reason, never explained, the normally fast Northrop averaged only 102 mph in the air— only two-thirds the speed that had been expected. Fuel was dwindling.

Two of the flights from the plateau of snow were less than an hour long. A three-day blizzard buried the grounded airplane and kept the men in their sleeping bags while the temperature dropped from +15° to –5°. The sextant went awry and the stove leaked. Under the storm's blanket the plane was barely visible. The fine, dry snow sifted into everything, including the tapered tail of the airplane. Using a bucket and food mug, Ellsworth spent most of a day removing it while jammed headfirst among cables and bracing.

The last hop brought the weary explorers within sight of their goal—the Ross Sea with its slate-colored water in contrast to the endless expanses of white. But after thirteen days, with twenty hours and fifteen minutes of flying, the last drop of 466 gallons of Texaco aviation fuel was gone. The Wasp began to sputter, and Hollick-Kenyon brought the *Star* down in a landing only 16 miles from the Bay of Whales. After three years, she had finally made the first transcontinental crossing of Antarctica.

The aerial journey was over, but it took Ellsworth and Kenyon another ten days to find the ghostly stove pipes that marked the buried location of Byrd's abandoned Little America. Digging down, they smashed a skylight and gratefully tumbled into an empty radio shack. It was another full month before the Australian ship *Discovery II* found them, to be soon followed by the arrival of Sir Hubert Wilkins with the *Wyatt Earp*. Late, and bucking ice, the Earp had proceeded as fast as possible to the planned rendezvous at Little America. Wilkins had been correct in his assumption that Ellsworth and his pilot were not really "lost."

Lincoln Ellsworth, suffering only a frostbitten foot, shipped out on *Discovery II* for Australia, leaving Wilkins and the pilots to wind up the expedition. *Texaco 20* was put ashore and fitted with skis. A party from the *Earp* shoveled out the *Star*, and she was flown the last short hop to Little America. Both planes came back to the United States on the *Wyatt Earp*, which docked in Brooklyn.

Polar Star was perhaps the best-known of the early Northrop airplanes. In Ellsworth's words: "She was good as new but far too dear a relic in my eyes to be permitted to grow old and go to aviation's boneyard." He gave the Gamma to the Smithsonian Institution on April 25, 1936.

One last journey awaited the *Polar Star*. From Long Island, Lincoln Ellsworth and Herbert Hollick-Kenyon were to fly her to the presentation ceremonies in Washington. But a Department of Commerce inspector took a good look at the wrinkles in the Gamma's metal-skinned fuselage and forbade the flight. After much persuasion, Kenyon was allowed to make the short ferry flight alone. Probably no airplane has ever been transported so many miles, something like 65,000, to make just one successful 2,500-mile flight.

Today, below Cape Northrop on the Palmer Peninsula, the maps of Antarctica show that some of the old names have been replaced. But there is still a vast stretch of "Ellsworth Highland," with a section of it called "Hollick-Kenyon Plateau." And at Washington's National Air and Space Museum, Lincoln Ellsworth's old *Polar Star* is the only Northrop Gamma in existence.

In good physical shape, wiry Lincoln Ellsworth, at fifty-eight, had one more stab at the continent of Antarctica to make. Critics had belittled his epic 1935 journey in the *Polar Star*, saying it was only a partial crossing of the Antarctic. Ignoring unfriendly geographers, Ellsworth launched a new private venture in 1938 to try to claim a goodly slice of the Antarctic for the United States.

With financing by a new Ellsworth Trust, the explorer's old converted herring trawler *Wyatt Earp* was readied for more pounding into the ice packs, and the services of Sir Hubert Wilkins were again engaged as adviser-manager. "Red" Lymburner went along as pilot, and this time there were two airplanes; a little Aeronca K on floats and a big Northrop Delta 1D on skis.

Ellsworth bought the Delta in April 1938, from George F. Harding of Chicago, who had used it for three years as an executive transport. It was re-engined and converted to a two-place job; the other seats went out and gas tanks to hold 553 gallons were installed. Sent to Sydney and then on to South Africa in the *Wyatt Earp*, the Delta left Capetown with the new expedition in October, heading south. Ellsworth had announced his intention of making a flight from Enderby Land, but switched his objective to Wilkes Land, several hundred miles farther on. He then told Wilkins of his land-claiming intentions. The latter, who had kept his Australian citizenship, mildly objected, pointing out that the area was already part of Australia's allotted Antarctic sector. But Ellsworth persisted.

Early in January, Lymburner, flying the Aeronca, made reconnaissance flights in the vicinity of the Rauer Islands and the Vestfold Hills of eastern Antarctica, on the opposite side of the continent from Ellsworth's previous aerial exploration. The Canadian pilot located a long frozen fjord, and the *Earp* beat her way in to sling the ski-shod Delta out on the rough, precarious ice. One test hop was made immediately, but conditions precluded a takeoff with any great load.

When Lymburner, with Lincoln Ellsworth beside him in the cockpit of the Northrop, got off the ice on January 11, 1939, he had fuel for little more than a six-hour round trip. Enjoying fine weather, the pair flew inland over an unbroken expanse of featureless snow that sloped gradually upward. Visibility was roughly 150 miles in every direction,

but no mountains were seen. Ellsworth called this interior tract the American Highland, a name it still bears, and duly dropped a cylinder that was supposed to establish the claims of the United States. When Red turned the Delta back at the end of their range of fuel, the flyers estimated they were 350 miles from the ice shelf at the coast. (On the basis of this flight over the Australian sector, Ellsworth ultimately claimed some 81,000 square miles of the Antarctic for America. Today, under international treaty, the United States neither makes nor recognizes territorial claims to Antarctica.)

This single foray over the unknown continent was the sum total of flying by the 1938–39 Ellsworth Expedition, and the explorer's last journey in search of new lands. When the *Wyatt Earp* arrived in Sydney in February 1939, both she and the Northrop Delta were sold to the Australian Commonwealth.

The last Ellsworth expedition. Northrop Delta and float-mounted Aeronca K reach Antarctica in 1938 aboard the trusty Wyatt Earp.

"Red" Lymburner and Lincoln Ellsworth with the Delta, ready for the explorer's last flight over the Antarctic Highlands, January 11, 1939.

7

ON AIRWAYS AT HOME AND ABROAD

I t took time for The Northrop Corporation to get going on the design and development of new airplanes. As a Douglas subsidiary, with additional brain and manpower resources, the plant on the south side of old Mines Field concentrated at first on building the first two Northrop Gammas. During the winter of 1932–33 the aviation press was full of construction plans for Meteor Man Hawks's new airplane and Ellsworth's ship, "built to assault the Antarctic." The publicity brought dozens of inquiries, plus some prospective airplane purchasers who arrived in person at the California factory. Among them was Jack Frye, by then Transcontinental and Western Air's twenty-nine-year-old vice-president. As the airline's operations manager, he was looking for a more com-modious version of Northrop's Alpha mail plane, which TWA had been flying. Couldn't there be an enlarged Alpha—longer, wider, with more wingspan, more horsepower, more speed?

Nine months after the two well-publicized Gammas were completed and flown, Jack Northrop produced a fourth Greek-letter ship, the Delta. It was what Jack Frye had asked for in a modern, all-metal transport, capable of carrying eight passengers behind a pilot who perched up front under a sliding canopy behind a 710-hp Wright Cyclone engine.

Pan American Airways' subsidiary Aerovías Centrales flew Northrop Delta on Mexico City–Los Angeles route.

First-built Northrop Delta was leased to Transcontinental & Western Air for four months.

The first Northrop Delta was finished in May 1933. It was a big chunky ship with seven windows on each side of the fuselage. Except for the trousered landing gear and metal skin, it resembled a larger version of the wooden Lockheed Orion, then popular with the infant airlines.

After fifty hours of testing over a three-month period, the Department of Commerce certificated the Delta, but reduced the passenger load to six. Canny Jack Frye first leased the airplane, so that TWA could make its own valuation. Some of his mail pilots preferred sitting in the open to the rear, as in the Northrop Alpha and the Consolidated Fleetster, but Frye contended that visibility was much better during takeoffs and landings from up front, as in the Lockheed Orions and the Delta.

Northrop's new entry in the airline transport field was put on TWA's mail and express routes, flying without passengers. It was rumored that the carrier was buying fifteen of them. Through no fault of the airplane, the TWA lease on the first Delta proved short. After a forced landing because of a broken propeller, the ship was repaired and put back on the Los Angeles–Kansas City run.

Then, during the evening of November 10, 1933, veteran TWA pilot Harlan Hull, eastbound out of Albuquerque, radioed that he had an engine fire at 6,000 feet and that the cockpit was full of smoke. Sliding back the canopy as the firewall collapsed, with flames and molten aluminum spewing around him, Hull bailed out. Twenty-four burned holes in his chute pack were later counted, and Hull consid-

ered himself lucky to suffer only minor cuts and bruises. The Delta and nineteen charred and battered sacks of mail were scattered over a mile of New Mexico desert.

Despite the loss of the prototype, TWA might have bought more Deltas. But the twin-engined new Douglas DC-1 was going through its paces, and this series of aircraft promised to provide the ideal airliner for the future, which was soon to arrive.

Northrop's second Delta, powered by a Pratt & Whitney engine, was ordered by another growing airline giant, Pan American Airways, Inc. Pan Am handed the new plane over to a Mexican subsidiary, Aerovías Centrales, S.A., which had been flying a mixed fleet of secondhand Fokker F-10A trimotors and Fairchild 71 cabin planes.

On April 26, 1934, pilot Harry C. Goakes and seven passengers made the inaugural flight from Mexico City to Los Angeles for Aerovías Centrales in the Delta, using Grand Central Air Terminal in Glendale as the port of entry. The line, with an eight-hour city-to-city flying schedule, was in competition with Líneas Aéreas Occidentales, which had begun a parallel international service two weeks before. LAO, a project of periodic airline operator Walter Varney, flew speedy Lockheed

Captain Harry Goakes, first passengers, arrive at Glendale's Grand Central Air Terminal on inaugural Aerovías Centrales Delta flight from Mexico City.

Orions. Aerovías Centrales countered with the Delta, a Consolidated Fleetster, and two fast Orions.

Like TWA's leased Northrop Delta, Aerovías Centrales' airplane flew only briefly. Nine months after its purchase, and only ten days after introducing the Mexico City–Los Angeles service, that old bugaboo, an engine fire, destroyed the plane on the ground. Pan Am had to introduce twin-engined Lockheed 10 Electras to compete with Varney's LAO.

Mexican label from A.C.S.A. line speeded recognition of airmail letters.

A third Delta airline customer was the Swedish A.B. Aerotransport, of Stockholm. Under a March delivery date in 1934, the company bought a fast eight-passenger job, and it was an aborted entry in the MacRobertson Race to Australia later that year. As A.B. flew expanding scheduled routes, the Delta became a familiar sight at the major European aerodromes. One record-breaking flight linked Stockholm and Paris in four hours and forty minutes. Named *Halland*, the plane's normal shuttle routes linked Sweden, Denmark, and Germany.

Four months later, in June 1934, the Swedish Delta was joined by another Northrop airplane. Although exported as a Delta 1E, the ship was more in the configuration of Lincoln Ellsworth's Gamma, the *Polar Star*. It was acquired by A.B. Aerotransport for use as a night mail plane, with a cargo compartment forward and a tandem cockpit

with sliding canopy to the rear of the fuselage. The Swedes called it a Gamma and named the plane *Småland*. Unhappily, after only a few days in operation, this "Delta/Gamma" developed aileron flutter and lost a wing over Almhult, Sweden, in July 1934. The pilot and radio operator left safely by parachute. Seeking the cause of the accident involved an early instance of cooperation between investigators of both nations, together with The Northrop Corporation. A.B.'s Delta meanwhile continued to speed passengers on European air

Sweden's A.B. Aerotransport flew Delta to new records on European airline routes.

routes and eventually was sold to the Spanish Republic.

Back in the United States, at Transcontinental &

Ill-fated, Hornet-powered Småland, *a night mail plane for Sweden.*

Opposite: *Air baggage labels issued by the five airlines that flew Northrop Alphas, Gammas, and Deltas.*

Western Air, the twin-engined Douglas transports were soon to go into service, but there was still a need for bigger and better mail-express-cargo planes. Jack Frye's airline bought a single-cockpit Northrop Gamma 2D in 1934. In February of that year, during a controversy over alleged collusion by the air carriers in bidding for subsidized airmail routes, the government had canceled all current contracts and attempted to have the U.S. Army Air Corps fly the mails between the larger American cities. When the routes were restored to civilian contractors, Frye seized the opportunity to show the public just what the airlines could do in the way of fast transport of mail. Personally flying the new Gamma, the soon-to-be TWA president restarted commercial airmail service on the night of May 13, 1934. Toting 335 pounds of mail and 85 pounds of express, he flew from Los Angeles to Newark with a single stop, setting a new airline speed record of eleven hours and thirty-one minutes.

Concurrent with the introduction of "modern" twin-engined, low-wing transports on the nation's principal airways came a directive from the Director of Air Commerce. Effective October 1, 1934, passenger-carrying single-engined aircraft were not to be operated on scheduled airlines of the United States except during daylight hours. The mail planes, most of them powered by one engine, could carry on at night, but not with passengers. The predictable result was that the major airlines of the nation just did not order any more single-engined airplanes and began to phase out the ones they were operating.

Still, TWA bought two more Gammas the same month the directive went into effect and flew mail, express, and freight in them for over a year. They were among the last fast transports in which the pilot sat alone with his precious cargo and hurtled through the black skies, showing the traditional Postal Service scorn of "rain or snow or gloom of night."

President Frye cracked up TWA's record-breaking Gamma himself, during a forced landing in Arizona. Another was sold to The Texas Company and sent to Cape Horn in the abortive "search" for Lincoln Ellsworth. The third was retained by TWA as a research airplane.

When TWA resumed flying mail in 1934, Jack Frye set a new transcontinental speed record with TWA Gamma.

Factory-new Gamma went to TWA for studies of icing, turbulence, engine efficiency, etc.

Beginning in January 1936, this last ship was used to test de-icers on its three-bladed propeller and wings, plus various radios, gasoline analyzers, and turbo-superchargers.

Much of the flying under actual conditions fell to Jack Frye's special assistant, TWA pilot D. W. "Tommy" Tomlinson. Two cramped observer's seats were installed in the Gamma's cargo bin and the plane was officially designated TWA's Experimental Overweather Laboratory. Tomlinson made substratospheric flights across the country, breathing in an oxygen mask at heights of from 20,000 to 35,000 feet. The idea was to study conditions at these levels, in anticipation of carrying passengers at higher altitudes in pressurized cabins. Much of the work was devoted to engine research, learning performance and speed differentials under actual conditions, as well as monitoring fuel consumption.

TWA's "Tommy" Tomlinson, who carried out experiments for the airline in the substratosphere.

Big Gamma was TWA's Experimental Overweather Laboratory.

Tomlinson was often accompanied by James Heistand, development engineer for TWA, who had his own set of instruments in the observer's compartment of the "overweather" Gamma. Thirty-six instruments told what was going on in the airplane and a camera took automatic photos of the illuminated panel at every 1,000 feet. Tomlinson and Heistand, with framed radio mouthpieces stuffed under their noses and tubes of preheated oxygen in their mouths, found they could wear light summer clothing, even at –30°. Helmetless Tommy, in the exposed cockpit, had to tuck a handkerchief over his bare head as he flew the Gamma higher and higher toward the sun. For more than two years the experimental work continued, with the Northrup shuttling back and forth across the continent.

On one flight in April 1938, Tomlinson left Kansas City for Newark, watching all the recording gadgetry, but unaware he had a 90-mph wind on his tail. Short on oxygen, he missed the Newark range signal and found himself some 150 miles out over the Atlantic, headed for Europe. Hastily backtracking and low on fuel, Tommy brought the "laboratory" well inland before making a forced landing near Princeton, New Jersey.

TWA's research Gamma was at the forefront of giant strides in airline development, schedule maintenance, smooth flight, and travel safety. Officials began talking and planning future air transports "with fifty-passenger capacity and wings of 150 feet from tip to tip." The foresight of Jack Frye, the experimental flying of Tommy Tomlinson, and the rugged service given by their Northrop Gamma are due great credit for making today's airline flights possible.

That last Northrop Gamma of TWA's, the "laboratory," was finally sold in 1940 to The Texas Company, where it continued as an experimental ship. At high altitudes, Texaco's Aubrey Keif tested oil flows and the temperature requirements of the company's lubricants. The plane ended up with the Army Air Corps in World War II.

TWA's "laboratory" became Texaco 36 to test lubricants.

Though only three airlines flew passengers in the six to eight seats of the Northrop Deltas, there were other customers for the airplane. A growing market existed for "executive aircraft "—airplanes devoted to fast transport of the pillars of industry, company heads, figureheads, and key personnel.

Purchased in July 1934, the first "executive" Northrop Delta was *The Richfield Eagle*, acquired to carry officials of both eastern and western headquarters of the Richfield Oil Corporation. When the company got into financial difficulties, William Duffie was appointed receiver and found the airplane handy to enable him to preside over reorganization meetings in both New York and Los Angeles.

Delta of Hal Roach Studios sits outside the Northrop factory hangar.

Only surviving Northrop Delta was originally The Richfield Eagle.

Powel Crosley, Jr., head of the Cincinnati-based Crosley Radio Corporation, had a five-place Delta for personal transport. His private aircraft insignia, a white C and red lightning flash on a triangular blue field, was painted just below the cockpit. Inside the two-tone brown of the cabin was a couch along the right side and two chairs, all upholstered in handsome red leather. To the rear in the Crosley ship was a fully equipped lavatory and a big baggage compartment.

Hal Roach Studios, the California maker of movie comedies, paid $33,263.31 for a new Northrop Delta in 1934. The company flew it only four months before selling it to Erle P. Halliburton of Los Angeles. Halliburton was an Oklahoman and former airline operator whose main business involved a profitable process for cementing oil wells. On frequent trips between California and the Midwestern oil fields, Halliburton rode in style.

Another Delta transported Boston executive William H. Danforth for more than three years. It was destroyed in a spectacular Miami hangar fire along with thirteen other planes.

Then there was the May company's airplane, a Delta used by the department-store family, Morton May of St. Louis and Wilbur D. May of Los Angeles. The latter sported a stylized red-and-orange triangle as his private insignia.

George F. Harding, an Illinois state senator and

head of the Chicago Real Estate Loan and Trust Company, liked to fly and own fast airplanes. He engaged a series of pilots-for-hire to fly his friends and himself on business and pleasure trips. Among the senator's hobbies was the collection of medieval military artifacts, most of which he picked up in his travels. Some of the six seats of Harding's Northrop Delta were often occupied by upright suits of armor and chain mail. It was this airplane that Harding sold to his fellow Chicagoan Lincoln Ellsworth, for Ellsworth's last Antarctic expedition.

The Executive Deltas, as they came to be called,

Executive Delta for William Danforth of Boston was powered by Pratt & Whitney's Hornet engine.

Senator George Harding's Delta flew the Chicago executive and his coats of armor, ended up in Australia.

Seward Webb Pulitzer's Delta with racing number for the 1935
Bendix Race. It was a non-starter.

were all built to the purchaser's requirements. They differed in seating arrangements and finished detail. One later model was flown briefly by Bruce Dodson of Kansas City and then went to Seward Webb Pulitzer of the publishing family. Based on Long Island, the plane was entered in the 1935 Bendix transcontinental air race, but a hard landing at Pulitzer's hands resulted in "a slight buckle of the center section." The Delta was still under repair at the Northrop factory when the rest of the race contestants took off in the foggy dawn for Cleveland.

The final Northrop Delta Executive was built to order for the United States Coast Guard and delivered in February 1935. It was not, as might have been expected, an austere, stripped-down ship but a plush seven-place job with a price tag of $41,909.20. The press described this Delta transport as "one of the most luxurious and refined planes ever placed in use by any branch of the Services."

The Coast Guard, in peacetime, was under the jurisdiction of the United States Treasury Department, and President Franklin D. Roosevelt's Secretary of the Treasury was Henry Morgenthau, Jr. A longtime Roosevelt friend, supporter, and appointee, the Secretary had requisitioned his first state-owned airplane back when FDR was governor of New York and Morgenthau his conservation commissioner. Ostensibly for Coast Guard staff

transport, the spick-and-span Executive Delta was kept ready for any trips Morgenthau felt moved to make. The Coast Guard had the Secretary's seal emblazoned on the fuselage, but carried the airplane on its records as a prosaic RT-1. Sometime during the second Roosevelt administration, Secretary Morgenthau's dazzling Northrop Delta came to grief. When sold to aircraft broker Charles Babb in October 1940, the plane had only 1,100 hours total time. Unfortunately, the plane's "gears, left wing and center section were buckled and torn," and it had "no engine, propeller, instruments or accessories." Charlie Babb paid the taxpayers $1,400 for the hulk and rebuilt it, a typical profit-making operation.

In January 1935, The Northrop Corporation built a Gamma 2E, similar to those it had been supplying as attack bombers to China. Frank Hawks, the holder of many speed records, had severed his connections with Texaco and was doing free-lance work. Northrop hired Hawks to take the 2E on a promotional tour of the South American republics, accompanied by factory superintendent Gage Irving.

The pair were in Buenos Aires making preparations to demonstrate the Gamma to the Argentine navy when they received a cablegram requesting the immediate return of the airplane. Though surprised, Hawks was pleased. Here was an opportunity to set more speed records, intercontinental this time. He plotted out a route and proposed a tight schedule, while Irving undertook to service the Gamma, both in the Argentine and along the route to California.

Hawks and Irving left unlit Morón airfield out-

Treasury Secretary Henry Morgenthau's plush Coast Guard Delta.

side Buenos Aires at 3:30 A.M. on May 5, cruising at 19,000 feet over the Andes to Santiago, Chile. They set a new record of an even four hours. This was the first leg of a full three-day trip to Los Angeles,

Northrop Delta No. II

The Delta was one of the aircraft featured on cards found in packages of H. J. Heinz's Rice Flakes.

which broke speed records all the way. In a little less than forty hours of flying time the military Gamma was flown 8,090 miles up the Pacific coast of South and Central America.

There was one heart-stopper en route. Leaving Cristóbal in the Canal Zone at 3:00 A.M., Hawks took the Gamma up to 18,000 feet to try to avoid the turbulence and steady downpour of a tropical rainstorm. But he forgot to turn on the carburetor heat until too late. The pounding pistons of the Cyclone engine slowed and then quit. Frank leaned the mixture, backfired the engine, and tried every trick to get a restart as he watched the altimeter unwind. Down, down, with uncertain terrain below. At last, after losing 12,000 feet, the big radial began to sputter, caught, and roared to life. Land, when the flyers could see it, was on the left rather than the expected right. The storm had blown the plane clear across the Isthmus of Panama and put it out over the Gulf of Mexico.

The trip up from Buenos Aires was Frank Hawks's last major record-smashing flight. He never inquired why the Gamma was so urgently needed back at the Northrop factory. Six months later, without a bill of sale or an export certificate, the same airplane was ferried east, dismantled, and put on a freighter. It had been quietly bought for

After speedy trip from Buenos Aires, Northrop 2E was shipped to Russia.

testing and evaluation by the Union of Soviet Socialist Republics.

Despite criticism, Britain had not been entirely unaware of developments overseas. Right after the MacRobertson Race to Australia, the Air Ministry, "in accordance with a policy of acquiring examples of some of the more outstanding foreign types of aircraft from time to time," bought a Northrop Gamma 2E attack bomber. The ship underwent exhaustive testing for the Royal Aircraft Establishment at Farnborough. Designers, draftsmen, engineers, and mechanics went over every inch and feature of the Gamma. Pilots gingerly tried out the ship and decided, to their surprise, that the

Metal construction and de-icing equipment of Northrop attack bomber were evaluated by England's Royal Aircraft Establishment in 1934.

performance figures claimed by Northrop were realistic. With bombs removed, the 2E really did move along at the maximum speed of 226 mph. It could carry nearly 95 percent of its own weight as a disposable load and had a range of 1,500 miles while carrying 1,100 pounds of bombs. The Air Ministry's wallahs marveled at the multicellular wing and the "planked" Alclad skin, which was crimped up at the joints for stiffening.

Even irascible C. G. Grey, longtime editor of *The Aeroplane* and a champion of anything British, devoted six pages of his magazine to the newly purchased attack bomber. He reminded his readers that an English biplane had had metal-covered wings as long ago as 1923, and that flaps had been in use even longer. He cited Britain's fighter biplanes, the late-model Fairey Fox and the Gloster Gauntlet, as "faster than the Northrop."

"Though an excellent example of an obsolete type," the Gamma, the caustic editor conceded, was "quite a good airplane," and looked "very handsome with its shining exterior." Coming from C. G. Grey, that was high praise.

Royal Air Force officers who flew the Northrop at Farnborough and Martlesham Heath were generally enthusiastic. One of the two civilian test pilots posted to the Royal Aircraft Establishment was Arthur Edmond Clouston, a New Zealander who loved to fly.

Clouston was assigned to learn more about the reaction of airplanes to icing. He at first flew a huge Handley-Page Heyford, an ungainly-looking bomber with the engines mounted on the 75-foot upper wings; the lower wings and undercarriage dangled far below the fuselage. Flying deliberately into freezing clouds, the test pilot could keep this monster airborne until about 2 inches of ice built up on the wings, struts, wires, and propellers. Sinking to earth with the Heyford still under control, Clouston would be bombarded with pieces of melting ice at the lower altitudes and at one point was knocked momentarily senseless by a chunk that slammed against his flying helmet.

A solution to the danger had already been demonstrated in America—the B. F. Goodrich De-Icers, such as those installed on the Northrop Alphas and Gammas of Transcontinental & Western Air. These inflatable rubber sleeves on the leading edges of wings were now tried out in wintry English skies, attached to the imported Northrop 2E. Under Clouston's pilotage they proved very successful. Hot-air control of the carburetor kept the air-cooled engine purring contentedly, and when the bombardment of ice began on inflation of the rubber tubes, the pilot was protected under the greenhouse of the cockpit.

The Gamma 2L, shipped to England in 1937 to test Bristol aircraft engines.

When the senior scientists of the RAE belittled the importance of the de-icer tests, Clouston took off with a full-size camera and stayed in a black cloud until "the Northrop looked like something straight out of the Arctic." Then he slid back the canopy and stood up on his seat. Swaying in the bitter-cold slipstream, the test pilot snapped pictures of a good 3 inches of ice on the leading edge of the Gamma's wing before the de-icers were inflated. Up there where it happens, Clouston also found that ice would build up in the gaps between the engine cylinders and cause the engine to overheat. Despite his visual report, the scientists stated that this was "impossible." The pilot was not vindicated until he had burned out two perfectly good Wright Cyclone engines.

In later years, Flying Officer A. E. Clouston became a record-breaking racing and long-distance flyer, an air commodore, and commandant of the Empire Test Pilots' School. His months of flying the Air Ministry's Northrop Gamma at Farnborough remained one of the high points of a distinguished career.

Later, a second Gamma was exported to Great Britain for test purposes. This was the 2L Model, the very last of the Greek-letter series to be built. The plane was imported in September 1937 by the Bristol Aeroplane Company, Ltd. Bristol test pilots, flying out of the factory field at Filton, used the airplane as a flying test bed for the fourteen-cylinder, twin-row 1,400-hp Bristol Hercules engine. With refinements and increased horsepower, this engine was later used on such aircraft as the Beaufighter, Bristol Freighters, Short flying boats, Handley-Page Halifax, Avro Tudor, and Vickers Viking.

Basically a Northrop military design called the A-17 in the United States, Bristol's Gamma had a fixed landing gear, with wheel fairings, that was elongated to keep the propeller off the ground. This second British test plane, having served its purpose, was dismantled at the Bristol factory during World War II.

Down under in Australia, another Northrop made a small contribution to the Allied war effort. This was armor collector George Harding's old Delta 1D, which had flown over the Antarctic with Lincoln Ellsworth's last expedition.

A year after the war in Europe began, the Australian government took the Delta out of storage and flew it from Sydney to Essendon for a complete overhaul by Australian National Airways. With wartime registration to the Department of Civil Aviation, the plane was used to test radio and navigational equipment, being stored for a while in the same hangar as Sir Charles Kingsford-Smith's famous old Fokker trimotor, *Southern Cross*.

With the acceleration of the war in the Pacific Theater, the Americans arrived to help in the defense of Australia and to mount attacks against the Japanese to the north. In July 1942 the refurbished Ellsworth Delta was chartered to the Allied Air Forces Directorate of Air Transport and flown by USAAF pilots to Galeton on the Indian Ocean. The Aussies got her back when the Yanks were shifted closer to the fighting.

Impressed into the Royal Australian Air Force and flying out of the desert depot of Laverton, the Delta ferried airmen of two different squadrons for ten months—live warriors now, not just the trappings of knights of the Middle Ages. Finally, a tail-wheel collapse on takeoff in September 1943 extensively damaged the ship and she was slated to be "converted to components."

Though Ansett Airways sought to use her, there were just no replacement parts for the Northrop. So after ten years as a plush executive transport, stripped-down polar explorer, and courier of military personnel, the exigencies of global conflict sent the once-famous Delta to an Australian scrapyard.

The first-built Executive Delta, after service as *The Richfield Eagle*, was sold to Baker Oil Tools of Huntingdon Park, California, early in 1938. Purchased through broker Charlie Babb in 1941, the ship carried officials of Georgia's Le Tourneau Company, engaged in the building and sales of heavy earth-moving machinery. War years for the Delta were spent with the Minneapolis-Honeywell Regulator Company of Minnesota, whose executive pilot was Max Conrad, later famous for his long-distance world flights. Conrad, "the Flying Grandfather," bought the airplane himself and kept it for ten years. After more owners and a stint of service as a crop sprayer in Wyoming, the old Delta's last recorded owner was Richard M. Davis of Shawnee Mission, Kansas. Davis restored the airplane; its last inspection was in 1958. The only Northrop Delta in existence, the airplane is presently believed to be stored in Kansas.

The Richfield Eagle *proceeded to ownership by Baker Oil Tools . . .*

. . . *then Minneapolis-Honeywell Controls, with Max Conrad . . .*

. . . *and last served as a Wyoming crop duster.*

8

ADVENTURES IN THE CHINA TRADE

Though it generally brings to mind the gaudy, shark-toothed P-40s of World War II's Flying Tigers, the air war between China and Japan had its start a decade earlier.

There were air battles over Soochow and Shanghai in 1931–32, followed by an uneasy truce after Japan seized Manchuria. With Japanese naval aircraft able to overfly its airspace at will, China had to develop air power in order to face the potential invader.

T. V. Soong, Finance Minister for the Chinese Central Government at Nanking, hired a group of Americans to reshape China's military aviation and train Chinese pilots. The group was headed by retired USAAC Colonel John H. Jouett, with nine Army Reserve pilots, four mechanics, and a secretary. China's General Chiang Kai-Shek gave the so-called Jouett Mission full authority, and a Central Aviation Academy, using American instruction

methods, was established at Hangchow, in Chekiang province. Some 350 new pilots were trained.

When the Jouett Mission arrived in Shanghai in July 1932, China supposedly had 270 miscellaneous aircraft. During the next four years nearly 500 military airplanes were imported from the United States, Britain, Germany, Italy, and France. Some were new, some were second- and thirdhand, and a large number came as components, to be assembled in China.

Final arrangements for the establishment of a Central Aircraft Manufacturing Corporation (CAMCO) took place on October 1, 1934. The factory and shops were located at Shien-Chiao ["awakening village"], an airfield near Hangchow, and were to be formally operated by the Chinese

Northrop 2E. Prototype for the Chinese attack bombers.

Nationalist government. Contracts were made with Curtiss-Wright, Douglas, and United Aircraft in the United States. CAMCO was a branch of the Intercontinent Corporation of New York, of which thin, talkative William D. Pawley was the president. Pawley, with his two brothers, came to China to run CAMCO for the Chinese. Though kept quiet, this American involvement did much to disturb the predatory Japanese military establishment.

Consolidated Aircraft of Buffalo, which was selling China its small Fleet biplane trainers, acted as agent for The Northrop Corporation for sales in the Orient. For a light, low-level bomber, the Chinese ordered the Northrop Gamma 2E and its variants. Powered by a Wright Cyclone P-1820-F53 engine of 750 hp, the ship was armed with two .30 caliber machine guns in the wing and could carry a 1,100-pound bomb load. A semiretractable bomb-aiming pod and a gun port were located under the rear cockpit. The prototype 2E, the tenth of the Gamma airplanes to be built, launched Northrop firmly into the ranks of military aircraft contractors.

Carl Cover, a longtime Douglas test and demonstration pilot, showed off the Northrop attack bomber to the Chinese. Delivery date for the first one was February 19, 1934. Shipped entire were two 2Es, seven 2ECs, and fifteen 2EDs, for a total of twenty-two. Under the supervision of Ellis D. Shannon of the Jouett Mission, Chinese pilots of the 1st Bombardment Squadron were taught to fly the gleaming metal aircraft.

In 1935 the parts for twenty-five more 2Es were crated in California and assembled as Chinese bombing planes in Hangchow. Though primarily devoted to Curtiss-Wright aircraft, CAMCO arranged to assemble the Consolidated and Northrop airplanes. They were kept busy at repair work on all makes of the motley fleet of Chinese military and training planes.

In addition to the Gamma attack bombers, the Chinese government bought two Northrop Alphas in July 1935. Secondhand ex-TWA mail planes, they were exported and handled by Hong Kong aircraft broker James W. Fisher ("Fish Air"). To

Chinese air force Northrop readies for takeoff. Trousered fairings were removed to avoid problems with freezing mud.

what use these single-place ships were put is not known, but they were "to be disposed of" by January 1937.

It would be gratifying to report that the forty-nine Northrop airplanes in Chinese service hung up an outstanding war record, but such was not the case. The majority of the Northrop 2Es were destroyed in routine training accidents, often being flown by only partially trained Chinese pilots. Bad weather and poor, hastily prepared landing fields contributed to the attrition.

On primitive dirt-and-gravel airfields, the 2Es long, trousered landing gear would pack up with mud during taxiing and takeoff. In the air the mud would often freeze, so that during landing the airplane was foredoomed to a nose-over. The obvious remedy was to remove the trouser fairing, which, after a number of crashes, was done. CAMCO crews labored mightily to keep the Gammas airborne. But though the Northrop Gamma 2E was China's first all-metal, low-wing attack and bombing aircraft, the Chinese air force was just not properly prepared to use them.

As of January 1937, a British air attaché reported the Chinese Air Force to still have thirty-four Northrop Gammas in service. These were assigned to the 9th, 11th and 14th Light Bomber Squadrons based at Tsining in Shantung Province.

Henry H. "Hap" Arnold, who was to become a famous Air Force general in World War II, delivered a lecture at the United States Army War College late in 1937. Arnold's informants assured him the Chinese had "seventy Northrop 2Es as of September 1," an example of the faulty intelligence-gathering of the 1930s. When the Japanese began a new, full-scale attack on China, beginning with the "Marco Polo Bridge incident" at Peking on July 7, 1937, it was widely believed that the defending Nationalist government had over 600 airplanes. In reality, only ninety-one were fit for combat.

This figure, which included some Northrop attack bombers, was arrived at by Captain Claire L. Chennault, a new American adviser who arrived in China just before the 1937 hostilities broke out. The Generalissimo and Madame Chiang Kai-Shek, the latter being titular head of the Chinese air force, were appalled. With a group of American "adviser-instructors" he had gathered, Chennault volunteered to help direct Chinese military flying.

The first big assault was planned for Saturday, August 14, 1937. The targets were the airport being used by the Japanese to attack Shanghai, their soldiers' camp, and the Kung Da Textile Company building, a supply depot.

Under Group Commander Sun Tung-Kang, twenty-seven Chinese air force officers flying Northrop Gamma 2Es set out to bomb the Japanese bases. All three objectives were successfully hit and the Chinese aircraft all returned safely. Today the Republic of China celebrates August 14 as Air Force Day. The bombing missions of the Northrops

marked the first time that the Chinese carried out an air attack on an enemy.

Before the end of the month another flight of Chinese pilots was not as fortunate. They mistakenly attacked the British cruiser *H.M.S. Cumberland* and the American Dollar Line's S.S. *President Hoover*, which were approaching the mouth of the Yangtze River en route to Shanghai.

In the *Hoover* incident, Jung Yin-Cheng and Hsieh Yu-Ching of the air force's 2nd Group led seven Northrops on a bombing raid over Pai-Lung Harbor. With no practice in the bombing of shipping, and expecting a Japanese troop transport, the Chinese pilots chose to dive on the American liner. Their leader, suddenly recognizing the Stars and Stripes, pulled up without dropping his bombs, but others behind had already let go their 100-pound missiles. The ship was bracketed and damaged, and a seaman was killed. The Chinese government paid a $100,000 idemnity to the Dollar Line, and six Chinese Gamma pilots were jailed awhile for their mistake.

Under Claire Chennault's prodding, the Nanking government's Commission on Aeronautical Affairs finally took a good honest look at the situa-

Assembly of Northrop attack bombers at CAMCO's plant near Hangchow, China.

tion. It was obvious that more aircraft must be procured immediately. Even more drastic was the shortage of proficient pilots. Many of the best ones had been lost, and there was no time to train replacements. To meet the deficiency, squadrons of Russian aircraft, manned by Russian personnel, were called in by arrangement with Moscow.

In addition, a hasty decision was made to recruit not just "adviser-instructors" for the Chinese air force, but an "International Squadron" of "volunteers" to fight the Japanese. Chinese consulates and the Bank of China officials worldwide were alerted to hire foreign pilots willing to renounce their citizenship, if necessary, to come and fight for China.

Many out-of-work pilots applied, but few qualified or were chosen. Formed in October 1937, the Chinese Nationalist air force's "14th Squadron, Foreign Volunteers," was based at Hankow, soon to be the provisional capital of China. Across the field were the self-contained Russian units, flying Poli-

A dummy rigged to represent a Chinese Northrop in an effort to confuse Japanese attackers.

karpov I-15 and I-16 fighter planes and Tupolev SB-2 Bombers.

Never more than a token force, the 14th Squadron was composed of, appropriately, just fourteen pilots, supported by sixteen Chinese air gunners and ten Chinese mechanics. Colonel Chennault's group of adviser-instructors helped out occasionally, but they were "real Army" and didn't take too kindly to mercenaries. Under American Captain Vincent Schmidt as squadron leader, the pilots of the Fourteenth were from five countries. At least three had no military training or experience whatever.

The main aircraft of the foreign volunteers was an allotment of Vultee V-11 attack bombers, some thirty of which were delivered to the Chinese late in 1937. Filling out squadron strength were a handful of the remaining Northrop 2Es. These were ordinarily used to train pilots and gunners prior to flying the newer, larger, three-place Vultee, which had a retractable landing gear.

Japanese air attacks on Hankow and the squadron's airfield between the Yangtze and Han rivers quickly became so frequent that a considerable amount of the Fourteenth's time was spent in simply flying the aircraft in their charge off the field and out of harm's way. When an alert was given, they usually had a half hour in which to pick a handy airplane and make themselves scarce. These were orders; they had to try to save the com-

paratively few flyable airplanes that the Chinese possessed.

The first warning would be a soldier riding a bicycle down the field—a "harbinger of caution." A hoisted black flag indicated that the pilots should get their engines going. A red flag meant "Take off! The enemy is expected in twenty minutes!" Finally, when both black and red flags went up, the Japanese raiders were expected at any moment.

Lyman Voelpel, a Missouri boy who had 1,800 hours flight time, but only on light commercial aircraft, told of his baptism into military flying on joining the 14th Squadron in mid-January 1938. Voelpel was getting his first look at the Vultees and Northrops on the field at Hankow when the black flag was hoisted over the operations office.

"Chinba! Chinba! Chinba!" screamed the coolies. "AIR RAID!"

. . . the field instantly became a scene of chaos. Everywhere clouds of dust were kicked up as motors were started and propellers began turning. The airplane maintenance crews ran for shelter and some five hundred coolies of the labor force just milled around. At irregular intervals bombers and pursuit planes took off, some crosswind.

As I stood there, appalled by the obvious lack of system, Captain Schmidt hurried by. Seeing me, he wheeled and caught my arm.

"I'm handicapped by a lack of pilots," he sputtered. "The squadron has one more airplane than flyer. Would you take a chance and fly it in order to save it? If it's left at the airport the Japanese will destroy it."

Voelpel hesitated. Then:

"Come on, let's go. Of course I'll fly," I replied.

"Wait, the Vultees instruments are labeled in Chinese," he said.

"The Northrop would be okay. I've just looked it over."

"Take it!" he said.

We ran back to the Northrop. The motor was ticking over and a Chinese gunner was in the rear cockpit. Captain Schmidt boosted me into the front, pouring instructions and advice into my ear as we went. I was to stay close to the ground, no higher than fifty feet.

"I'll follow you in a Vultee," were his last words. "Stay alongside me. You haven't a map."

I gunned the ship to the runway and poured the coal to the engine. Up came the tail and I was in the air. I made my turn and saw Schmidt's machine close behind. Throttling back, I took a position on his left wing. He headed north, up the river, flying very low. He'd explained that it was difficult for air raiders to spot a ship against the ground, while it was easy to see one silhouetted against the sky. The men of the Fourteenth, flying bombers, were not in a position to offer combat to fast, single-engine fighters.

When Voelpel returned to the Hankow field an hour and a half later, an oil line in his Northrop broke on final approach and he landed fast without benefit of flaps.

The 14th Squadron did manage to stage a few air strikes against the Japanese, usually flying a formation of Vultees, six to eight of them, but often including a spare Northrop. One member, Elwyn H. Gibbon, an ex-USAAC pilot, put fifteen hours on 2Es during his four months with the squadron, including a raid on the railroad junction at Sin Siang on March 5, 1938. This involved a 600-mile trip—five and a half hours in the Northrop, with no heater. In February, Gibbon used a Gamma 2E to check out James W. M. Allison, a Texas soldier of fortune who had fought in Spain the year before.

Another member of the 14th had also been a fighter pilot for the Loyalists in Spain. He was twenty-five-year-old William Labussière, a Frenchman who took part in all of the squadron's air activities out of Hankow.

For the Foreign Volunteers, official "Mission No. 3" was laid down for February 27: a bombing raid on Loyang, to be undertaken by six Vultees flying north out of Hankow. Arriving early at the airfield, Labussière discovered that the propeller-pitch mechanism on his assigned ship was inoperable.

The only serviceable airplane that could be substituted was the 14th's last Northrop Gamma 2E ("coded '109' "). It had no bombsight, there were extended hours on the engine, and the ship had never been on a mission. Over Captain Schmidt's objections, Labussière decided to fly the plane and had the armorers transfer the bombs. There was no time to load the machine guns.

With Lieutenant Shou as crewman/gunner, Labussière reached Loyang after a three-hour flight. The target area was obscured by a gusting snowstorm. With low ceiling and minimum visibility, each plane went after a prearranged individual target. The Frenchman and Shou in the Northrop headed for a Japanese munition depot east of the city.

Mounting a diving attack, the eager Labussière pulled the manual bomb release. Nothing happened. With a second run on his target, he pulled harder and the release handle broke off in his hand. The bombs remained in their racks, under the wing between the wheels.

By this time all the Vultees had departed, leaving the pilot of the Gamma in heavy flak to make a third diving run on the ammo dump. The French flyer desperately pulled the emergency SALVO release to drop all the bombs at once. The target was hit.

Half an hour later, Labussière caught up with the others at their rendezvous point, to be met with frantic gestures. One of his bombs remained, hanging down in the rack, held by a rear lug and automatically fused. The Vultees circled. While his squadron mates watched, Labussière threw the Northrop into a steep vertical dive above the barren countryside, then pulled up sharply. Both he and Lieutenant Shou nearly blacked out. On the third try the menacing package fell free.

An unforeseen sequel to this incident took place when Labussière received a notice from the Commission on Aeronautical Affairs that he was fined $300 (U.S.) for dropping a bomb on returning from an air raid. The family of a lone Chinese victim on the ground had been indemnified in the amount of $5 (Chinese)—actually a few cents. The French bomber pilot protested, and payment of his fine was finally, after much paperwork, revoked. *C'est la guerre!*

Because of misunderstandings, jealousy, and dissatisfaction on both sides, the 14th Squadron, Foreign Volunteers, was disbanded on March 22, 1938. William Labussière stayed on to do further flying for the Nationalist government, but thereafter flew only French airplanes. The aircraft of the 14th were dispersed to other, all-Chinese units.

The Japanese had their own Northrops. This navy Gamma was later flown by Manchurian Air Lines.

Within a few months all the Northrop Gamma 2E attack bombers were gone from the skies of China.

On the other side of the Asian conflict, the Japanese were well aware of China's Northrops when they began to arrive early in 1934. But it was over a year before the Japanese navy purchased a Gamma of its own. This was a Model 5A, powered by a 775-hp Wright Cyclone engine.

Built, experimentally licensed, and sold in October 1935, this airplane received no approved type or export certificate. It was hurriedly shipped out the same month, with the customer's name left unspecified. Arrived in Japan, it was coded BXN-1 by the Japanese navy and used "for a study of modern aviation engineering." Flight evaluation followed, and during the tests the ship apparently was cracked up in a rice paddy.

A second Gamma, again a hush-hush export in September 1936, had a longer, more useful career. This was another experimental model, a Gamma 5D, which the Japanese navy coded BXN-2. This one was powered by a Pratt & Whitney 550-hp engine, turning a three-bladed propeller. After the navy's flight testing, the airplane was handed over to the Nakajima Aircraft Manufacturing Company at Koizumi. Here its study by designers was said to have been "very helpful" in construction of aircraft that culminated in the Type 97 carrier-based attack bomber, or Nakajima "Kate."

Still later, the Japanese Gamma 5D was passed on to the military-run Manchurian Air Lines, whose photographic division used it for aerial reconnaissance. Occasionally flown out of Hong Chien airport, the gleaming trousered monoplane was a rare Manchurian bird. Whenever the Japanese air cadets who trained at Hong Chien in 1939 heard the distinctive bark of its Pratt & Whitney, they always flocked out to watch the ship.

Though by this time the Chinese had lost all their Gammas, the speedy Japanese example was utilized by the Kantoh-Gun (local army forces) to make aerial mapping of another potential enemy's territory—that which lay to the north, beyond the border with the Soviet Union.

PLANES FOR SPAIN

n July 1936, a group of Spanish army generals launched an uprising against the Spanish Republic, which led to nearly three years of civil war. This conflict was used by those who assisted the belligerents—Italy, Germany, Russia, and, to some extent, France—as a testing ground for aircraft and weapons of war with which they would soon be battling each other in World War II.

Under siege, the legitimate government of Spain sought to buy aircraft to combat those supplied to the rebels (or "Nationalists") by Italy and Germany. Cautious France supplied a few, but then withdrew into a farcical policy of "nonintervention" with Great Britain. The Soviet Union eventually sent airplanes and the men to fly them, with payment in Spanish gold. Meanwhile, the Loyalist government alerted its embassies and agents in Europe and North America to buy anything in the way of aircraft that could possibly be used to fight a civil war. Coming at a time of depressed world economy, it made a bull market for used and obsolete airplanes. In addition to purely Spanish agents, both diploma-

tic and commercial, the Communist International was asked to procure airplanes for the Spanish Republic. Unscrupulous arms dealers played prospective buyers against each other. Duplication of effort resulted in the aquisition, at highly inflated prices, of a motley collection of airplanes—castoffs, demonstrators, single-engined ex-airliners, and business executive aircraft that had flown well past their prime. In the United States, these included four Northrop Deltas and two Northrop Gammas.

At the time, antiwar and isolationist sentiment was prevalent in America, which led to "neutrality" legislation. Mandatory embargoes were placed on the sale of arms to warring countries. In the case of the Spanish fighting, a civil war, President Franklin D. Roosevelt first appealed to American businessmen and arms dealers to refrain from selling to

Once the Executive Delta of radio maker Powel Crosley, Jr., this Northrop was captured on the high seas and impressed by the Spanish Nationalists.

either side. The President's "moral embargo" worked for a few months, but the opportunities offered for substantial profits proved too much.

In December 1936, The Vimalert Company of Jersey City, New Jersey, applied for a permit to export secondhand airplanes, including two Northrop Deltas. Robert Cuse, president of Vimalert, had bought the former executive transports of Powel Crosley, Cincinnati radio pioneer, and department-store man Wilbur D. May of Los Angeles.

Openly defying Roosevelt's moral embargo, Cuse planned to ship the Northrops and sixteen other former transport aircraft, plus 411 used airplane engines, to the Spanish Loyalists. He started to assemble the $2,777,000 order, and to get the airplanes aboard the Spanish freighter *Mar Cantabrico*, which lay at Pier 35 in Brooklyn. Legislation extending the nation's Neutrality Acts to include "the unfortunate civil strife in Spain" was hastily prepared in Washington.

Feverish activity in Brooklyn resulted in eight crated airplanes and *one* engine being slung aboard the *Mar Cantabrico* as deck cargo. With Congressional passage of an embargo act to cover arms for Spain on January 6, 1937, the ship immediately cast off and proceeded down New York Harbor.

Onetime May Company Delta suffers a nose-up in Spain. Plane had been seized by the Nationalists aboard the Mar Cantabrico.

President Roosevelt was unable to sign the lawmakers joint resolution until some forty hours later, by which time the *Mar Cantabrico* was well out in the Atlantic and had won her race against Congress.

It was a Pyrrhic victory, for the *Mar* never reached her destination: Bilbao in Loyalist Spain. She was intercepted 125 miles north of the Basque Coast and boarded by men from the Nationalist cruiser *Canarias*. Her cargo became war booty for the rebels.

Put ashore at El Ferrol, the two Northrop Deltas were uncrated, assembled, and flown to Nationalist air force bases, where they were used for a while as part of the transport service, Grupo 43. The former May Delta suffered a nose-up accident, presumably at Seville, while the ex-Crosley ship flew out of León. Both Northrops, with replacement parts unavailable, were shorn of their wings. Minus engines, they served as ground offices and crew rest lounges at Nationalist air fields.

Another attempt to circumvent the American embargo on planes for Loyalist Spain was more

successful. Los Angeles aircraft broker Charles H. Babb had quietly acquired options on nineteen used American transport planes during the fall of 1936. Among them was a Northrop Delta 1D, formerly the property of Erle P. Halliburton, the oil-well-cementing-process man. In December, broker Babb exercised his options and two days afterward sold the airplanes to Rudolf Wolf, a naturalized citizen and nominally a New York City dealer in burlap and jute.

"Somewhere in Spain, 1937." One plush Northrop Delta served as a pilot's lounge.

Far from the oil fields, the former Halliburton Northrop went to the Spanish Republic in 1937.

Former Swedish airline Delta went into service with LAPE, the semimilitary transport group run by the Spanish Loyalists.

Skirting the publicity and uproar that accompanied the proposed Cuse shipment direct to Spain, dealer Wolf quietly obtained export licenses for his airplanes, consigning them to a Dutch firm, with France the ultimate destination. Then he dropped dead.

With remarkable presence of mind and the appeal of a distraught new widow, Mrs. Wolf incorporated the burlap dealer's firm and within ten days was issued new export licenses. While the harried Cuse and the *Mar Cantabrico* occupied the front pages of the city newspapers, Rudolf Wolf, Inc., using two vessels, shipped out the nineteen airplanes. The Delta's wings went on one ship and her fuselage became deck cargo on the passenger liner *President Harding*.

Off-loaded at Le Havre, the Northrop was assembled and tested by a pair of American aviator-technicians whose source of pay was soon traced to the Spanish embassy in Paris. An Air France airline pilot ferried the ship to the private airfield at Toussous-le-Noble, where it was certificated and licensed by French authorities. After several months, though reportedly damaged by saboteurs in league with the Spanish Nationalists, this Northrop was flown to Republican Spain. Its use is said to have been as a VIP transport and "for bomber training."

A fourth Northrop Delta arrived in Spain under still more mysterious circumstances. This was the Swedish Model 1C, the *Halland*, which had been in airline service with A. B. Aerotransport. Despite an embargo on aircraft exports to Spain imposed by Sweden, and without any export permit or certification, the airplane was somehow spirited off to the Iberian peninsula. *Halland* was reportedly sold in May 1937 to Beryl Markham, the lady from Kenya who had made the first woman's east-west solo flight across the Atlantic Ocean the previous September. British registration was allotted but never applied. Nor was a sale to the Royal Flight of Iraq ever confirmed. Instead, the eight-place Swedish Delta turned up in Spain as a small workhorse airliner, flying for the militarized national airline Líneas Aéreas Postales Españoles. As one of the LAPE fleet, the plane was used to transport Spanish government officials, its usual pilot being José-María Carreras y Dexeus. Among other trips, Carreras flew Spanish Foreign Minister Julio Alvarez del Vayo to Geneva, where the latter bitterly protested the "nonintervention" apparatus, approved by the tottering League of Nations, that was strangling Loyalist Spain.

Two Northrop Gammas arrived in Spain by circuitous routes, to be incorporated into the Spanish Republican air force. One was the big ex-TWA mail plane that had been to the Antarctic as *Texaco*

20 for the Ellsworth "search" of 1935–36. A single-place ship with cockpit to the rear, it was peddled through a Long Island middleman to Colonel Gustavo León of the Mexican air force. León assured the State Department's Munitions Control Board that the Mexican government would be using the Gamma "on official business."

The other Gamma, a Model 5B that had its two-seat cockpit well forward, was intended for a "goodwill tour" as a demonstrator when it left the Northrop factory in October 1935. Demonstrations were obviously of a military nature, as bomb racks hung from the underside of the airplane.

After engine changes and several months languishing in storage, the Gamma 5B appeared in Buenos Aires in September 1936. There, flying out of Morón and Palomar airports, it was put through its paces for the Fuerza Aérea Argentina by free-lancing demonstration pilot Eddie Allen, no stranger to Northrops. Over a three-month period, Eddie put another hundred hours on the ship, but no immediate sales resulted. Acting Department of Commerce inspector John T. Shannon reapproved

TWA's mail carrier became Texaco 20, *went to the Antarctic, and then served as a Republican patrol plane during the Spanish Civil War.*

the airplane and issued a permit to ferry it north, for purchase by Henry G. Fletcher, a British aircraft distributor in Mexico City. Since the sale was made outside the United States, the Munitions Control Board did not investigate the matter. In actuality, both Northrop Gammas were bought with money from the Spanish embassy in Mexico City. They were given licenses in the name of Lieutenant Colonel Rafael Montero, a known agent of the Spanish Republic. Flown to Veracruz, the potential warplanes were stored in a Pan Am hangar to await shipment to Spain during the summer of 1937.

Military Northrop Gamma 5B was stored unsold in South America until peddled to the Spanish Republic via Mexico.

It was nine months before Mexican President Lázaro Cárdenas, who had promised the Roosevelt administration he would *not* send aircraft to Spain, was presented with a *fait accompli*. The two Northrop Gammas, together with eleven other American-built airplanes, had been shipped out of Veracruz the day after Christmas. Their carrier, the Spanish ship *Ibai*, put the planes ashore at Bordeaux in France. After another six months of delay, they at last were flown off to the Spanish Republic.

The single-place Gamma, which some Spanish pilots mistook for a Boeing Monomail, arrived in mid-August 1938 and was incorporated into the Escuadrilla de Vultee, Grupo 72, commanded by Captain Carlos Lázaro Casajust. The ship's usual pilot, flying out of Los Alcazares on the Costa Blanca in Murcia, was Lieutenant Joaquín Tarazaga Moya. The Spanish lieutenant flew the big Northrop on the Motril and Tereul fronts, escorting Russian-built SB-2 Katiuska bombers on raids, and concurrently defending the Mediterranean coast.

Tarazaga recalled: "I was in love with this airplane . . . never flew a plane so fine to handle . . . always the maneuvers responded to perfection . . . it gave me the impression of going up in an elevator."

By order of Comandante Juan Macho, Tarazaga's Gamma was not evacuated with other Republican aircraft at the end of the Spanish Civil War in March 1939. The other Gamma and one or both of the Republicans' Northrop Deltas may have been flown to French Algeria at the end of hostilities, eventually to be handed over to the Franco forces as the *de facto* government of Spain. Their fate in the hands of the victorious Nationalists is not known.

10

BULWARK OF DEFENSES

Right from the start, Jack Northrop and his business colleagues had in mind the United States Army as a good customer for his airplanes. Although the Army's Air Corps in 1930 was painfully small, and Congressional appropriations even smaller, there was a possible market for sizable and repeat orders of aircraft. The main product of Northrop's then parent company, Boeing, was Army and Navy fighter aircraft. What the Northrop people had to offer was something new for the Army: a low-wing all-metal monoplane. At that time the brass were not thinking of a monoplane as a fighting aircraft. But a fast command transport plane, something that could carry a couple of generals and high-ranking officers from air base to air base at 158 mph in comfort—well, that was worth looking into. Speed was the important thing, and the Northrop Alpha offered an abundance of it.

On an inspection trip to California in March 1930, Major General James E. Fechet, chief of the Army Air Corps, made the rounds of the aircraft manufacturers. At United Airport he struggled into a parachute and flew in the prototype Alpha. Fechet was flown by his trusted pilot Captain Ira C. Eaker. Jack Northrop, Ken Jay, and Eddie Bellande watched a bit nervously, knowing how much depended on approval by the Air Corps men. General Fechet and Captain Eaker returned with happy smiles.

Experimentally licensed for flying without passengers, the second and at the time the only Northrop Alpha was flown to Wright Field in Ohio.

Major General James E. Fechet and Captain Ira C. Eaker (in cockpit) of the U.S. Army Air Corps flew the first Northrop Alpha in March 1930.

Army tested the second Alpha at Wright Field in Ohio and cracked it up, but placed an order.

Tested by the USAAC pilots in July 1930, it was damaged in a forced landing within a week. The shops at Wright repaired the ship before returning it to the factory.

As a further temptation for the Army, Northrop took this second Alpha and its other demonstrator out of circulation for a month in the late fall of 1930. Number two, which had already been at Wright Field, was put on loan for the personal use of General Fechet, while the other went to Assistant Secretary of War for Aeronautics F. Trubee Davi-

Three Alphas were purchased for the USAAC in 1931 and designated Y1C-19s.

son. Instead of a lumbering Fokker or a rackety Ford, Alphas flew the top general and the secretary to appointments and vantage points where Army maneuvers could be observed. What Fechet and Davison thought of Northrop's generosity is not recorded. But within four months an order was placed for three military Alphas. Powered by Pratt & Whitney Wasp engines and equipped with radios, the first Northrop aircraft sold to the Air Corps went at a bargain price: $15,814.89 each.

The original Army Alpha, designated in the "cargo" category by the Air Corps as a C-19, was delivered at Wright Field on May Day 1931. With its two sister ships (Y1C-19s), the Alphas usual station was either Wright or Bolling Field, which served Washington, D.C.

For over a year the three C-19s, finished as four-place jobs, served Army officers much as the "executive transports" just coming into popularity served

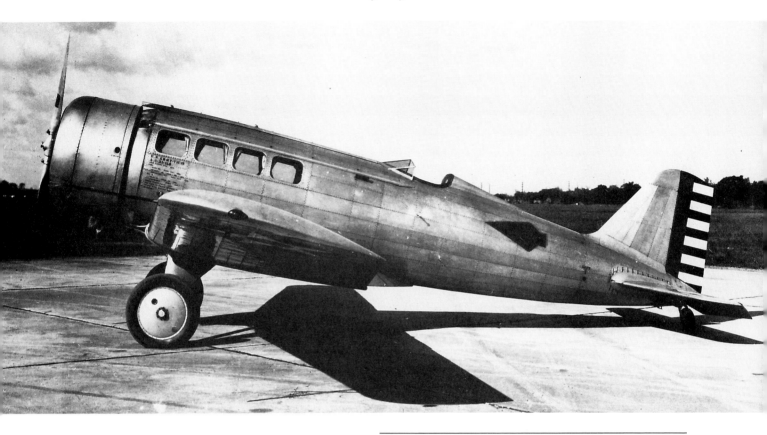

Air Corps Y1C-19 used for liaison and speedy transport of Army brass.

civilians. First lieutenants and captains, anxious to build up flight time out of Bolling Field, vied for the privilege of escorting some doughty general to a distant destination. After jockeying the Alpha, a number of pilots of the peacetime Army, seeing only niggardly appropriations ahead and the opportunities to achieve flight status diminishing, decided that their future lay in commercial piloting.

The Air Corps pilots' love affair with the Alpha was marred by a fatal accident in March 1933. Flying his father and another major from the Judge Advocate General's Office to Washington, Lieutenant James E. Willis, Jr., crashed in a fog near Petersburg, Virginia.

The other two Y1C-19s were relegated to communications and liaison duties with the squadrons based at Selfridge Field in Michigan, Langley in Virginia, and Pope Field at Fort Bragg, North Carolina. One old Air Corps pilot recalls flying in a load of fresh fish for the mess at Middletown Air Depot in Pennsylvania. The Alpha's cabin had a definite savor of the sea for weeks thereafter.

Surprisingly, the remaining Army Alphas survived forced landings, minor and major crack-ups, and rough treatment at the hands of dozens of military pilots for eight years. Not until 1939 were they dismantled, crated up, and shipped to schools

of aeronautics in New Jersey and Louisiana. Even there the Y1C-19s soldiered on. Eager young men took them apart and reassembled them as part of their training.

Northrop's second model, the little single-place Beta, was carefully scrutinized by the Air Corps when delivery pilot Eddie Allen stopped off at Wright Field in February 1932. There was no actual testing or demonstration of this, a civilian sports plane, but discerning planners in the Army's Matériel Division could see the Beta as a "monoplane fighter."

Despite accusations of incompetence and lack of foresight, the Air Corps' matériel people did know what was going on in the field of aeronautics; they simply had little money to spend on research and development. A USAAF report of Captain J. G. Taylor in September 1933 describes the Northrop Delta, which men from the Matériel Division had examined:

". . . The commercial transport development in the United States during the past year has been based on the general idea of speed and still more speed. Commercial operators realize that speed is necessary in order to successfully combat the older and more established means of transportation. Practically all the commercial transports have jumped their top speed to a point between 180 and 200 mph, with the latter figure their goal. At these speeds cleanness of design has become imperative and for this reason monocoque, low-wing monoplanes, internally braced, with purely cantilever wings and tail surfaces . . . have become the fashion. . . . [The Northrop Delta] puts the pilot's cockpit forward, the fairing for this cockpit has been carried right on back to the tail section and allows 6 or 8 inches additional headroom for passengers; two front seats face to the rear and six to the front. The entire airplane is very trim and neat, and the manufacturer's figure of 217 mph does not seem unduly exaggerated. . . .''

By 1932 the new Northrop company, The Northrop Corporation, now affiliated with Douglas, was building the two original Gamma models at the Los Angeles Municipal Airport (Mines Field) in Inglewood. Military contracts were no less important to the survival and development of Northrop/Douglas than they had been to Northrop/Boeing/United. The next two Northrop airplanes, built simultaneously, were the first Delta, reported on by Captain Taylor, and a military version of the Northrop Gamma, styled for attack and light bombardment.

The Northrop Gamma 2C, the company's entry into the more warlike aspects of military aviation,

Northrop 2C became Army's YA-13, then XA-16.

was finished in May 1933. Powered by a 735-hp Wright Cyclone engine with a two-bladed propeller, the 2C had the tandem cockpits moved forward. As a civilian airplane, licensed experimentally, it was delivered to Wright Field in July by test pilot Carl Cover. The Air Corps kept it for testing for almost a year, a not uncommon practice. Dozens of Army pilots checked out in the trousered two-seater, now called an attack bomber. During the months of testing in Ohio, the Gamma was once sent back to the factory for alteration, notably a more triangular-shaped fin and rudder, plus some internal modifications.

Since the Gamma 2C was not yet an official United States military type, Northrop was free to offer the ship for export, and did. Any production of a promising line of military airplanes was bound to attract the attention of other nations—those that wished to intimidate a weaker neighbor, as well as the weaker neighbor that felt it must provide defense against takeover by a belligerent. The bulk of Northrop Gamma 2 Cs went to China. Meanwhile the prototype languished at Wright Field under a bailment contract (that is, a contract involving delivery of goods on trust).

Final acceptance for the Army's first Gamma did not come until July 26, 1934, at which time the USAAC purchased the airplane, complete with a new Wright Cyclone engine, for $80,950—quite a contrast to the Army's "cheap" Alphas of 1931. The state of Air Corps airplane procurement at the time is brought home by the fact that this was only the twenty-seventh airplane for which purchase was arranged during the fiscal year just ending.

The Gamma was given the USAAC designation

YA-13. Its armament consisted of two .30 caliber machine guns in each wing and another in the rear cockpit, and it carried a 1,100-pound bomb load under the center section between the fixed, trousered landing-gear struts.

Not satisfied with the large-diameter Cyclone engine on the YA-13, the Army again returned the airplane to the factory in January 1935. Now a slimmer, twin-row 950-hp Pratt & Whitney Wasp engine was installed, and the Army designation for the ship became XA-16. Further testing showed that the airplane now had too *much* power and should either have a bigger tail or a smaller engine.

With the XA-16 purchased but not fully acceptable, Northrop submitted another demonstrator to the Army in hopes of a contract for attack bombers. This was the Gamma 2F, with an even slimmer and lighter 825-hp Twin Wasp, Jr., engine, a revised tail, and a lowered, extended cockpit canopy. It also had the first retractable landing gear on a Northrop airplane for the Air Corps. With a streamlined flap ahead, the wheels were made to retract rearward into bulging fairings below the wings. The plane was also fitted with a three-segment split flap on the trailing edges of the wing.

This type of gear might have been acceptable to the Navy, but the Army balked. The Gamma 2F went back to Inglewood for rebuilding. It emerged with neatly faired, half-panted fixed landing gear.

Military Gamma 2C/YA-13/XA-16 ends up in a Long Island junkyard.

Even with its modifications the Gamma 2C or XA-16 never went into production for the Air Corps and ended its days as an instructional airframe at Roosevelt Field on Long Island.

Instead, it was the Gamma 2F, after all *its* modifications, that was chosen. At Northrop, on the day before Christmas 1934, the last mail brought an official letter of intent from the War Department, announcing allocation of $2,047,774 to the purchase of 110 attack bombers, to be known as Northrop A-17s. Joy in the little California factory was boundless. After four and a half years of show, tell, furnish, and fix, Northrop finally had a U.S. Army contract.

Frugally, the much-modified Gamma 2F/A-17 prototype became the first airplane of those in the contract, and was officially delivered on July 27, 1935. Tooling up, together with design approval and production delays, took another five months. Beginning in December the first of the production A-17s was rolled out of the factory. It was followed, over a period of a year, by the rest. From a small company with a tiny design staff and a few dozen employees who virtually hand-built each airplane, Douglas's little Northrop Corporation subsidiary went to mass production and 1,000 employees.

The Northrop A-17 had four .30 caliber guns in the wing roots and a single .30 caliber in the back cockpit where the gunner rode, facing either forward or rear. There was no lower gun position or hole in the floor for bomb aiming in this model. No longer hanging below in racks, twenty 30-pound fragmentation or antipersonnel bombs were in-

Northrop A-17 in service.

ternally loaded and could be sent on their way by means of chutes.

All through 1936 the A-17 attack bombers rolled out of the Inglewood factory, now beginning to be called El Segundo, after the plant was moved half a mile east. Resplendent in bright paint—yellow wings and tail surfaces, with blue fuselages—they went through the customary period of evaluation at the Matériel Division at Wright Field and testing

Lineup of A-17s at March Field in California.

by the Technical Training Command at Chanute Field in Illinois. The majority of the new Northrops went to equip the 3rd Attack Group at Barksdale Field in Louisiana and the 17th Attack Group at March Field in California, only a short ferry hop from the factory.

As A-17 production proceeded, Northrop continued experimentation with the backward-retracting landing gear that had been tried on the prototype Gamma 2F. Finally tinkered into a form in which the wheels came up fully, it made the airplane heavier, but promised increased speed with the decreased drag. Installation of an 825-hp Pratt & Whitney R-1535-13 engine gave the improved Northrop a top speed of 220 mph and a greater bomb-carrying capacity, and added another 100

miles to the airplane's range. This plane would be designated the Army's A-17A.

Since the Air Corps was satisfied with the performance of the A-17s flying out of Barksdale and March, it was a logical step to order more of them in fiscal 1936. The War Department ordered a hundred of the improved A-17A. The first one was delivered in August 1936. Because of some mechanical design problems and new government specifications laid down after production began, the A-17As came out of El Segundo in fits and jerks, and the last of the Air Corps' 129 airplanes was not taken on strength until September 13, 1938.

Production was further slowed during this period by growing disputes and confrontations with the labor force. With animosity widespread, the War Department refused to accept any more Northrop-built airplanes until the workers' problems had been settled. This led, on April 5, 1937, to Douglas's taking over complete financial control. After further dispute and an employee strike, Douglas dissolved The Northrop Corporation as of September 8, 1937. From then on, the manufacture of the A-17A and its successors was continued by the reorganized El Segundo Division of the Douglas Aircraft Company. Most of the employees stayed on, but Jack Northrop himself resigned effective January 1, 1938.

Two airplanes were given special attention in the Northrop/Douglas production line and completed and delivered even before the first regular A-17As. These were three-seat unarmed staff transports, designed for the top brass. Called an A-17AS, the first had a 600-hp direct-drive Pratt & Whitney R-1340-41 nine-cylinder radial engine and a three-bladed propeller. It was delivered July 17, 1936, as the personal airplane of Major General Oscar Westover, chief of the Air Corps.

Five days earlier, Brigadier General Henry H. "Hap" Arnold, Westover's assistant chief, had been given his Northrop A-17AS, but he had to be content with a geared engine and a two-bladed prop.

The "command" Northrops, with the distinctive Capitol-dome insignia of Bolling Field and the general's stars of the chiefs, were immaculate and scrupulously maintained. Personally flying out of their Washington headquarters, Westover and Arnold made inspection trips all over the nation, observed winter and summer maneuvers, and generally supervised the Army's expanding Air Corps.

General Westover piloted his "two-star Northrop" for more than two years. On September 21, accompanied by Sgt. Samuel Hynes, his crew chief, the general made a short hop from March Field over to Burbank, California, for a visit to the Lockheed Aircraft facilities. Attempting to land on the old, narrow airport adjacent to the factory in his A-17AS, Westover overshot, turned back, slipped off on one wing, and spun in. Both the chief and Hynes died in the crash and ensuing fire, which consumed the airplane and a parked car, and set an adjacent house ablaze. General "Hap" Arnold succeeded Westover as chief of the Air Corps.

In 1939 two of the Northrop A-17s were used by the National Advisory Committee for Aeronautics in experiments at Langley Field, Virginia. One of these was a test of a new laminar-flow airfoil, which built up and nearly doubled the depth of the wing.

Northrop A-17A, 34th Attack Squadron, "A" Flight Commander's airplane, 17th Attack Group. Oakland, California, 1938.

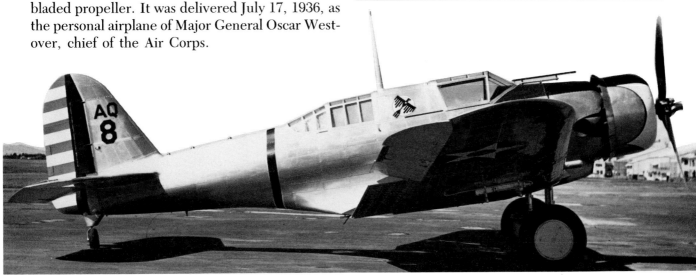

NACA decided its wind tunnel could give better data. Tests of an elongated cowling and nose spinner that contained blowing ducts for engine cooling on the ground were more successful. The Langley people referred to the airplane as "the nose-blower Northrop."

The A-17s of Barksdale Field's and March Field's attack group squadrons were gradually supplemented and replaced by the newer and speedier A-17A attack bombers. The older planes were transferred to training commands and then to lesser duties as transports and hacks with other scattered units.

What was it like to fly the Northrop A-17?

The following, excerpted and condensed from an account by Second Lieutenant Boardman C. Reed, tells of a flight made on January 11, 1941, from McChord Field, Tacoma, Washington:

. . . easing the throttle back to high idle, I note the oil temp is slowly climbing back toward operational limits. . . . It was a great feeling to be a young Air Corps officer . . . not a worry . . . the Battle of Britain was off in another world and Pearl Harbor merely the name of some faraway naval base. . . .

Cowl flaps full open, instruments "in the green" . . . throttle back and I nod to the crew chief to pull the chocks. Easing on a little power we begin to roll and I pick up the big hand mike.

"Aah, McChord Tower, this is Army 35-129, give me taxi instructions." The new, condensed radio discipline was almost upon us.

"Okay, A-17, you're clear to the runway, following those B-18s."

This was the only A-17 on the bomber base. I watch the big silver bombers from my own 34th Squadron lumber along the taxiway toward the northeast end of the field and follow well behind them . . . "essing" constantly with a touch of alternate brake pedals to see around the big blind nose . . . got to get used to the feel of an A-17, seeing as how I'd never soloed one before. . . . The B-18s buzz off. . . . I quarter into the wind . . . set brakes . . . cowl flaps in trail . . . 1,750 RPM . . . engine instruments quivering under their normal green arcs . . . check mag switches: LEFT 70 drop, RIGHT 50 drop, BOTH . . . check carburetor heat . . . cycle the hydraulic propeller . . . throttle back . . . check flight controls for free movement . . . canopy locked open . . . pull the goggles down over my eyes . . . check my watch . . . call the tower . . . "Clear to go" . . . head into the wind on the main runway . . . and give her the gun. . . .

The big, 750-hp Twin Wasp, Jr., bellows . . . the three-bladed Ham Standard disappears into a silver arc . . . nose swings left a little . . . add a bit more right rudder to hold her straight . . . rolling smooth, fast and getting light . . . tentatively ease back on the

stick ever so slightly, and the big blue-and-yellow Northrop leaps into her element.

Reduce manifold pressure and RPM to climb power . . . level off at seven thousand over green earth, blue water, and pretty white clouds . . . cruise power . . . ease mixture control back nearly halfway with a sharp eye on the tach, then forward a freckle when the RPM first starts to drop . . . cowl flaps closed . . . recheck instruments . . . going to try a few stalls.

Ease back on the big military throttle . . . increasing pressure on the stick grip . . . airspeed drops off as the nose rises above the horizon . . . 70 mph and falling . . . a slight buffet, then a shudder . . . stick full back, wing stalls and the nose drops abruptly . . . walk the rudder to hold her straight . . . ease the stick and throttle forward and we're flying again . . . nothing to it . . . just like a rocking chair . . . now the same thing in both right and left turns. . . . Next, an experiment with a secondary stall by jerking the stick back sharply, at low speed . . . in a flash we're over on our back . . . keep that in mind at low altitude and in the traffic pattern . . . roll out smoothly and regain altitude . . . try a couple of gentle stalls with full flaps . . . very nice . . . bring mixture, RPM, and manifold pressure up to climb power again . . . the deep, heavy bark of the exhaust stack and the cool, crisp air reminds us to slide our canopies closed . . . 10,500 feet . . . level off at cruise power.

From earlier flights in Army Northrops, Lieutenant Reed visualizes the cockpit to the rear, as the gunner might be thinking:

You settle back, raise your goggles, shift slightly on your firm parachute seat-pack. . . . You also have stick, rudder, engine, and prop controls, but doubt you could land the big brute sitting so far back with practically no forward visibility. You can scan the rear panel; a few basic instruments . . . they're all up front . . . just an altimeter, airspeed, and compass. . . .

You note the distance separating pilot and gunner . . . must be three feet or more. . . . How would you talk to each other if the interphone went out? . . . . Then you notice the flex cable on the right side with pulley and crank for each man and a spring-loaded clip for holding notes; primitive but practical! Near the relief tube you discover the lever under your seat for rotating and facing the rear (*after* you remove and stow the control stick) to fire the .30 caliber machine gun (*if* it were installed). The A-17 would have been a hot attack ship in World War One . . . even ten or fifteen years later, maybe . . . but [in] 1941, with neither armor nor self-sealing tanks, it would be a flaming coffin. . . . You're glad this flight is just for fun. . . .

Lieutenant Reed resumes his own musings:

. . . wonder how this compares with the old Northrop Gamma? After all the A-17 is a development by the same engineers . . . more power . . . or even the Northrop Delta cabin job . . . always wanted to get a hop in one . . . still do . . . and here I am flying an Army Northrop . . . biggest, most powerful ship I've ever soloed, so far. . . .

Time to return and shoot a couple of landings. . . . "Hello, McChord Tower? This is Army 35-129 entering your pattern from the northwest. Give me landing instructions, please."

Mixture RICH . . . prop pitch HIGH RPM . . . throttle 16″ or 17″ on the manifold pressure gauge . . . canopy open and goggles down . . . wheels down . . . (Ha! they're *always* down!) . . . little less throttle . . . base leg, turning final . . . full flaps . . . 85 mph . . . over the fence . . . chop the throttle, ease back on the stick . . . a little more . . . more. . . . tail wheel touches and the mains follow instantly . . . rolling smoothly and slowing down . . . flaps UP . . . stay off the brakes until ready to turn . . . taxi back and take it around the pattern a couple of more times . . . the crew chief is watching . . . waiting for us on the ramp . . . taxi up and swing around . . . hold the toe brakes . . . Mixture IDLE CUT OFF . . . prop clanks to a stop . . . Switch OFF . . . wheel chocks in place . . . radio, generator, and master switches OFF . . . fill out Forms 1 and 1A . . . "No problems, Sergeant, you keep a clean airplane" . . . Chute over my shoulder, helmet and goggles in hand, I walk away. . . .

In the rush of world rearmament and the development of new concepts of air power, the Northrop A-17/A-17A was a victim of early obsolescence. Although following the American war maneuvers of 1938–39 the plane was declared to be "the most effective ground attack aircraft yet devised," the new Air Corps thinking was toward the advantages of two-engined airplanes for attack and bombardment. Though a good, dependable aircraft, well liked by its pilots, the A-17A was in first-line service for less than three years.

By 1939, all the remaining A-17A attack bombers in the USAAC were declared surplus. World War II had begun in Europe, and the British and French, facing Germany, were desperately in need of *any* military aircraft. Ninety-three of the American Northrops were sent to El Segundo for new engines and refurbishing by the Douglas Company. Released for sale, they were snapped up by a French purchasing commission. In France, the Air Ministry had been impressed by the dive-bombing of the Luftwaffe's "stukas" over Poland and wanted airplanes, new or used, with similar capabilities. Ferried east with temporary civil markings in wash paint, the A-17As were stranded when the French armies capitulated to the Germans in June 1940.

Great Britain took over the French orders, and two lots of A-17As were crated up and sent by sea to England. Under the name Nomad, the Northrops were evaluated by the Royal Air Force. Even in dire straits and under daily German attack, during this confused period of the war the British could conceive of no role for what had recently been America's first-line attack bomber.

Northrop Nomad as refurbished by Douglas and delivered to the Royal Canadian Air Force during World War II.

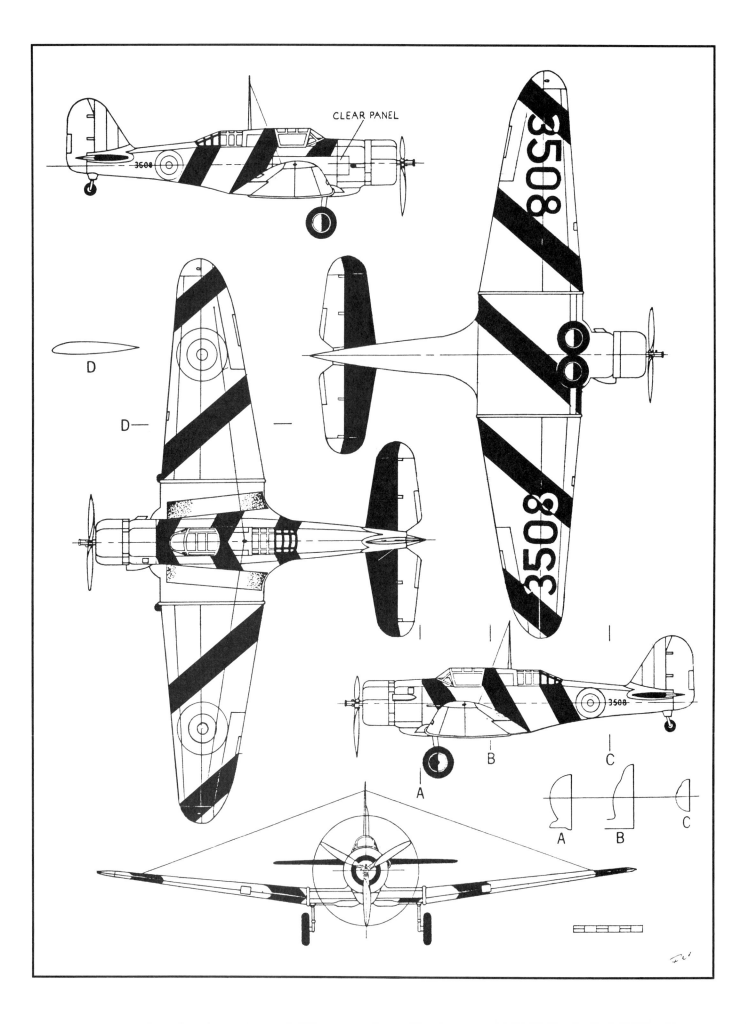

CLEAR PANEL

3508

3508

3508

D

D

A

B

C

A

B

C

Opposite: *Three-view of Canadian Northrop Nomad (former A-17A).*

All but four of the RAF's Nomads were reportedly redelivered to the South African air force for use as trainers and target tugs. In the United States, the remaining thirty-two A-17As of the French order were supposedly to go aboard the French aircraft carrier *Bearne* for transport to Free French soil in Martinique.

In actuality, still in their temporary U.S. ferry marks, the planes were hustled over the border into Canada, where the Royal Canadian Air Force took them on strength in August 1940. Also called Nomads by the Canadians, they were used as conversion trainers and to give check flights for the many civilian pilots who offered their services to the RCAF. Major and minor crashes reduced their numbers. The survivors were modified in 1941, becoming target tugs for air-to-air practice firing, and were assigned to No. 4, No. 6, and No. 9 Bombing and Gunnery schools in Quebec and Ontario. Painted yellow, they were made further distinguishable by wide black stripes diagonally painted across the wings and fuselage.

Though not considered a particularly outstanding aircraft, the Canadian Nomads provided reliable service in mundane chores, some logging flight times of up to 3,000 hours. After four and a half years of wartime service, the last RCAF Northrop Nomad was struck off strength at Uplands in June 1945. None went to ground schools and none were made available to civilian purchasers; they all were immediately scrapped in the "rush to normalcy" which followed the end of World War II.

Of all the Northrop-built military airplanes of the 1930s, only those of the Chinese air force, the secondhand civilian planes of the Spanish Civil War, and the Norwegian N-3PBs (discussed in chapter 12) appear to have ever fired a shot or dropped a bomb in anger.

The Douglas Aircraft Company's El Segundo Division went on to produce a number of military variants of the basic Northrop A-17 design. The name died hard. Although the former corporation had passed completely out of existence, the subsequent Douglas-built aircraft have usually been known as Northrops, and for a while they even continued the original series of constructor's numbers initiated in 1932.

Douglas-built was the 8A series of aircraft for export, continuing the basic USAAC A-17 configuration with many modifications. An engineless Douglas 8A-1 went to Sweden in April 1938, where it served as the pilot model for 103 others built with British Pegasus and Hercules power plants. Thirty 8A-2s—an A-17 with the old Gamma-style external bomb racks and Wright engines—were shipped in 1938 to Buenos Aires, for incorporation into the Fuera Aérea Argentina. The same year, the Cuerpo de Aeronáutica del Peru ordered ten 8A-3Ps, again with the Wright engine but with the Gamma-type retractable lower gun position. Three of the order were flown from California in a little less than twenty-five hours; the rest went on a slow boat.

The Dutch bought eighteen 8A-3Ns, similar to the Peruvian jobs, late in 1939, only to have them wiped out in the German invasion the following spring. In 1940 the government of Iraq got fifteen Model 8A-4s, a further version of the Peruvian planes. They are believed to have all been destroyed by the Royal Air Force in the little-known action taken to crush an Iraqi uprising under Rashid Ali.

Finally, there was a Douglas 8A-5 model, with a 1,200-hp Wright Cyclone engine—the most powerful of the lot. Armament was added, too: an extra

Northrop/Douglas 8A-5, one of five delivered in 1940 to the Norwegian Air Force Training Center in Canada.

pair of .50 caliber machine guns in the wings, and upper *and* lower guns for the rear cockpit. The aircraft could carry 1,200 pounds of bombs externally, plus thirty 30-pound bombs in the chutes inside.

Thirty-six of this last and most formidable of the Northrop/Douglas attack bombers were ordered by the Norwegian government early in 1940. After Norway was overrun, five of the planes were delivered to the Norwegian air force training center in Canada. The balance were taken over by the USAAC. Though termed the A-33 because of their attack configuration, the airplanes were never armed and served out their brief military lives as prosaic advanced trainers.

Simultaneously with its efforts to win an Army contract, The Northrop Corporation wooed the United States Navy. The Navy's Bureau of Aeronautics was interested in new fighters, particularly monoplanes, and the service's major suppliers, Boeing, Curtiss, and Vought, were hastening to comply. Against this well-entrenched competition, on a prototype order of May 8, 1933, Northrop produced a trim, single-cockpit fighter. It was called, in Navy parlance, the XFT-1.

Jack Northrop conceived the Navy plane as a scaled-down version of the big Gamma, and it looked it. A team headed by Edward A. Heinemann engineered the ship into reality. Powered by a 625-hp Wright R-1510-20 engine, the XFT-1 was

only the Navy's second type of experimental monoplane fighter. Sturdy, cleanly streamlined, with neat, trouser-faired landing gear, it was fitted for two .30 caliber machine guns mounted just ahead of the cockpit, firing through the propeller. Two 116-pound bombs could be hung below the center section.

Finished early in January 1934, the Northrop XFT-1 was first flown the same month by Vance Breese, and was delivered east to Anacostia Naval Air Station in February. Evaluation by naval pilots showed the Northrop could do 235 mph at 6,000 feet. This made it the fastest thing on Navy wings. It had the lethal "look" of a fighter and promised good performance. Still, the service test pilots, used to slower, more readily maneuverable biplanes, found flying the XFT-1 a bit tricky. Even when it was fitted with split flaps, landings were difficult to control. Tail buffeting occurred during spin tests, and there were misgivings about forward visibility for an airplane expected to be able to fly off the decks of the big new airplane carriers.

Twice the XFT-1 was returned to Northrop for modifications. The second time it got a twin-row Pratt & Whitney R-1535-72 engine, the heavier weight of which meant reducing the useful fuel capacity to only 80 gallons.

Now called the XFT-2, the shiny metal fighter again made the journey to Anacostia, but bad spin characteristics still marred the otherwise improved performance. It was slated for return to the factory once again. While being ferried across the ridges of the Alleghenies on July 21, 1936, the XFT-2 ran

Navy experimental fighter XFT-1.

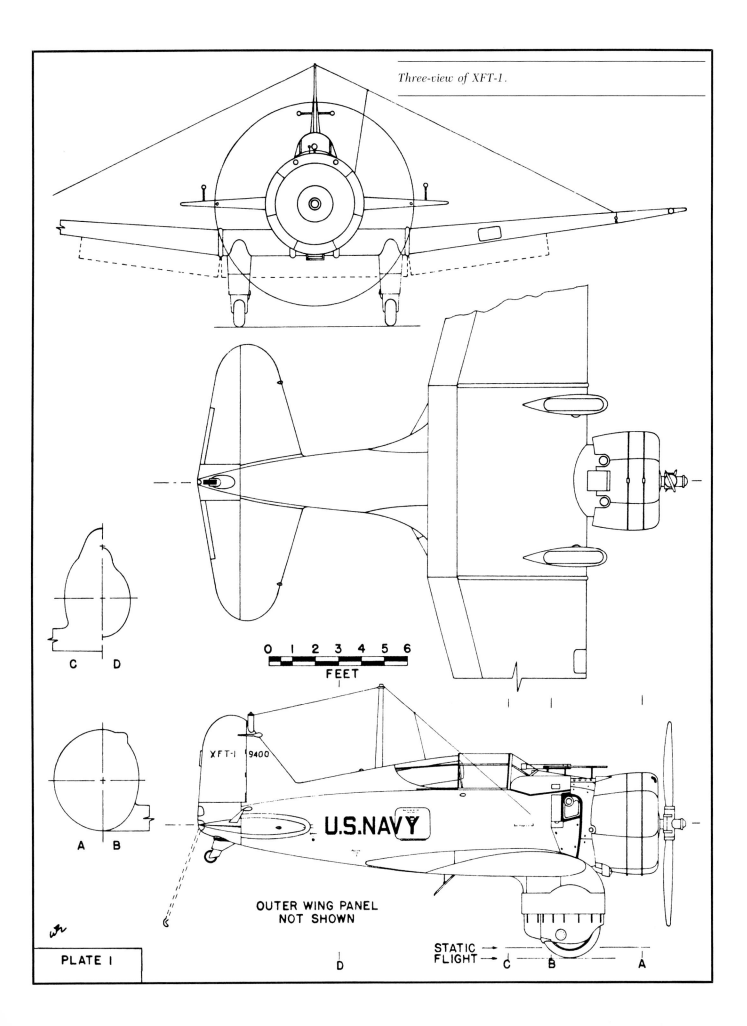

Three-view of XFT-1.

0 1 2 3 4 5 6
FEET

XFT-1 9400

U.S.NAVY

OUTER WING PANEL
NOT SHOWN

C   D

A   B

STATIC
FLIGHT

D   C   B   A

PLATE 1

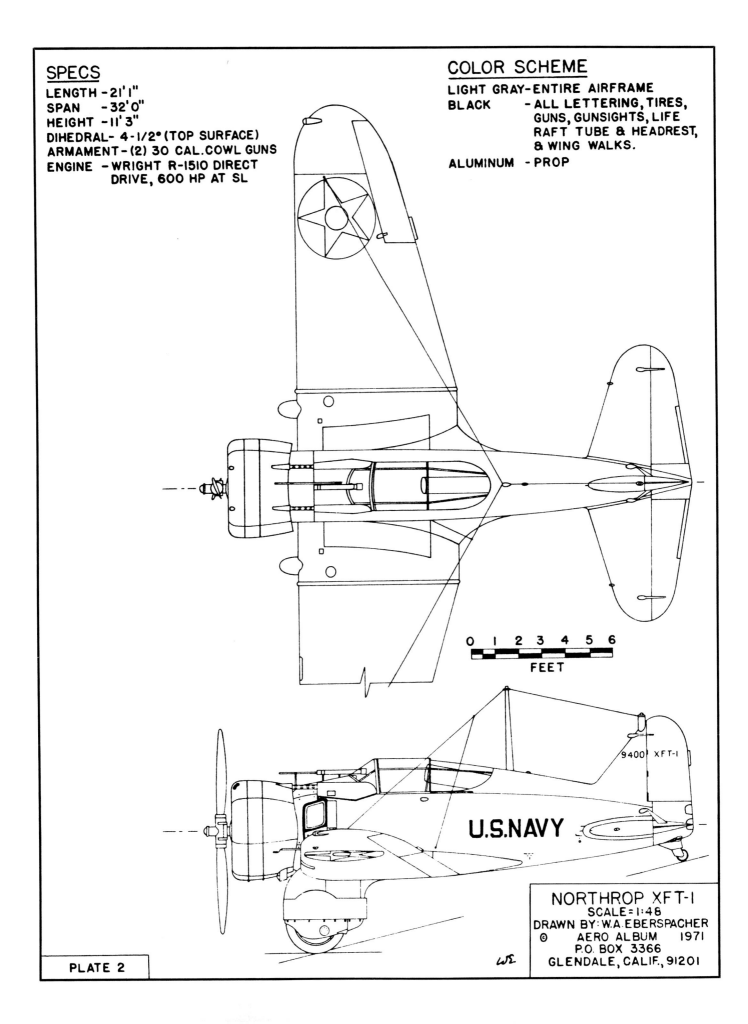

SPECS
LENGTH – 21'1"
SPAN – 32'0"
HEIGHT – 11'3"
DIHEDRAL – 4-1/2° (TOP SURFACE)
ARMAMENT – (2) 30 CAL. COWL GUNS
ENGINE – WRIGHT R-1510 DIRECT
DRIVE, 600 HP AT SL

COLOR SCHEME
LIGHT GRAY – ENTIRE AIRFRAME
BLACK – ALL LETTERING, TIRES,
GUNS, GUNSIGHTS, LIFE
RAFT TUBE & HEADREST,
& WING WALKS.

ALUMINUM – PROP

9400 XFT-1

U.S. NAVY

0 1 2 3 4 5 6
FEET

NORTHROP XFT-1
SCALE = 1:48
DRAWN BY: W.A. EBERSPACHER
© AERO ALBUM 1971
P.O. BOX 3366
GLENDALE, CALIF., 91201

PLATE 2

into turbulence. As was prophesied by the Navy test pilots, a spin did it in.

In addition to fighter planes, the Navy needed other types of aircraft. In June 1934, the Bureau of Aeronautics set up specifications for a new carrier-based dive-bomber and invited manufacturers to bid on its design and construction.

For Northrop, dive-bomber competition would come from new naval biplanes built by the Curtiss, Great Lakes, and Grumman companies, and monoplanes from the drawing boards of Brewster and Vought. Jack Northrop and Ed Heinemann's team set to work. As for the Navy fighter of the previous year, they used the Northrop Gamma as a basis. This time they introduced a retractable landing gear—one that folded backward into large, protruding pods below the wings. In theory, should the landing gear give trouble, the plane could be skidded in on the pods. The split flaps were to be used either in the conventional manner or as the dive-braking system desirable in a dive-bomber. Northrop and Heinemann submitted convincing performance figures with their proposal.

The Navy liked it. It chose the design over those of the other five competitors and gave Northrop an order for a prototype in November 1934. This was just ahead of the Army order for A-17s, which came the next month. Working on orders for both the services simultaneously had both advantages and disadvantages. The first Navy dive-bomber, the XBT-1, was completed the following summer. Only one major problem came up during the ensuing test program, which began August 19, 1935. It was discovered that the use of the dive brakes produced a terrific buffeting action on the tail surfaces. Pieces threatened to shake off.

Running out of remedies, project engineer Heinemann submitted the problem to the National Advisory Committee for Aeronautics. After a series of wind-tunnel tests at NACA's laboratory at Langley Field, the committee recommended that the flaps be perforated. Accordingly, holes were drilled in the flaps of the prototype—large ones—and Vance Breese, on testing the ship, reported immediate improvement. Not only was the tail buffeting eliminated, but diving speed could be still further reduced, if desired. It was natural to call the new control surfaces "swiss-cheese" flaps, a name which stuck from then on.

The prototype Northrop XBT-1 was finally accepted by the Navy on December 12, 1935. This led, after minor modifications, to a contract for fifty-four airplanes, which was awarded nine months later. Mass aircraft orders for China, the Army, and now the Navy tripled Northrop production.

The number of Northrop BT-1s ordered suggests that they were to equip three aircraft carriers. In the event, as they were delivered to the fleet, thirty-six of them became the bombing squadrons of two flattops.

The eighteen airplanes of Bombing Five (VB5) aboard the U.S.S. *Yorktown* were identified by their red fins and rudders and the insignia of a winged head of Satan. The six three-plane sections of Bombing Six (VB6), flying off the U.S.S. *Enterprise*, had blue tails and a distinctive leaping wild goat insignia.

After flying Boeing and Curtiss fighting biplanes off pitching decks to make simulated dive-bombing runs, the carrier pilots at first found the Northrops slow and awkward to handle. One description compared landing the monoplane on the *Yorktown* to "guiding a winged bathtub to safety atop a storage tank." The airplane's designation, BT-1 (Bomber/Torpedo), was occasionally corrupted to "bastard terror."

Despite the teething problems and continuing efforts to solve stall characteristics, the BT-1 was gradually accepted by the pilots and crews of the *Yorktown* and *Enterprise*.

Northrop BT-1 of UB-5, U.S.S. Yorktown, *Oakland, California.*

One of the Northrops was delivered with an experimental fixed tricycle landing gear, a forerunner of airplanes to come. This novel BT-1 had struts and wheels moved back and a nosewheel with an anti-shimmy device stuck far forward, but still clear of the whirling propeller. At Anacostia, while practicing dummy carrier landings, a naval pilot suffered engine failure and was nearly overcome by gasoline fumes. He managed a dead-stick crosswind landing and passed out. The "tricycle ship" continued rolling and collided with another plane. There were no casualties, but tests of the tricycle landing gear were curtailed for a while. Douglas rebuilt the airplane as a DB-19 and eventually sold it to the Japanese navy.

At one time the Navy's Bureau of Aeronautics contemplated adapting Northrop BT-1s as parasite aircraft, to be carried on dirigibles. But loss of the Navy airships *Akron* and *Macon* and then the German commercial zeppelin *Hindenburg* led to cessation of the naval lighter-than-air program.

The last aircraft on the Navy contract, completed in July 1938, had a 1,000-hp Wright XR-1820-32 engine installed and the wheel pods were replaced with a simple fully retractable landing gear which folded into the wing. This was the Northrop XBT-2.

The standard Northrop BT-1s were kept in first-line service on the two aircraft carriers and naval air stations until early 1941, after which they were transferred to advance training bases, notably at Miami, Florida. They were replaced by direct descendants of the Northrop XBT-2, built by Douglas as the SBD-2. Known as the Douglas Dauntless, it would become America's most successful dive-bomber of World War II.

After Northrop won its attack-bomber contract in 1934, the company was spurred to make its entry into still another military field, that of fighter aircraft.

The Matériel Division of the Army Air Corps early in 1935 announced a design competition for a new single-place pursuit airplane. American aircraft manufacturers were invited to submit not just designs, but full-scale prototype airplanes built with their own money. The goal was an eventual replacement for the Boeing P-26, the stubby externally braced fixed-gear fighter which had been the Army's principal fighter plane for three years. Curtiss was entering its Model 75, and the new Seversky Aircraft Corporation had a single-seat version of its SEV-2XP amphibian in the works.

Northrop put Ed Heinemann and his team on the project. It had to be done quickly, as competition evaluation at Wright Field was slated to begin May 27, 1935. Fresh from design and development of the XFT-1 carrier fighter for the Navy, the Heinemann team came up with a neat variant sporting fully retractable landing gear, the Northrop 3A. Powered by a 700-hp, fourteen-cylinder Pratt & Whitney Twin Wasp, Jr., engine, the 3A pursuit plane for the Army was only 150 pounds heavier than its Navy counterpart.

The USAAC fighter competition deadline was postponed until August, but despite great haste, the Northrop 3A was not completed until July. The ship was given preliminary testing at Mines Field and then ferried east. The first commentary from the Matériel Division's people confirmed Northrop's own quickly made test reports: the plane was "rather unstable and prone to spins." Back to California went the speedy, streamlined little fighter, in the hope that some miraculous and quick solution to the stability problem could be found. Due to be Army-tested again as the XP-948, the Northrop pursuit entry got some new modifications just before it was due to return to Wright Field.

Late in the afternoon of July 30, 1935, Arthur H. Skaer, an Air Corps reservist and pilot for Northrop, took the fighter prototype for a test hop. He was last seen over Málaga Cove near Palos Verdes Estates on the Pacific. No trace of either airplane or pilot was ever found.

The disappearance of the prototype put Northrop out of the competition for a new Army pursuit plane. To regain a little of its interest in time and money and offset the agonizing loss, the design rights and plans of the 3A were sold to Chance Vought Aircraft of East Hartford, Connecticut, long a manufacturer of naval scouting aircraft. The Northrop fighter design reappeared as the Vought Model V-141, but failed to win any acceptance from the Air Corps. A modified version, the V-143, with longer fuselage and redesigned tail, was brought out for the military export market and demonstrated in South America by Eddie Allen. It was eventually sold to the Japanese and has erroneously been reported to have inspired the famous Zero fighter.

The Northrop Corporation had extreme good fortune in receiving contracts from both the Army's Air Corps and the Navy's Bureau of Aeronautics.

While awaiting word on acceptance of the Northrop attack bomber in 1934–35, the company went after still another military plum. This was an Army competition for a new advanced training airplane.

The entry from El Segundo was called the Northrop Gamma 2J, a private-venture three-seater with standard Gamma wings, but a new, elongated fuselage and the fully retractable landing gear being tried and tested on what would become the A-17A attack bomber.

Completed in December 1935, the Gamma 2J lost the advanced-trainer competition to North American Aviation's NA-26 (BC-1). The 2J was kept by Douglas as an all-round work plane for six years, until sold locally in 1944.

Other military uses of early Northrop airplanes are four which served with the United States Army Engineers during World War II.

In 1941, Charlie Babb, whose aircraft brokerage firm now operated on both coasts, dusted off the wreckage of a couple of Northrop airplanes he'd had lying around for a while. There was the TWA No. 16, the airline's first Gamma, in which Jack Frye had survived a forced landing in Arizona, and the damaged old former Coast Guard Delta in which Secretary Henry Morganthau once had flown in style. A third ship was the former Russell Thaw/Guggenheim Gamma, which had been wrecked while owned by Bernarr Macfadden. And Babb bought intact and complete the Northrop Delta formerly flown by Seward Webb Pulitzer.

Charlie Babb had all four airplanes fixed up and sold them to the Army Engineers in 1942. During the war the Corps of Engineers operated all over the world, in theaters of war and far from them. Some of their projects have never been fully documented.

One of the engineers' projects was Canol, the Canadian oil pipeline considered vital to defense.

On this the ex-Pulitzer Delta and the Macfadden Gamma were flown by both the Army Air Transport Command and a private contractor, Bechtel-Price-Callahan Company, transporting supplies and men to the project. On completion of the Canol work and of the Alaskan Highway project, the planes were considered surplus. It is reported that "on orders from some bullet-headed general," the Delta and Gamma, together with four other obsolete but still flyable airplanes, were simply bulldozed into a pile and burned.

The TWA single-place Gamma and the former Coast Guard Delta were transferred to Babb's New York City affiliate and then to the Engineers and probably went overseas. The Gamma was laconically reported by Babb as "wrecked in Africa."

A fifth World War II "draftee" was the well-known Northrop Gamma used as TWA's Experimental Overweather Laboratory by Tommy Tomlinson and later for lubricant-testing as *Texaco 36*. The Texas Company sold the ship directly to the War Department in October 1942 and received $11,225 for it. The big Gamma was given an Air Corps serial number and an Army designation—the one and only UC-100.

Presumably put to use transporting cargo, the UC-100 was assigned to Duncan Field in Texas, where it soon suffered an accident. The Gamma was repaired, but a "shortage of parts" was duly noted. In September 1943, the nine-year-old Northrop, pioneer in substratospheric flying, was "surveyed"—i.e., scrapped—at Kelly Field, Texas. This was the only single-place cargo airplane to be carried on the all-time roster of the United States Army Air Corps.

Gamma 2J2 as tested by USAAC. Rejected, it became a Northrop company hack.

11

MAP THE BUSH, SCOUT THE SEA-LANES

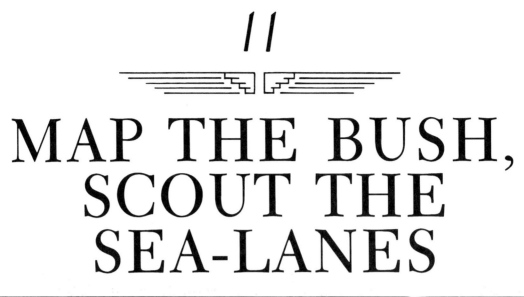

O n the St. Lawrence River at the foot of Viau Street in Montreal was the factory, floating dry dock, and ship basin of Canadian Vickers, Ltd. As a subsidiary of England's Vickers armaments firm, it had built a variety of aircraft, flying boats in particular. On becoming Canadian-owned in 1927, the Montreal plant undertook the manufacture of Fairchild FC-2s, Fokker Super-Universals, and then Bellanca CH-300s, all under license arrangements.

During the 1930s Depression, manufacturing at Vickers barely sputtered along. For years, manager Richard J. Moffett and a permanent staff of three kept projects going. The Aircraft Department repaired Bellancas, designed floats, built an aluminum patrol boat, and even turned out pipe for

paper mills and stainless-steel kettles for a local brewery.

By 1935, the Royal Canadian Air Force had become interested in the acquisition of a high-speed aircraft adaptable for photography—one that could be mounted on floats for operations in mapping the far north of Canada. There was a lurking thought that the aircraft could, if necessary, be modified for military use.

Dick Moffett consulted with the RCAF and government officials in Ottawa. After a survey of current Canadian, English, and American airplanes,

Northrop Delta on floats, newly built at Canadian Vickers' Montreal factory.

the consensus favored the Northrop Delta. It was a period of "Buy British" sentiments, or at least "Buy Empire." Rather than buy Deltas direct from Northrop in California, why not build them in Canada? Moffett immediately obtained first a sales and then a manufacturing license. The Aircraft Department at Vickers would produce a "Canadian Delta" for the RCAF.

The bare components of one airplane, called a Delta 1D-8, were shipped from Inglewood to Montreal. Vickers had no hydraulic press and no experience whatever in manufacturing metal aircraft. The fixed price included tooling, and so Moffett and his increased engineering and working staff proceeded to build three more Deltas, using the parts from California as pilot models. The planes were built by hand-forming, using wooden blocks faced with steel and laboriously bending over the Alclad flanging. Though Canada was a major aluminum producer, the alloy had to be imported from the United States by special permission.

Working on the unheated assembly floor of the factory, the Canadians formed and fitted the fuselage halves together and rounded out wing curves and fillets. They added a larger, upward-opening freight door and designed and fitted the arrangements for photography. They adapted the Delta to fly on twin Vickers Type 75 floats, with which a top speed of 195 mph might be obtained. For operations on snow they used the Vickers Type F streamlined skis that had been developed by the Canadian National Research Council. These were equipped with the Ferrier trimming gear, which kept the skis level in flight.

With the plans from Northrop came design details for the Gamma 2E, in which the Chinese air force had mounted armament. A .30 caliber Browning machine gun was installed in *one* wing of the Canadian Deltas and bomb racks were fitted in the portion of the planes that retained the trousered undercarriage. The men at Vickers were cautioned not to mention these warlike appendages, but the RCAF was happy to make a few simulated bomb runs and loose a few rounds of ammunition over remote areas.

In 1936 the Vickers company could not afford a test pilot of its own. Fairchild pilot A. S. Schneider flew the first float-equipped Delta off the St. Lawrence River on August 21. Among others who made the initial flights in the succeeding ships were Herbert Hollick-Kenyon, who had piloted Lincoln Ellsworth's Northrop Gamma in the Antarctic, and the colorful French-Canadian bush pilot Romeo Vachon.

The Vickers Delta introduced Canada to all-metal aircraft production. The employment and knowledge gained in building twenty Northrops set the Vickers' Aircraft Department on the road to full capacity of its works during World War II, during which the company moved to Cartierville and became Canadair, Ltd.

At Rockcliffe, Ontario, a Canadian Delta is tested with three-ski landing gear.

The first Vickers Delta, on floats, was delivered to the Royal Canadian Air Force's Ottawa Air Station at Rockcliffe on September 1, 1936, followed by two more in October. Three Fairchild A3 automatic aerial cameras were mounted to the rear of the cabin, pointing downward and to the sides. Additional sister ships for use in the aerial survey program continued to emerge from the Montreal factory. The RCAF worked them north as the ice melted from the lakes of Ontario, Quebec, and the Northwest Territories and returned them to a fixed base in the fall. Detachments of two planes with a six-man allotment worked out of Ottawa, eastern Canada, and the west coast. One squadron, No. 6 GP (General Purpose), maintained communications, flying supplies, and surveyors in support of the photo planes in the north. To aid in the photography, it was found expedient to add extra windows to the sides below the cockpit and in the cabin floor.

Even before the lights went out in Europe, the RCAF had recalled all the photo aircraft and dispatched No. 6 GP Squadron's six float planes to Sydney, Nova Scotia. One Vickers Delta on wheels was assigned to No. 1 Fighter Squadron and used to train pilots who would fly Hawker Hurricanes, those built in Canada by the Canadian Car & Foundry Company of Fort William, Ontario.

A pair of Vickers-built Canadian Deltas as delivered to the RCAF.

By the time Canada declared war on Nazi Germany in September 1939, there were twelve Vickers Deltas in service, all photo planes. With the strength of the RCAF at low ebb, every airplane was required for defense. The machine guns went into *both* wings now, and an upper gun position to the rear was installed. Two Deltas were hurriedly fitted with a "turtleback" fairing ahead of the upper gun port. This caused so much buffeting that it was soon replaced by a plain hatch with a glass window.

Of the six planes dispatched to the defense of Sydney on August 27, 1939, one came to grief. Overflying Maine, Delta 673, flown by Flight Sergeant J. E. Doan and Leading Aircraftsman D. A. Rennie, force-landed with engine trouble. Parts were ferried by two other Deltas, which enabled Doan to get back over the Canadian border to Lac Megantic, Quebec. By September 14 a substitute engine had been fitted to 673. Doan and Rennie took off to join their squadron mates in Sydney. There were ample reports of the roar of the Cyclone's exhaust along the inhabited parts of their presumed route, but the airplane never reached Sydney. A grid-pattern search for the missing men was carried out for two months and then reluctantly abandoned.

Nearly nineteen years later, in July 1958, the wreckage of the Delta was discovered in the deep New Brunswick woods, some forty miles north of Fredericton. No trace of the pilot and crewman was ever found, and Doan and Rennie are listed as the

Royal Canadian Air Force's first casualties of World War II.

Flying out of North Sydney, the Delta squadron, now No. 8 BR (Bomber Reconnaissance), ranged out over the Atlantic to Sable Island and north to Newfoundland's Strait of Belle Isle. The float installations made for the placid lakes and rivers of the Canadian north were twisted in the ocean swells and their fittings were corroded by salt water. As reported by one Delta pilot, takeoffs and landings in Atlantic waters had to be made along the swell, no matter what the direction of the wind. Should a takeoff be attempted against an ocean swell, "the noise of popping rivets would be very much akin to machine-gun fire."

Because of a suspected spin problem, an antispin parachute was installed in the elongated tail cone of three of the RCAF Deltas. These and those built later had a redesigned vertical fin and rudder, which was tapered and moved farther forward on the fuselage.

During the summer and fall of 1940, eight more Vickers-built Deltas were taken on strength by the Royal Canadian Air Force. In No. 8 BR Squadron, they were gradually replaced by Canadian-built Bristol Bolingbrokes. Some of the Deltas were transferred to the west coast and flown out of Patricia Bay Air Force Station near Vancouver, British Columbia, by No. 120 BR Squadron.

By August of 1941 the commanding officer at Patricia Bay didn't know what to do with the Deltas. He wrote that they were "taking up space in the hangars." Dual-control instruction was ruled out, as there were no brakes for the right-hand seat. The CO recommended that the airplanes be used for target towing, radio training, or general communications duties. The Secretary of Defense thought otherwise. He decreed that all remaining Deltas were to be relegated to Canada's training schools, as instructional airframes. They could provide a quick course in modern metal aircraft construction. The last three, lashed to flatcars, trundled across the continent from British Columbia to St. Thomas, Ontario, in January, 1942.

Of the twenty Canadian Vickers Deltas, five were destroyed in accidents (three of them fatal), two were removed from service, and the remaining thirteen were sent to schools. Disassembled and reassembled over and over by students, these examples of Canada's first stressed-skin low-wing monoplane survived at some instruction centers as late as February 1945.

The incomplete and damaged parts of RCAF 673, recovered from the New Brunswick wilderness, are today retained, as the last vestige of a Canadian Vickers Delta, by the National Aviation Museum, now located at Rockcliffe, Ontario.

Below: *Canadians elongated the Delta's tail cone and redesigned the fin and rudder.*

Overleaf: *Three-view and exploded drawing of Canadian Vickers–built Northrop Delta.*

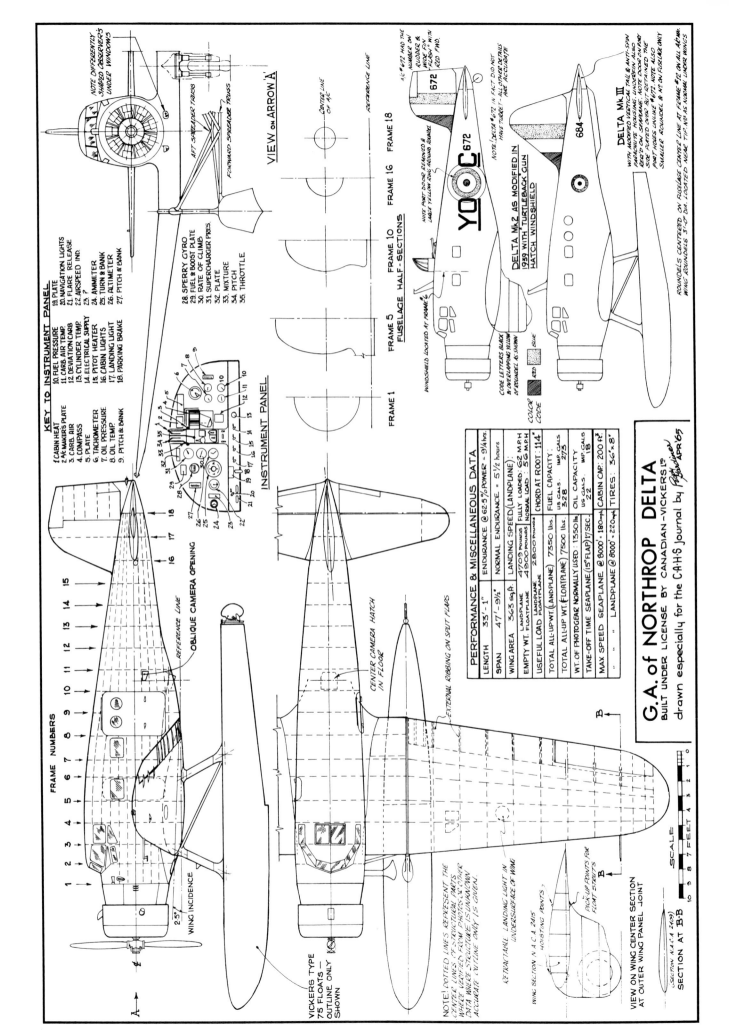

NOTE DIFFERENTLY SHADED OBSERVER'S UNDER WINDOWS

VIEW ON ARROW 'A'

AFT SPREADER TRUSS
FORWARD SPREADER TRUSS

CENTER LINE OF A/C
REFERENCE LINE

A/C #672 HAD THE NUMBER ON RUDDER & HELD FIN WITH FLAP FWD.

NOTE: DELTA #672 IN FACT DID NOT HAVE TURRET - ALL OTHER DETAILS ARE ACCURATE.

672

DELTA MK.2 AS MODIFIED IN 1939 WITH TURTLEBACK GUN HATCH WINDSHIELD

684

DELTA Mk. III

WITH MODIFIED VERTICAL TAIL & ANTI-SPIN PARACHUTE HOUSING ON RUDDER. ALSO SQ. PLATED OVER BUT RETAINED THE PART HOLES UNLIKE #672. NOTE ALSO SMALLER ROUNDEL & Nº ON FUSELAGE ONLY

ROUNDELS CENTERED ON FUSELAGE CENTER LINE AT FRAME #12 (ON ALL A/C)·WING ROUNDELS 31'-0" DIA. LOCATED NEAR TIP, Nº's NORMALLY UNDER WINGS

FRAME 1   FRAME 5   FRAME 10   FRAME 16   FRAME 18
FUSELAGE HALF-SECTIONS

WINDSHIELD LOCATED AT FRAME 'G'

CODE LETTERS BLACK IN OVERLAPPING YELLOW OF ROUNDEL AS SHOWN

COLOR CODE
■ RED   ▒ BLUE

KEY TO INSTRUMENT PANEL

1 CABIN HEAT
2 A/c MAKER'S PLATE
3 CARB. AIR
4 COMPASS
5 PLATE
6 TACHOMETER
7 OIL PRESSURE
8 OIL TEMP.
9 PITCH & BANK
10 FUEL PRESSURE
11 CARB. AIR TEMP.
12 DEVIATION CARB
13 CYLINDER TEMP.
14 ELECTRICAL SUPPLY
15 PITOT HEATER
16 CABIN LIGHTS
17 LANDING LIGHT
18 PARKING BRAKE
19 PLATE
20 NAVIGATION LIGHTS
21 FLARE RELEASE
22 AIRSPEED IND.
23 ?
24 AMMETER
25 TURN & BANK
26 ALTIMETER
27 PITCH & BANK
28 SPERRY GYRO
29 RATE OF BOOST PLATE
30 RATE OF CLIMB
31 SUPERCHARGER PRES.
32 PLATE
33 MIXTURE
34 PITCH
35 THROTTLE

INSTRUMENT PANEL

FRAME NUMBERS

1 2 3 4 5 6 7 8 9 10 11 12 13 14 15

16 17 18

REFERENCE LINE
OBLIQUE CAMERA OPENING

2.5°
WING INCIDENCE

VICKERS TYPE 75 FLOATS — OUTLINE ONLY SHOWN

CENTER CAMERA HATCH IN FLOOR

EXTERNAL RIBBING ON SPLIT FLAPS

NOTE! DOTTED LINES REPRESENT THE CENTER LINES OF STRUCTURAL PARTS WHERE VERIFIED FROM PHOTOS & OTHER DATA WHERE STRUCTURE IS UNKNOWN ACCURATE OUTLINE ONLY IS GIVEN.

RETRACTABLE LANDING LIGHT IN UNDERSURFACE OF WING

WING SECTION N.A.C.A. 2415
HOISTING POINTS

PICK-UP POINTS FOR FLOAT STRUTS

B
B
B

VIEW ON WING CENTER SECTION AT OUTER WING PANEL JOINT

SECTION N.A.C.A. 2409
SECTION AT B-B

SCALE
10 9 8 7 FEET 4 3 2 1 0

PERFORMANCE & MISCELLANEOUS DATA		
LENGTH	33'-1"	
SPAN	47'-9½"	
WING AREA	363 sq.ft.	
ENDURANCE @ 62.5% POWER = 9¼ hrs.		
NORMAL ENDURANCE = 5½ hours		
LANDING SPEED (LANDPLANE):		
EMPTY WT. LANDPLANE	4709 POUNDS FULLY LOADED:	62 M.P.H.
FLOATPLANE	4900 POUNDS NORMAL LOAD:	56 M.P.H.
USEFUL LOAD LANDPLANE	2800 POUNDS	CHORD AT ROOT: 114"
FLOATPLANE		
TOTAL ALL-UP WT. (LANDPLANE)	7350 lbs.	FUEL CAPACITY:
TOTAL ALL-UP WT. (FLOATPLANE)	7500 lbs.	US GALS. 328 IMP. GALS. 273
WT. OF PHOTOGEAR NORMALLY (USED) : 1550 lbs.		OIL CAPACITY
TAKE-OFF TIME SEAPLANE (15° FLAP) 17/SEC.		US GALS. 22 IMP. GALS. 18
MAX SPEED SEAPLANE @ 8000' 180 mph		CABIN CAP: 200 ft³.
" " LANDPLANE @ 8000' 220 mph		TIRES: 36"×8"

G.A. of NORTHROP DELTA

BUILT UNDER LICENSE BY CANADIAN-VICKERS LT⁰.

drawn especially for the C.A.H.S. Journal by Peuviner APR 65

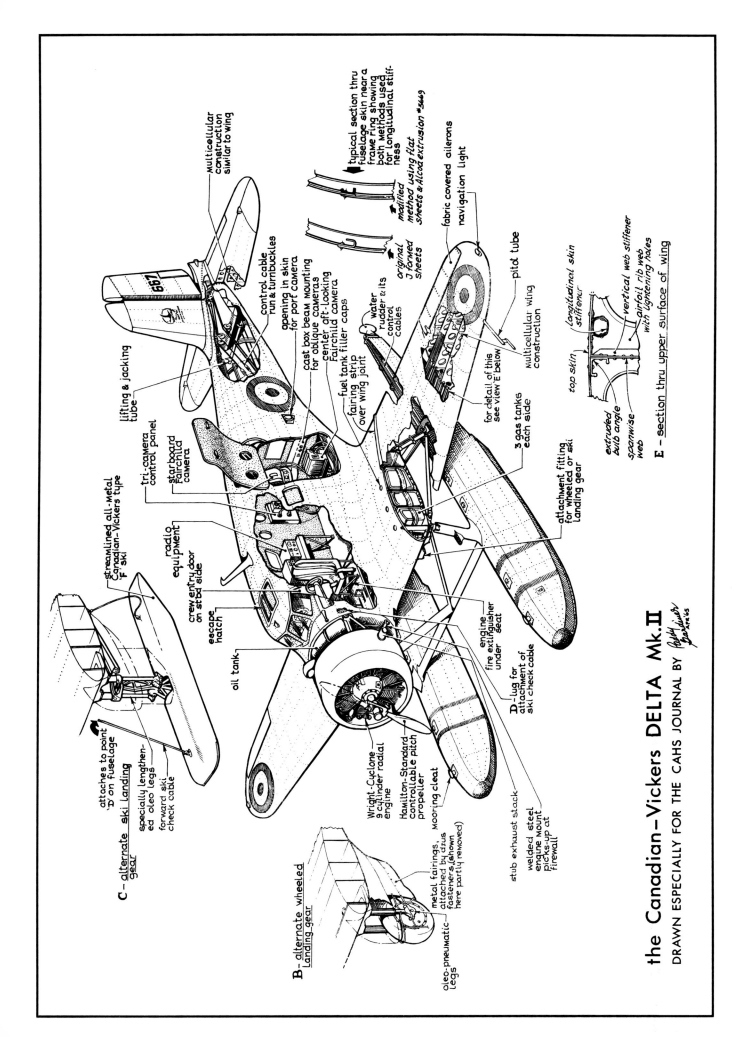

the Canadian-Vickers DELTA Mk.II

DRAWN ESPECIALLY FOR THE CAHS JOURNAL BY

multicellular construction similar to wing

typical section thru a fuselage skin near a frame ring showing both methods used for longitudinal stiffness

modified method using flat sheets & Alcoa extrusion #3649

original J formed sheets

fabric covered ailerons

navigation light

control cable run & turnbuckles

opening in skin for port camera

cast box beam mounting for oblique cameras

center aft-looking Fairchild camera

fuel tank filler caps

fairing strip over wing joint

water rudder & its control cables

pitot tube

multicellular wing construction

for detail of this see view 'E' below

3 gas tanks each side

attachment fitting for wheeled or ski landing gear

lifting & jacking tube

tri-camera control panel

starboard Fairchild camera

radio equipment

crew entry door on stbd side

escape hatch

oil tank

engine fire extinguisher under seat

D-lug for attachment of ski check cable

Wright-Cyclone 9 cylinder radial engine

Hamilton-Standard controllable pitch propeller

mooring cleat

stub exhaust stack

welded steel engine mount picks-up at firewall

C - alternate ski landing gear

streamlined all-metal Canadian-Vickers type 'F' ski

attaches to point 'D' on fuselage

specially lengthened oleo legs

forward ski check cable

B - alternate wheeled landing gear

metal fairings, attached by dzus fasteners (shown here partly removed)

oleo-pneumatic legs

E - section thru upper surface of wing

top skin

longitudinal skin stiffener

vertical web stiffener

airfoil rib web with lightening holes

extruded bulb angle

spanwise web

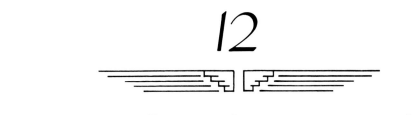

12

PATROLS IN THE DENMARK STRAIT

After his resignation from Douglas Aircraft's El Segundo Division, John K. Northrop spent several unencumbered months determining what to do next. He wanted a company staffed with competent engineers—one that would be small and free from the chores of never-ending production. The idea was to develop advanced designs. Northrop's dream of a real flying wing had been kept in abeyance for a decade.

Starting again, Jack Northrop established Northrop Aircraft, Inc., in August 1939. Associated with him in this company were some of the best people in their fields. La Motte Turck Cohu had served as president of American Airlines and gone on to TWA. As an experienced financial manager and labor-relations man, Cohu became chairman of the board and general manager.

Northrop's longtime associate Gage H. Irving, who had transferred from active flying to plant op-

erations, became vice-president and assistant general manager. Northrop himself was named president and chief engineer.

To this trio were added Edward Bellande—the Eddie Bellande who had first flown Northrop's Lockheed Vega and the Avion back in the '20s—and another well-known test pilot, Moye Stephens.

As secretary of the new company as well as flight chief, Stephens scouted southern California in search of a factory site that could be bought or rented at a reasonable rate. He shortly leased a 72-acre piece of property at Hawthorne, California, to the southwest of the Los Angeles Municipal Airport at Inglewood.

Northrop Aircraft, Inc., with six employees,

Northrop N3PB is test-flown over Lake Elsinore in California.

114

started business in the old yellow-painted Hotel Hawthorne. In the space of six months a new 122,000-square-foot factory was built, adjacent to a new mile-long airport, christened Northrop Field.

Since war had broken out in Europe, practicality dictated that Jack Northrop's conception of a pure aeronautical engineering, research, and development company would have to be shelved, at least for a while. La Motte Cohu ascertained that there was considerable business to be had making parts for the bigger and busier aircraft manufacturers who held contracts with the Army and Navy and the foreign powers already battling in Europe.

From San Diego, Major Reuben Fleet's Consolidated Aircraft gave Northrop a subcontract early in 1940 to build tail sections for its PBY-5s. This was soon extended to include engine cowlings and seat installations for the Navy planes. (Later the company would be firmly into manufacturing, with British and American orders for the Vultee V-72 Vengeance, a single-engined dive-bomber, built under royalty arrangements with Vultee.)

With Britain and France at war with Germany and neutral nations in danger of being drawn into the conflict, the overseas sale of airplanes looked good to Cohu and Northrop. A good friend of both, Bernt Balchen, had carefully watched the assembly of the first Northrop Gammas back in 1933. Now Balchen induced a purchasing commission from his native Norway to have a look at the spanking-new Northrop plant in Hawthorne.

Commander Kristian Ostby of the Norwegian naval air force had a specification for a coastal reconnaissance and torpedo bomber, one that could be flown closely along his country's rocky, fjord-indented coast. Ostby's specification of March 7, 1940, called for a patrol bomber on floats with a maximum speed of 200 mph, a 1-ton weapons load, and an operational range of 625 miles. Northrop and his new engineering team of Walter Cerny, Francis Johnson, Ray Gaskell, and Tom Quayle set to work on it, together with project engineer Fred Baum.

The team already had a design for a Northrop 8A with increased weight and improved performance, called the Model N-3 attack bomber. Hasty provisions were made for ski or float gear. The design was shown to Commander Ostby, who suggested minor changes and improvements, and in just five days Northrop had its first contract for its own new airplane. Twenty-four Northrop N-3PB (Patrol

Bomber) seaplanes were to be delivered to the Norwegian navy over the next ten months. The price was $57,325 each, less engine, propeller, and armament.

The N-3PB certainly showed its ancestry—right back to the seaplane for Wilkins of 1928 and the Northrop Alpha of 1930. But it was much bigger and far more powerful. On the nose was to be a Wright Cyclone GR-1820-G205A engine, rated at 1,200 hp for takeoff. The big twin Edo floats were neatly faired to the wing with massive streamlined pedestals. Though Oerlikon and Fabrique National machine guns were to have been mounted in the wings, they were not available. Four Colt .50 caliber MG-53As were substituted. From both ventral and dorsal openings of the gunner's rear cockpit a .30 caliber Colt MG-40 flexible gun protruded. The lower gun fired through a hinged hatch and was to be manned by a third crew member. All five bomb racks were placed below the center section of the wing and between the floats. This would later be the position to hang three depth charges.

Had it not been for the appendages of war, the Northrop N-3PB was probably the cleanest and most attractive pure seaplane since the days of the Schneider Cup speed racers. The comparatively few people who ever saw one were apt to breathe appreciatively and murmur: "Beautiful!"

Less than a month after the Norwegians contracted for their new patrol bomber, Norway was attacked by Germany. Resistance continued until June and, with the removal of the government and royal family to London, was carried on under military and naval officers and men who had managed to escape from the country. Determined to fight on in exile, the Norwegians continued their airplane contracts in the United States.

After nine months, with a day of grace, the Northrop factory finished its first patrol bomber for Norway. On completion, it was trucked out to Riverside County and assembled on the north shore of Lake Elsinore, an inland body of water some 65 miles to the southeast of Hawthorne. A small lakeside airport provided an assembly area. On December 22, 1940, the sleek new Northrop was first flown off the lake. The engineering test pilot was Vance Breese, whose own monoplane Jack Northrop had helped design back in 1926. The services of Breese were now in great demand; he flew many of the initial test flights for Lockheed, North American, and Vultee.

Breese got the Northrop up on step and lifted easily off Lake Elsinore, circling over the canyons in the valley north of the Santa Ana mountains. Subsequent testing and evaluation flights occupied him for several weeks. Breese and others who subsequently flew the ship reported no real difficulties; it had good stability, easy handling, and excellent takeoff and landing characteristics. Pilots shied away from acrobatics. Those who tried them found the N-3PB a bit sluggish with the bulky pontoons hanging upside down at the top of a loop.

An acceptance team of twelve Norwegian "businessmen," led by Commander Ostby in pinstripe mufti, took over the first seaplane at Lake Elsinore on February 5, 1941. After getting to know the ship, the group flew the first six production aircraft up to Jericho Beach at Vancouver, British Columbia, where an ice-free advanced training base was established by the exiled Norwegians.

Though the terrain resembled that of their native country, winter training in the fog-shrouded Strait of Georgia brought only disaster to the men from Norway. Used to flying lighter, slower biplanes, they found it took time to master the heavy, high-powered Northrop monoplane. An accident off Vancouver in February killed two Norwegian flyers. Within a month another N-3PB crashed on

Norwegian patrol bomber on duty in Iceland during World War II.

takeoff at Patricia Bay, leaving only one survivor of its crew of three. The remaining four Northrops were flown east to Toronto, Ontario.

Shared with the army units training fighter pilots for service in England, the leased base at Toronto's Island Airport on Lake Ontario was called Little Norway. Here, half a world away from the fighting, Norwegian pilots and crewmen-in-exile continued their flying training in preparation for future battles. At Little Norway the Norwegian vice admiral, Hjalmar Riiser-Larsen of the Marinens Flyvevaben, arranged with his British and Canadian hosts to send a reconnaissance squadron of Norwegians to Iceland.

Iceland had been occupied by British forces in May 1940, as a precaution against German attack after Denmark and Norway were overrun. By the next spring the operations of German U-boats far out into the North Atlantic had expanded and Allied merchant ship losses were steadily mounting. On Iceland, the British had only three squadrons—one each of Fairey Battles, Lockheed Hudsons, and Short Sunderland flying boats. Only the last could operate off water.

British Coastal Command and the Fleet Air Arm began negotiations to replace this mixed and inadequate force with the Norwegians' new consignment of Northrop patrol bombers. They formed the first free Norwegian operational unit to be created within the Royal Air Force: No. 330 Squadron, established April 25, 1941.

The new squadron's CO was Commander Hans A. Bugge, who had followed through with evaluation testing of the N-3PB all the way from balmy Lake Elsinore to storm-swept Iceland.

After the arrival of the crews at Reykjavík, there was an anxious month of waiting. Shipped across the United States by rail, the new squadron's entire batch of eighteen Northrop N-3PBs, including spare parts, ammunition, and bombs, were all loaded on the Norwegian freighter *Fjordheim* at New York, destined for Iceland. The month of May already showed a drastic rise in shipping losses, and only a single torpedo from a German submarine could have wiped out this particular Norwegian war effort. Bugge and his men were on tenterhooks until the *Fjordheim* appeared in Reykjavík's outer harbor with its precious cargo.

The Norwegians always called the planes "the Northrops." They were soon being assembled in Iceland's only seaplane hangar on the outskirts of the capital. This relic had been built by a defunct German company. It was called "Balbo Hangar" because of its use by General Italo Balbo's Savoia-Marchetti S-55 seaplanes during their 1933 Flight from Rome to the Chicago World's Fair. Except for what this hangar could accommodate, all repair and maintenance had to be done in the open, out in the extremes of Icelandic weather.

Though bought by Norway and delivered with national markings, No. 330 Squadron's Northrops were soon repainted with standard British roundels and coded GS with a following letter. The squadron's Royal Air Force badge featured a Viking ship and the motto *Trygg Havet* ("Safeguard the Ocean").

The British were reluctant to fully commit their Norwegian allies—unsure of the capabilities of the men and their untried American aircraft. The first mission assigned was a two-plane, two-hour big-brother job; only one plane was ready. Pilot Lieutenant A. Stansberg, navigator H. O. Rustad, and wireless operator T. Hansen escorted a merchant convoy which was passing to the south of Iceland on June 23, 1941.

On becoming operational, 330 Squadron was deployed into three flights. Six Northrops were flown out of Reykjavík, three from Akureyri to the north, just below the Arctic Circle, and three from the village of Dudareyri, nestled in a fjord on Iceland's east coast. The remaining six airplanes were kept in reserve at Balbo Hangar.

The squadron's first brush with the enemy came on August 27, when Qm. Conrad Helgesen's crew in an N-3PB sighted the conning tower of a U-boat. In a dive from 900 feet all three depth charges failed to release, much to Helgesen's disgust. Half an hour later he spotted another periscope dead ahead. This time the pilot opened fire with his machine guns while the crew managed to drop the charges manually. The explosives landed just ahead of where the submarine had crash-dived. Helgesen circled the area for nearly an hour, but no debris or oil slick appeared on the rough seas below. Yet again, one of Admiral Doenitz's "wolf pack" had escaped.

Keyed up, the squadron sent out three Northrops the next morning. Ranging the choppy waters, Qm. Hans Olai Holdo came upon a surfaced German sub about to attack a British destroyer guarding four trawlers. Or so it seemed. Diving to attack, Holdo braced the enemy vessel with two depth charges, which landed fifty feet on either side and blew the sub almost clear of the water. On his climb out, the pilot got an urgent radio signal from the destroyer. Unknown to Holdo and his crew, the German had surrendered the previous day and was awaiting a boarding party. (Towed to Reykjavík and refurbished, the sub became the H.M.S. *Graph* of the Royal Navy.)

Still keen, the Norwegians resumed patrol and within a half hour sighted the conning tower of another submarine. Holdo dove again, his wing Colts clattering, and let go his remaining depth charge. As in Helgesen's attack the previous day, there was no evidence of damage inflicted on the enemy. Holdo pounded his fist on his knee in frustration and turned back to base. As if two unsuccessful attacks were not enough excitement for one day, the Northrop was "halfway to Greenland" before the crew realized they had a faulty compass. Turning, they managed to reach the safety of a tiny fishing village on Iceland's barren west coast before running out of fuel.

Stalking a seldom-seen quarry, with daily patrols in some of the world's worst weather, 330 Squadron repeated such incidents again and again as its planes ranged the gray skies from the Faeroes north to Jan Mayen Island, far up in the Arctic Sea.

Following Germany's attack on Russia in June 1941, the Allies instituted the far-north shipping route to supply the hard-pressed Soviets. The convoy ships welcomed the Norwegian escort planes, identifiable by their prominent floats and big British bull's-eyes. But when the planes turned back there was no air cover for shipping the rest of the 500 miles to Murmansk.

Back at Canada's Little Norway, one of the N-3PBs taking off from Toronto Harbor crashed into a ferry boat, with two casualties. The remaining three were sent to join the others on the Iceland patrols.

When not escorting convoys, the Northrops were pressed into a multitude of wartime tasks, as transports, ambulances, and camera planes and for air-sea rescue and iceberg spotting. The ocean patrols continued as long as the U-boat menace existed. Occasionally a German reconnaissance aircraft, flying from a captured Norwegian base, appeared in the surveillance area and was promptly engaged. With six guns, the Northrop mounted considerable firepower, but had difficulty bringing it to bear when a lone Focke-Wulf 200 Condor or Junkers 88 turned and sped off for home. In eight such encounters, hits were observed, but there were no confirmed downings.

An equal number of attacks on German submarines was also inconclusive. Perhaps the greatest contribution of the little squadron was not destruction of the enemy but, by its continued presence, the deterrence of enemy attacks on shipping.

Of the twenty-one Northrops flown by 330 Squadron, eleven were lost in accidents, four with their crews. On April 25, 1942, the squadron was a year old and celebrations were planned. That day the commanding officer, Commander Hans Bugge, took off with the first and original N-3PB, planning a wide-ranging anti-submarine sweep. No trace of his aircraft or crew was ever found, and the commemorating cake went uneaten.

Parts of some of the wrecked planes were salvaged and used to keep the others flying. One entire ship was cannibalized. In the summer of 1942 the squadron began to receive Catalina MkIII (PBY-5A) amphibians as replacements, but patrols using both aircraft continued. One by one the Northrops were called in to Reykjavík and grounded.

For over a year and a half, from June 23, 1941, to March 23, 1943, 330 Squadron's Northrops flew a total of 1,011 sorties with 3,512:52 hours of flying time. Contrary to wartime propaganda and press releases, the N-3PBs made no confirmed "kills" and did not take part in the highly publicized sinking of the German battleship *Bismarck*.

In 1940, Colonel Kristian Ostby had brought the Norwegian navy's patrol bomber specifications to Northrop. Years later, as a retired 4,000-hour pilot, he echoed the thoughts of the crews that flew from Iceland on those long, cold, tedious sweeps above the gray Atlantic and Arctic oceans, stating that "the N-3PB is the very finest aircraft I've ever flown."

When the Norwegians were transferred south to the Shetland Islands in the spring of 1943, 330 Squadron had ten Northrop N-3PBs remaining. With the speedy attrition of war they were already considered obsolete. No more were being built, and there were no spare parts. Orders came down to scrap them.

On April 21, 1943, Lieutenant Wsewolod W. "Sevi" Bulukin took one of the last remaining Northrops on what was to be its final flight from Budareyri air base to the Balbo Hangar boneyard. Forced down by a blizzard that swept Iceland's south coast, Bulukin managed to land on the fast-flowing glacial River Thjorsa. The plane's starboard float was wrenched off and the airplane was carried downstream to lodge some 120 feet from the west bank of the river. Both the pilot and a passenger, Qm. L. Rustad, managed to scramble ashore.

Ten years later some parts of the plane were still above water, but chunks, including the engine and tail sections, had been ripped off by local farmers in misguided attempts at salvage. Then the hulk disappeared completely, packed solid with sand and clay, on the river's bottom.

In Norway, the Northrops' contribution to the war effort was half forgotten. At the end of the war, two N-3PBs that had been stored in Iceland were sent on to their original country of destination. Presumably they were to be kept for eventual museum display. But hardheaded Norwegian naval air force officials ordered them sold for salvage, one in 1949 and the other in 1956. That left only the sad remains at the bottom of the River Thjorsa.

In Iceland, the Northrop was not forgotten. Iceland has an active aviation historical society, and its members, particularly Ragnar J. Ragnarsson, who had chronicled the history of No. 330 Squadron, were well aware of the wreck in the river. In 1977 the society, with the Icelandic Life Saving Association's rescue team and the Explosive Ordnance Disposal Group from the U.S. Navy's air station at Keflavik, located the airplane, using a mine de-

tector and divers. The divers reported that the water visibility was limited to less than 2 inches!

It was estimated that salvage would cost about $500,000. That kind of money was not forthcoming, but a campaign, involving volunteer efforts in four nations, was launched to recover the last N-3PB from its watery grave.

Ragnarsson and other key instigators of the project looked for sponsors and donators of equipment, and found them. In August 1979, a thirty-five-man team set up camp on the riverbank, ready to work

Parts of last Northrop N-3PB are recovered from the River Thjorsa in Iceland after thirty-six years.

long and hard under the midnight sun. When flotation bags proved incapable of raising the clay-impacted wreckage, a 90-foot crane from a nearby hydropower construction job was pressed into service.

When the carcass of the N-3PB surfaced after its thirty-six-year entombment, what remained was

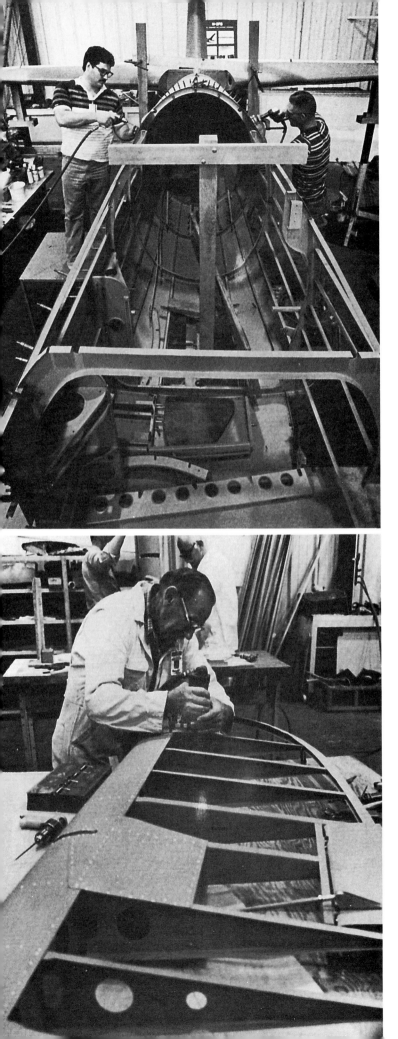

found to be remarkably preserved. Even the Exide battery would still hold a charge.

Disassembled and crated, the wreckage of the Northrop was stowed aboard a Norwegian air force C-130H Hercules for the trip to California, where it was to be worked on in the same Northrop assembly hangar in which it had been built. Three hundred and forty volunteer Northrop employees and retirees lovingly restored the airplane to its original appearance. Nearly 75 percent of the parts had to be refabricated, using computer-calculated processes to form many new sections, some based on the pieces to which they had been originally connected.

Extensive use was made of old photographs. Midway through the restoration project a box of 1,800 original N-3PB drawings turned up in an old Northrop storage warehouse. Completed on March 10, 1980, John K. Northrop's eighty-fifth birthday, the new-old patrol bomber was rolled out at Hawthorne with appropriate ceremony. In addition to the principal recoverers and restorers, over a hundred individuals, organizations, and companies in Iceland, Norway, England, and the United States contributed money, time, materials, and equipment to the project. The actual contributed cost was a trifling 1 percent of the $500,000 first estimate.

Today, the last Northrop N-3PB, after having been exhibited at Hawthorne, San Diego, and Reykjavík, has an honored place in Norway's Air Force Museum.

At the Northrop factory in Hawthorne, California, the battered relic is slowly restored and rebuilt.

13

THE FLYING WING
(1939)

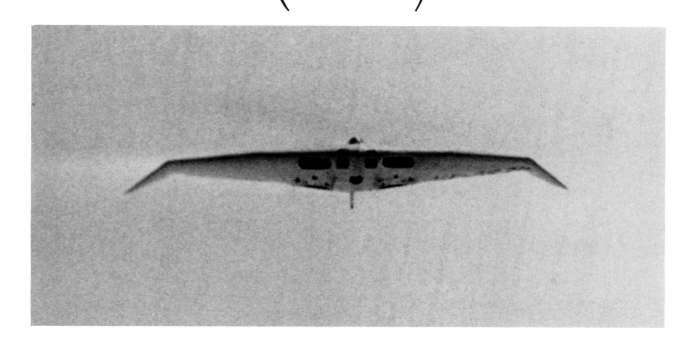

What Jack Northrop, one of aviation's greatest designers, had envisioned all along, since as far back as 1923, was a flying wing. It would be an airplane consisting of a wing and nothing else. No fuselage, no appended fin and stabilizer; everything contained in the wing itself—pilot, engine, controls all enclosed in a neat, streamlined entity.

Such an airplane seemed impossible. Neither birds nor anything else in nature flew like that. And yet Northrop was forever folding and creasing paper to make gliders, doodling sketches and scribbling calculations on odd scraps. He was convinced that putting everything into a thick airfoil *was* practical, and more than that, more efficient than the design of a conventional airplane. The only protrusions need be some means of propulsion, and if the jet engine was perfected, even that could be eliminated.

A fragile balsa, cardboard, and tissue model, built under Northrop's direction, pointed the way to go. The little 33-inch glider had miniature hinged wingtips, cardboard flaps, and elevons to provide balance and control. As the designer tried out his theories of stability in flight the little model became battered and tattered from many hand launches across the room and down the hall.

With his new company established at Hawthorne and well into profitable contracts and subcontracts, Jack Northrop at last had the freedom to break with traditional aircraft design. While Northrop Aircraft, Inc., was first subcontracting to build PBY tail sections, a company airplane of its own that had no tail at all was taking shape.

N-1M in ghostly flight over the Mojave desert.

John K. Northrop and pilot Moye Stephens with the N-1M, the "flying wing" of 1940.

Northrop himself wrote: "We . . . concentrated our efforts on an all-wing aircraft, by which I mean a type of airplane in which all of the functions of a satisfactory flying machine are disposed and accommodated within the outline of the main supporting airfoil."

Northrop now had Walter J. Cerny as assistant chief of design to supervise the experimental program. What they quietly proceeded to engineer and build during 1939–40 was the N-1M, the first true flying wing to be manufactured in the United States.

The N-1M (Northrop Model 1 Mockup) was, as might be expected, unusual in appearance. From the front the thick, swept-back wing with the anhedral droop of the tips gave the impression of some prehistoric bird. At the rear of the wing the shafts from two submerged 65-hp Lycoming engines spun a pair of two-bladed pusher propellers. Mounted on tricycle landing gear, the ship also had a faired tail wheel, which prevented the plane from tipping back on the ground as well as providing a small amount of directional stability. Northrop employees nicknamed it *The Jeep*, after a popular cartoon character.

Like his old Lockheed S-1 and the Vegas of the 1920s, Northrop's N-1M was molded of wood; it had spruce ribs overlaid with mahogany plywood. Both the flaps could be operated simultaneously as air brakes or to increase the angle of glide.

On completion, *The Jeep* was trucked over the mountains to Baker Dry Lake in the Mojave Desert for testing. The 38-foot bright yellow "wing" appeared from above to be some strange bug on the red-brown terrain. Vance Breese, strapped into the diminutive cockpit, inadvertently made the first flight on July 3, 1940. During a taxi run at high speed, the airplane bounced into the air, flew several hundred yards, and then settled back on all four wheels. More, hesitant test flights followed.

Jack Northrop lost no time in reporting the encouraging hops of the little N-1M to his friend General "Hap" Arnold, the Army Air Corps chief. Ultimately, Northrop foresaw, there could be a huge flying wing. In his opinion, money was being wasted in the building of bigger and bigger airplanes with conventional fuselages. In 1940, the war in Europe was going against Britain and France

Nicknamed The Jeep, *the experimental airplane originally had drooping wingtips.*

was overrun. It was conceivable that a new long-range bomber might be necessary to combat Nazi Germany from Canada or the United States. The flying wing from Northrop might have to be America's answer to the threat. General Arnold and his planning staff sifted through the reports from the Mojave very carefully.

Succeeding Vance Breese, whose services were in great demand, Moye Stephens went back into active flying, continuing the N-1M evaluation tests. Stephens found the Lycoming engines couldn't get *The Jeep* much more than 5 feet above the dry lake. Dr. Theodore von Karman of the California Institute of Technology suggested extending the trailing edge of the elevons back to a meeting place of the two sections of air flowing over the thick wing. In straight-line flights the plane then reached a ceiling of about 10 feet.

The wooden construction made adjustments to the N-1M possible at the test sites. Changes were made to the dihedral, flaps, and sweep of the wing and to the droop of the hinged outer tips. The engines were changed to 117-hp Franklins, and three-bladed propellers were installed. This doubled the horsepower but led to problems of overheating. To get the plane airborne, Stephens had to

run the engines to capacity limits, and beyond. As the program continued, the retractable landing gear was given wheel covers. Also, with no significant loss in stability, the drooping wingtips were replaced with straight ones.

Despite the engine difficulties, which he felt could be overcome, Jack Northrop concluded that the flying-wing concept, as demonstrated by the N-1M, was practical and workable. He thought the next logical step might be a medium-size, medium-range bomber. Hap Arnold and the Army Air Corps were thinking even bigger. By September 1941, the Northrop feasibility studies led to a confab with the Matériel Division at which an experimental flying wing with military capabilities was seriously discussed. It would weigh 140,000 pounds, thirty-five times as much as the little ship now parked out in the desert.

With hush-hush long-range bomber plans involved, the flight testing of *The Jeep* was accelerated. Tight security was established both at Hawthorne and up at the lake, and all information on

N-1M (Northrop Model 1 Mockup) at Baker Dry Lake, California.

the N-1M and flying wings in general was classified as of June 1941. Too late, it was discovered that Jack Northrop had filed the design with the patent office back in November. After routine publication of the patent details, Northrop and what was by then called the Army Air Forces had to release data and a photograph of the N-1M. It was discovered years later that the announcement led to increased

Below and opposite: After thirty years of storage, the Northrop N-1M *Jeep* was restored by the National Air and Space Museum and awaits display in Washington, D.C.

activity in the development of a German flying wing for military use, and to the world's first turbojet-powered flying wing, the Horten HO IX (Go 229), which first flew in January 1945. Internationally, the cat was out of the bag.

By November 1941, flown successively by Vance Breese and Moye Stephens, the experimental ship had made nearly fifty flights from Baker, Muroc, and Rosamond dry lakes. Since the "wing" could not be flown at altitude, it was towed by an Army C-47 over the mountains to Los Angeles Municipal Airport at Inglewood, where two more Northrop pilots and two Army Air Forces colonels made further test flights.

Favorable reports went regularly to Army headquarters and received the approval of General Arnold. Though Northrop's innovative N-1M was a puny, awkward, and exasperating airplane, by frequent alteration and redesign the basic soundness of the flying-wing concept was demonstrated.

The little yellow airplane itself was given to the Army Air Forces in 1945 and stored in Indiana and Illinois. Custody of the plane was assumed by the National Air Museum of the Smithsonian Institution in 1949, but *The Jeep* remained crated in two dusty boxes for thirty years.

Finally, Northrop's trail-blazing N-1M was carefully and fully restored by a team at the museum's Paul E. Garber Facility at Silver Hill, outside Washington, D.C. After 11,500 man-hours of labor, the brilliant yellow wedge of airplane emerged into the Maryland sunshine on March 4, 1983.

America's first true flying wing, the vindication of John K. Northrop's impossible dream, would join his Alpha and Gamma in the National Air and Space Museum, on display as milestone aircraft in the nation's heritage of flight.

EPILOGUE

BIGGER WINGS, NO WINGS, AND NEW WINGS

Any immediate development of more new airplanes by Northrop Aircraft, Inc., had to be shunted aside. The fledgling company was only a month old when World War II began in Europe, and the military and naval aircraft needs of the free world took precedence over all else. Even before the order for patrol bombers from Norway, La Motte Cohu and Jack Northrop had made arrangements with an old friendly competitor, Reuben Fleet of San Diego's Consolidated Aircraft, negotiating subcontracts that would keep their new factory busy.

Early in 1940, Northrop began building tail sections for Consolidated's PBY-5 naval patrol bombers. This was shortly followed by other subcontracts for PBY seating and engine cowls. Later in the year, Boeing awarded Northrop's plant in Hawthorne another subcontract for more cowlings of burnished sheet metal for the engines to be installed on their B-17E Flying Fortress bombers.

With France defeated and the Axis forces poised for attack across the English Channel, the beleaguered British were hard pressed for aircraft—any aircraft that might help fight off the expected invasion. One of the airplanes being built to British specifications was the Vultee V-72, called the Vengeance.

The Vengeance was a single-engined dive-bomber, the military refinement of a design that had its beginnings in the Vultee V-1 commercial transport of 1932–33. Designer Gerry Vultee, had eventually learned to fly and was killed in an Arizona plane crash in 1938. His company continued production of a succession of airplanes—sleek bombers and attack aircraft notable for retractable landing gear, greenhouses bristling with machine guns, and a characteristic high, truncated fin and rudder.

The British Purchasing Commission ordered 700

V-72s, far more than the Vultee factory in Downey, California, could handle. A new production line was set up in Nashville, Tennessee, and to further accelerate delivery schedules, Vultee subcontracted with Northrop for 200 of the Vengeances. By September 1940, the Hawthorne plant was gearing up to build $17 million worth of Vultee V-72s. To this was added an additional order for 200 similar attack bombers for the United States Army Air Corps. These were called A-31s.

The airplane was not theirs, it was a Vultee. But Cohu and Northrop's new aircraft-building organization had been formed at just the right time to be suddenly launched into the big time. War production saw Northrop grow over a two-year period from 100 employees to 4,700, working in plants of more than four times the original capacity. From nothing, Northrop at the height of Vengeance dive-bomber production ranked as the thirteenth-largest American aircraft manufacturer.

Hush-hush and under wraps, other things were going on at the burgeoning Hawthorne factory. Most employees had no idea that Northrop was engaged in anything but building V-72s, assembling PBY tails, and bumping out B-17 cowlings. In reality, Northrop's engineering teams were laboring day and night over a dozen wartime projects, for most of which there was extensive military financing.

As early as January 1941 an Air Corps requirement was sent out, with a $1,367,000 contract to back it up. This was for two examples of a practical fighter aircraft that could counter the expected German night bombing attacks on England. It would use the newly developed radar to locate the unseen enemy, and had to be large enough to carry not only the equipment but heavy armament as well.

The Northrop design team came up with the

XP-61, a twin-engined, twin-boom pursuit plane. A crew of three were housed in a pod mounted between the booms on the 66-foot wing, and the ship had a remote-control gun turret. The radar equipment was housed in the jutting nose.

The plane was called the Black Widow, the name stemming from recollections of the spiders that lurked in the closets of the old Hawthorne Hotel, where the engineers had set up their drawing boards. This was most appropriate, as the XP-61 was both lethal in appearance and deadly in performance as a weapon of war.

This formidable airplane was first flown from Northrop Field, adjacent to the Hawthorne factory, on May 26, 1942. Again it was Vance Breese who added another aircraft to his impressive list of first flights. An order for fourteen Black Widows for service testing followed. The testing resulted in both major and minor modifications. The production P-61 was not officially revealed to the public until the night of January 8, 1944. At a rally of war workers in the Los Angeles Coliseum, the black-painted Widow, trimmed with red markings, flashed by overhead in the glare of searchlights.

Operational service of the P-61 began the following summer, when the ship was assigned to the 18th Fighter Group in the South Pacific. Before the year was out, Black Widows were flying with night fighter squadrons in both the Pacific and European theaters, scanning the skies for enemy intruders. All told, Northrop built 674 Black Widows in various versions, right up to the day of Japanese surrender.

Neither the design nor even the existence of other supersecret airplanes on which Northrop engineers worked was ever revealed until long after the war. As might be expected, the bulk of them had to do with the new concept and development of the Flying Wing, a name which the company adopted and eventually registered as a trademark.

That all-wing principle had been well proved and shown to be feasible by the successful flying of the N-1M in 1940–41. In September 1941, Northrop submitted preliminary designs for a Flying Wing bomber, an airplane four times the size of the diminutive N-1M. The Army contracted for two of them, the XB-35s, a secret project which was not to be completed until the 1945–50 period. In military reasoning, a long-range bomber of this type might be needed to attack a victorious Germany from bases in Canada and the United States, or again by

that time it might not be needed at all.

To get flight research data, Northrop engineers, using the N-1M configuration, designed a version with two Menasco engines and a 60-foot wingspan. Called the N-9M, it was virtually a flying scale model of what the big Flying Wing bomber would be. Four of the planes were built. The first flight took place two days after Christmas 1942, right beside the busy Northrop factory in Hawthorne.

Though one of the N-9Ms was destroyed in a fatal accident early in the program, the remaining planes were flown for hundreds of hours, gathering feasibility and flight characteristic data for use in Flying Wing development. That big bomber of the future was always the ultimate goal in Jack Northrop's mind.

Over a three-year period, the N-9Ms became a common sight over Muroc Army Air Base. (Not of Indian origin, "Muroc" is "Corum," the name of an early settler, spelled backward.) Visiting officers often rubbed their eyes in disbelief at the sight of what appeared to be three batlike paper gliders flying overhead in formation. The fourth airplane, powered by two 330-hp air-cooled Franklin engines, had a fuel tank removed so that Dr. William P. Sears, Northrop's chief of aerodynamics, could ride along to make personal observations. Two of the "Flying Scale Models" were painted with a yellow underside and a blue top so that ground observers could ascertain if the airplane was being flown upside down or right side up.

Also at Muroc during the war years of 1943–45, a Nazi espionage agent might have seen any one of a number of weird, wild, and wonderful airplanes which sprang from the fertile minds and ink-splotched drawing boards of Northrop's engineering teams. All were conceived in answer to Army Air Corps ideas and directives, and all used some version of the Flying Wing concept.

There was the XP-56, a big stubby bullet of a plane, with extended ventral and dorsal fins but no real tail. It was powered by a buried Pratt & Whitney Double Wasp engine of 2,000 hp, swinging counter-rotating pusher propellers. Viewed from the side, standing tall on its retractable landing gear, it appeared incapable of flight.

The XP-56 was the world's first all-magnesium, all-welded airplane to get airborne. This was made possible by Northrop's patented Heliarc welding process, in which a jet of helium kept the light and tricky magnesium alloy from bursting into flame.

Only two XP-56s, sometimes called Black Bullets, were built.

Rocket propulsion, which had been under development in Germany for many years, also came up for Army Air Corps scrutiny. Known until 1947 only as Northrop Project 12, with no details, was another series of three of the Flying Wing breed of airplane.

These "wings," smaller even than the N-1M, were first tested as gliders. They were towed aloft by a Lockheed P-38 fighter and usually released at an altitude of about 13,000 feet. To reduce aerodynamic drag on the airplane, which was only 12 feet long, the pilot was required to lie prone in the cockpit, like Orville Wright at Kitty Hawk.

One of the Rocket Wings (the MX-334) was fitted for installation of a new XCAL-200 rocket engine, under development by the Aerojet Corporation of Azusa, California. The fuel was oxidized by nitric acid in a cast-aluminum combustion chamber. With this plane, lying flat on his stomach alongside the engine, test pilot Harry Crosby was towed to 8,000 feet on July 5, 1944. In a pass over Muroc Dry Lake the tow line was released and Crosby triggered the rocket motor. With flame and black smoke the MX-334 picked up speed and accomplished America's first military rocket plane flight. Though it lasted only three and a half minutes, the journey was called "an unqualified success."

Next in the line of Northrop exotic airplanes came the JB-1 (MX-543), the Power Bomb. This one, under development in answer to Germany's V-1 rocket bomb, was a Flying Wing even shorter (only 10½ feet long) than the Rocket Wing. A tiny, racy-looking teardrop fuselage sat between two bulbous bomb pods (one ton of explosives in each), in the center of the 29-foot wing. Harry Crosby tested it successfully as a towed glider.

The idea was to have a pair of General Electric Type B turbojet engines and a preprogrammed guidance system replace the pilot. Set on course from approximately 200 miles away, this American "buzz bomb" with its 4,000-pound bomb load was supposed to make a dive at the end of its run, zeroing in on a predetermined target. In theory, the MX-543 was to be launched from a 400-foot railroad track.

By the end of 1944, this kind of weapon was not needed, and the attention of military planners had shifted to pulse-jet engines. America's unmanned-flying-bomb project was closed out.

A final fighter/interceptor, a swept-wing job, stemmed from an Army Air Force idea that verged on the suicidal. A plane was to be built with heavy magnesium structure and steel armor plating, designed to dive on enemy bombers and slice off their tails. Northrop responded with XP-79B or MX-365. It could only be described as a flying ram. At first the installation of two rocket engines was considered, but because of their high fuel consumption, the prototype was fitted instead with Westinghouse turbojets. As in the MX-334 Rocket Wing, the pilot lay prone, stretching his legs to the foot pedals that controlled the air brakes. This airplane never got a chance to prove its worth as a vengeful slicing machine. The Flying Ram made its first and only flight on September 12, 1945. A climbing turn became a roll, a stall, and a spin, and Northrop's resourceful veteran test pilot Harry Crosby perished in an aborted bailout.

During World War II, Northrop built some 1,131 aircraft of its own design as well as fulfilling extensive subcontracts and carrying out secret experimental projects. After the surrender of Japan, some $21 billion in war contracts was summarily canceled, and the company lost 90 percent of its military sales virtually overnight. What next?

Fortunately for Northrop, one airplane was continued in production at Hawthorne after hostilities ceased. This was the F-15 Reporter, a long-range photoreconnaissance plane. With room for six cameras, it was a twin-engined, twin-boomed airplane, an extension of the Black Widow and later escort fighter designs. The Army Air Forces ordered 175 of them in June 1945, even before Northrop had flown the prototype. In the event, only thirty-six were built, but the contract kept the vastly curtailed Northrop work force busy.

Only one foray into the civilian/commercial airplane field marked Northrop's post–World War II activities. Jack Northrop and his engineering staff were prepared to design whatever there was a market for. What would the airlines, ready to expand on a global basis, be needing?

Boeing, Douglas, Lockheed, Convair, and Martin already had new airliners under development or ready to go into production. Northrop picked up some piecework, such as converting wartime Douglas C-47 cargo transports into civilian passenger-carrying DC-3s.

Of all the air transport companies, only one showed any interest in a possible "airliner" from

Hawthorne. The president of TWA, Jack Frye, had been a Northrop friend, buyer, and booster since the days of the Alpha and the Gamma. And Frye's specifications had led to the development of Douglas's DC series, in which Northrop's multicellular wing had played such a great part.

Frye had South American expansion and affiliations for his airline in mind. He suggested that Northrop design and build a modern trimotor transport plane that could operate from the grass fields and short runways of Latin America, as well as those of the emerging African and Asian nations. A Flying Wing commercial transport was all well and good for TWA's passengers, but not until it had been fully tested and perfected by the military.

La Motte Cohu of Northrop enthusiastically took up Frye's suggestion and scouted the market possibilities during a junket to Brazil. Jack Northrop is described as "lukewarm" about the project, but assigned the trimotor transport to his engineering staff and as usual put some of his own energies into it.

The result was a high-winged conventional passenger/cargo monoplane, which Cohu had dubbed the Pioneer. With two 800-hp Wright Cyclone engines in the wing and another on the nose, the ship could tote 5 tons of cargo. Northrop's vice-president and director of sales John Myers often made 400-foot takeoffs and 600-foot landings with the trimotor. A big airplane, with an 85-foot wingspread and broad, fixed landing gear, the Pioneer was inevitably touted as a replacement for the Ford Trimotor, many of which had found their way to south-of-the-border countries. The commodious fuselage was stressed-skin monocoque, first used by Jack Northrop sixteen years previously, in his first Alphas.

The Pioneer was test-flown for a year, but airline sales did not materialize. As the doubters had accurately predicted, there were just too many surplus military transport planes available, readily convertible for sale to the smaller airline operators, at home and abroad.

The pioneering Pioneer had its huge fin and rudder modified, which led to a fatal accident when a dorsal fin came loose and smashed the tail surfaces of the airplane. Nevertheless, the Air Force came through with a $5,500,000 order for twenty-three of an improved version called the C-125 Raider. These were tested as assault transports, replacing the wartime gliders, and also for Arctic rescue

duties. The Raider of 1949–50 had a redesigned tail assembly and 86½-foot upswept wings.

At no time did Jack Northrop and his engineers at Hawthorne lose sight of their major objective, the full-size Flying Wing. This was their dream plane, and for Jack the dream had been there for twenty years.

Because it was so radically different, and even though smaller test planes had proved the principle and shown the design to be practical, the advent of a full-size Flying Wing was received with awe amounting to disbelief.

The two Flying Wings (termed XB-35s) ordered by the USAAC back in November 1941 and under development at Northrop all during World War II were to be four-engined pusher-propeller-driven structures with massive 172-foot wings, no fuselage, and no empennage. During the war, the XB-35 program moved slowly, because of more pressing concerns, and it was not until June 25, 1946, that the first full-size Flying Wing was scheduled for flight. Built in secrecy at Hawthorne, the airplane was rolled out and positioned on the runway beside the plant. Though the men and women who had worked on the "big bat" were requested to stay inside, it was too much to ask, and the runway was lined with employees, eager to see "their" airplane take the air. Jack Northrop had read the "stay at work" memo and watched from the window of his office.

Test pilot Max Stanley was at the controls. He'd never flown anything so big, to say nothing of its being unconventional. He called the control tower and received clearance, and the Flying Wing rolled down the runway. Slowly at first, she inched up to 75, then 100 mph. At 115, the 200,000-pound bomber was off and flying in a cloud of smoke and dust. The waiting workers let out a spontaneous, collective "Oh my God!" One of them remembered: "It was like the Dowae stunt planes we had when we were kids. No tails! Launched from a slingshot! WHOOOSH!"

Forty-four minutes later a sweat-drenched Stanley put the big plane down at Muroc Dry Lake and called Jack Northrop to report that his Flying Wing had indeed flown—and "No bugs—no squawks!"

Like any program so drastically new and different, the B-35 bomber program at Northrop proceeded slowly, with test after test and painstaking improvements. It was a year before the second Flying Wing was delivered to Muroc. Another four months saw a new version take the air with the original test crew, blasting off from the Hawthorne factory field. This was the YB-49, powered by eight General Electric TG-180 jet engines and equipped with four small fins for greater lateral stability. Air Force officers who flew them declared the four prototype Flying Wings to be "among the cleanest, most troublefree and most ready-to-fly new bombers ever received from aircraft contractors."

Meanwhile, Northrop's competitor Consolidated-Vultee had built a huge intercontinental bomber of its own, the XB-36. This was of conventional configuration, 200 tons of airplane with six pusher engines. But to most observers, Northrop's Flying Wing appeared to be the bomber of the future. Though the feature was not planned, the very thin profile of the airplane, flying toward a target at 500 mph, proved difficult to detect on radar. It was an attribute not appreciated at the time; the possibility that an aircraft might sneak up on an enemy at such a speed, undetected, was inconceivable.

Despite a disastrous accident at Muroc on June 5, 1948, the Air Force decided to put Northrop's bomber into production, and thirty RB-49A Flying Wings were ordered. The airplanes were to be built in expanded facilities at Consolidated-Vultee's Fort Worth, Texas, bomber plant, which was owned by the government. Eleven unfinished Wings from the original 1943 order remained at Hawthorne and were to be converted to the improved version. Consolidated's work on its conventional B-36 was to be terminated, and the firm would subcontract from Northrop to build B-49s. It appeared to be a clear competitive victory for John Knudsen Northrop and his Flying Wings.

Like so many victories, this one was short-lived. Though the details are controversial, it would appear that in July 1948, Jack Northrop was summoned to a meeting with Secretary of the Air Force Stuart Symington, at which Floyd Odlum, chairman of the Atlas Corporation, was also present. Atlas was a major Consolidated-Vultee shareholder.

Out of the blue, Symington demanded that if Flying Wings for the Air Force were to be built, the Northrop company must be merged with Consolidated-Vultee. Symington further issued a veiled threat of reprisals in the event that this was not accomplished. The thought of such a forced merger or takeover was a shock to Jack Northrop. It was

unacceptable to him and to his stockholders. They voted to turn the proposition down. Six months later, in a complete reversal, the Air Force canceled the production contract for thirty RB-49 Flying Wing bombers and transferred allotted funds to continue the production of the Consolidated B-36. Cited were deep budgetary reductions, changing requirements, and adverse technical analysis. Cancellation was not enough. The Air Force eventually scrapped every completed and uncompleted Northrop Flying Wing bomber in existence—millions of dollars' worth of airplanes. They were government property, of course, but even the reams of test reports and historical paperwork were destroyed, some of it on orders of a later Northrop management group in a conscious effort to erase memories and forget the whole thing. Jack Northrop later said "We suffered vicious bureaucratic consequences."

Northrop Aircraft, Inc., had only one major customer, the United States Air Force, and with cancellation of the Flying Wings the company was fortunate to survive. Only two other aircraft were in production, a missile and a fighter.

Northrop's N-25 was the world's first on-line intercontinental guided missile. Sled-launched and flight-tested at Holloman Air Force Base in New Mexico, the sleek and secret strategic warhead carrier with no pilot was improved to become the N-69, which could sometimes be returned undamaged and reused after testing. This in turn led to the development of an astro-inertial navigation system capable of guiding a 5,000-pound missile to a target 5,000 miles away. Jack Northrop whimsically called it the SNARK system, after a mythical creature created by Lewis Carroll—"half snake, half shark." Over fifty Snarks were purchased and put on operational status by the Strategic Air Command.

Northrop's tactical fighters were preceded by a pair of tiny experimental test beds for jet engines. Called the X-4, or Bantam, and, more grandly, the Skylancer, the transonic fighter was only 23 feet long, with the swept-back all-wing configuration for which data were needed.

Powered by two Westinghouse 1,600-pound-thrust jet engines, the X-4 could fly at 680 mph, but was not designed to exceed the sound barrier. Among its better-known test pilots were Chuck Yeager of the Air Force and Scott Crossfield of NACA.

Jack Northrop's last design to see flight was a successor to his Black Widow of World War II. Developed as an all-weather fighter-interceptor, with two Allison Turbojet engines in the lower fuselage, it was given the Air Force designation F-89. The ground crews at Muroc (soon to be renamed Edwards Air Force Base) thought the upswept tail, high above the backwash of wing and engines, resembled that of a riled-up scorpion, and the name stuck. A tricycle landing gear and distinctive nondroppable fuel pods at the wingtips distinguished the Scorpion. Later, the pods were modified to house fifty-two rockets, which could be fired selectively or in salvo. The aircraft was first flown in August 1948, and 1,050 Scorpions were operated by the Air Force and the Air National Guard until the summer of 1969. It was the first airplane to fire an air-to-air nuclear weapon.

The Scorpion was Northrop's first production jet aircraft, and the last aircraft in which Northrop himself had a hand. Unhappy over the peremptory disposal of his Flying Wing bombers and the engineering personnel changes forced upon him by newly appointed management, Jack Northrop resigned from the company which bore his name in December 1952.

Northrop's early retirement by choice, at fifty-seven, severed his association with aircraft manufacture, but not with aviation. Ostensibly a golfing man of leisure with a beautiful home in Santa Barbara, he invested in real estate and prefabricated-housing ventures and renewed a youthful association with the Boy Scouts of America as an active official.

At Hawthorne, as an extension of its wartime training program, Northrop Aircraft had in 1945 established the Northrop Aeronautical Institute to teach engineering and the manufacture and maintenance of aircraft. Though a success, with student enrollment over 1,000, the school was up for elimination in 1953. The company needed space, and had decided to concentrate on building airplanes and missiles.

To save the school, Jack Northrop took the time and effort to gather financial backing. With its assets purchased, the educational facility was reestablished in Inglewood as the Northrop Institute of Technology, with Jack as chairman of the board of trustees. Today, Northrop University is a fully accredited four-year college, an institution of higher learning of which the founder was very proud.

After 1952, Northrop Aircraft, Inc., suffered more setbacks, management changes, and the ups and downs that plague a manufacturer with only one unpredictable customer. As the company moved to diversify its products, aircraft and missile building at Hawthorne became one of several divisions of the Northrop Corporation (1959). It produced such military aircraft as the T-38 Talon jet trainer, the N-156F Freedom Fighter, and the Skoshi Tiger, the F-5 tactical fighter. The United States and the air forces of twenty-two other countries flew the Tiger and its successors, the P-530 Cobras and the Navy's F-18 lightweight fighters. Development and building of aircraft at Northrop is an ongoing activity.

Outstanding among the products of the present-day Northrop Corporation is the controversial B-2 or Stealth Bomber. Under development for more than a decade under conditions of strict secrecy, with a hidden budget and a classification higher than Top Secret, the B-2 was planned as America's ultimate deterrent to attack, and is probably the last bomber that will carry a human crew. The "stealth" feature is achieved by a low radar image at both high and low altitudes, terrain-following capabilities, shielded engines, and virtual elimination of contrails. With a 6,000-mile range, it is what the Air Force wants. If ultimately put in production, 133 examples will cost some $69 billion.

When the prototype B-2 was rolled out at Palmdale, California, on November 22, 1988, the 500 carefully screened invited guests saw a flying wing. Indeed, the new Stealth Bomber is a vindication of Jack Northrop's concepts, which had culminated in the Flying Wing YB-49 of forty years before. It is a surprising re-creation of the graceful Wings of the late 1940s—with even the same wingspan, 172 feet. It was first flown successfully in Palmdale, California, on the morning of July 17, 1989.

Discredited, dismantled, chopped up, the plans and records obliterated, here was Jack Northrop's Flying Wing—come back and an actuality after all the dead years. Although details are still subject to security and production still very much in the future, the B-2 appears to be, at last, the airplane of Jack Northrop's fertile foresight.

Long ago he had watched the graceful gulls on the beach at Santa Barbara, and in retirement on the hilltop above the same city, Jack still enjoyed the marvel of bird flight.

It is now known that, in 1981, bedridden and

near the end of his life, Jack Northrop was given a special security clearance in order that Pentagon officials could tell him that the Air Force had finally recontracted with his old company to build a flying wing as the nation's flagship strategic bomber. He remarked, "I'll be satisfied when somebody does something with the flying wing to prove how good it is. . . . I still believe that this will happen."

At his old company this *has* happened, and the Northrop Flying Wing is once more a reality. The old designer would have been pleased.

Except for a belated revelation concerning the canceled Flying Wing bomber contract, Northrop

never committed more than snippets of his recollections to paper or tape. He told people who came to see him that he never kept historical records and as a "technically advanced high school graduate" he was simply "just lucky" in his work.

"We did what we pleased," he said, "and what we pleased was to make better airplanes."

At a testimonial dinner, Northrop's old friend Donald Douglas had what is probably the best and last word:

"Any formal education he lacked he didn't need. Jack Northrop was a man with a million ideas—all of them good. He was an innovator and a dreamer whose innovations succeeded and whose dreams became real. There is a little of him in every airplane that flies."

Wiley Post takes oath as airmail pilot, 1935, with TWA's "Over-weather" Northrop Gamma.

SUPPLEMENT A
Individual Histories of Aircraft,
1929 to 1937

Key:

Registered owners are in CAPITALS. Obvious middlemen, dealers, short-term operators, etc., where not important, have been omitted. Formal names are in italics.

c/n	= Serial number given by manufacturer (from the British "constructor's number," which is used internationally)
Type	= Designation given by manufacturer
Model	= Number or number and letter symbol, assigned by manufacturer
Reg.	= Registration (i.e., license) number assigned by U.S. Department of Commerce, Aeronautics Branch (later Bureau of Air Commerce, Civil Aeronautics Authority). U.S. prefixes:

C or NC   = Commercial
R or NR   = Restricted
X or NX   = Experimental
Ident. no. = Identification Mark Assignment Number (unlicensed)
N   = Indicates "United States" in world registrations; since 1948 used without second letter on all U.S.-registered aircraft

Mfg.	= Month and year or month, day, and year given by manufacturer as date on which aircraft was completed
Eng.	= Name, type, and c/n of original engine installed in individual aircraft
ATC	= Approved Type Certificate, with number; awarded after testing by U.S. Department of Commerce. Special and converted types were covered by ATC Memos, with group numbers (such as Gr. 2-490)

Other Abbreviations:

Acc.	= Accident
CAA	= Civil Aeronautics Authority, its predecessors, the U.S. Department of Commerce, Aeronautics Branch and Bureau of Air Commerce, or *its* successor, the Federal Aviation Agency
TT	= Total time
l/g	= Landing gear
lic.	= License
A.C.	= Serial number assigned by U.S. Army Air Corps

C/n 1

Type	Avion
Model	Experimental No. 1
Reg.	X 216H
Mfg.	5/29
Eng.	Menasco Cirrus Mark III #134/3
ATC	None

The original "flying wing," developed by John K. Northrop for THE AVION CORPORATION, 4515 Alger St., Los Angeles, CA. Northrop patented the design 5/10/29 (#1,929,255). Application for X lic. 5/11/29 as 2-place dual-control pilot and passenger ship. Lic. issued 5/31/29. Test-flown at Muroc Dry Lake, CA, by Eddie Bellande. Transferred 11/23/29 to NORTHROP AIRCRAFT CORPORATION, United Airport, Burbank, CA. Reapproved for X lic. 12/6/28, with engine now referred to as a British Cirrus. Publicly introduced 2/10/30. Flown first with engine as a pusher, then as a tractor. On 9/22/30, Northrop advised CAA that flights with this ship would be discontinued "pending numerous wind tunnel and laboratory tests." No further record.

C/n 1

Type	Alpha
Model	2
Reg.	X 2W
Mfg.	3/30
Eng.	P&W Wasp
ATC	None

The original Northrop Alpha, built by NORTHROP AIRCRAFT CORPORATION at Burbank, CA, during winter of 1929–30. Application for X lic. 3/11/30. Ident. no. assigned 3/15/30 and X applied. Acc. 3/27/30. Pilot Stephen R. Shore bailed out safely. Airplane demolished, near Glendale, CA.

C/n 2

Type	Alpha
Model	2
Reg.	X 127W, NR 127W, NC 127W
Mfg.	4/25/30

The second Alpha built served for almost two years as a demonstrator for the Northrop Corporation.

Eng. P&W Wasp #2246
ATC (381)

Approved for X lic. 4/25/30 to NORTHROP AIRCRAFT CORPORATION, Burbank, CA. Used as demonstrator and test ship. Taken to Wright Field, OH, for testing by USAAC 7/7/30. Damaged in forced landing 7/14/30. Repaired at Wright Field and returned to factory. Loaned to USAAC 10/9/30 for private use of Gen. James E. Fechet for 30 days. Returned to factory and extra stiffeners added to outer wings and hydrostatic fuel gauges installed. On display 5/30 fitted with teardrop wheel pants. Approved for NR lic. 10/10/30 and NC lic. 1/2/31 under ATC 381. Back to X lic. 1/12/31 for tests as seaplane on Edo "K" floats. Approved for NC as land- or seaplane 2/6/31. To X again 7/2/31 to test new-type landing gear as Alpha 4. Title transferred to STEARMAN AIRCRAFT COMPANY, Wichita, KS, 9/28/31, still as demonstrator and test ship. Lic. X 1/11/32 to test 10:1 blower for Wasp C 500-hp engine, for altitude performance. Sold 3/9/32 to TRANSCONTINENTAL & WESTERN AIR, INC., New York, NY. TWA Fleet No. 14. Converted to Alpha 4A by TWA as of 4/5/32. Lic. NC 4/15/32. Acc. Amarillo, TX, 4/16/32. Left wing and l/g damaged. Repaired. Acc. Near Portage, PA, 12/11/33. Pilot Dean Bur-

ford left via parachute. Airplane demolished, $73,000 consignment of diamonds recovered intact.

C/n 3

Type Alpha
Model 2
Reg. NS 1, NR 11Y, NC 11Y
Mfg. 11/30
Eng. P&W Wasp C #3162
ATC 381

Pilot-and-2-passenger airplane, tested by Edmund T. Allen. Sold 1930 to UNITED STATES DEPARTMENT OF COMMERCE, AERONAUTICS BRANCH, Washington, DC. Painted black and orange, flown by Asst. Sec. of Commerce Clarence M. Young. Lic. NS 1 to expire 12/15/31. Sold 4/16/31 to FORD MOTOR COMPANY, Dearborn, MI. Sold 4/20/31 to NATIONAL AIR TRANSPORT, INC., Chicago, IL. Flown briefly as 4-passenger, and relic. NC 11Y. Sold 11/27/31 to TRANSCONTINENTAL & WESTERN AIR, INC., New York, NY, as Alpha 4a. TWA Fleet No. 12. Sold 4/26/35 to FREDERICK B. LEE, New York, NY. Lee purchased floats from Bellanca of Dr. Richard U. Light, and planned a long-distance world flight that did not materialize. Sold 9/12/37 to HARRY V. SPAULDING, New York, NY, as

1POLM. Sold 1/20/38 to RICHARD E. CONLEY, Ridgefield, CT. Sold 12/20/40 to MURRAY B. DILLEY, JR., Kansas City, KS. Sold 5/16/42 to UNITED AIRCRAFT TRAINING, INC., Wichita, KS. Sold 5/12/45 to HAROLD V. LESLIE, Detroit, MI. Sold 9/18/45 to FOSTER HANNAFORD, Winnetka, IL. Last owner died in 1971 and plane acquired by EXPERIMENTAL AIRCRAFT ASSOCIATION, Hales Corners, WI. Completely rebuilt with TWA markings in 1975 by TWA and presented to NATIONAL AIR AND SPACE MUSEUM, Washington, DC. Since 1976 on prominent display in museum.

C/n 4

Type Alpha
Model 2
Reg. NR 999Y, NC 999Y
Mfg. 10/10/30
Eng. P&W Wasp C #2852
ATC 381

Lic. NR to NORTHROP AIRCRAFT CORPORATION, Burbank, CA, 10/10/30 for pilot and 6 passengers. Loaned 10/9/30 for 30 days to USAAC for personal use of Asst. Sec. of War F. Trubee Davison. Approved 11/11/30 for NC lic. Sold 4/13/31 to TRANSCONTINENTAL & WESTERN AIR, INC., New York, NY. TWA Fleet No. 5. As of 5/7/31 converted to Alpha 3 at factory under ATC Gr. 2-335. As of 9/6/31 converted to Alpha 4 under ATC 461. Acc. 5/5/32, Kansas City, MO. Converted to Alpha 4a by TWA at Kansas City as of 6/9/32. Acc. 11/15/34 near Newhall, CA. Pilot George Rice suffered minor injuries. Airplane washed out.

C/n 5

Type Alpha
Model 2
Reg. NC 933Y
Mfg. 11/10/30
Eng. P&W Wasp SC #3198
ATC 381

A pilot-and-6-passenger ship, approved for NC lic. 11/12/30 to NORTHROP AIRCRAFT CORPORATION, Burbank, CA. Sold 4/13/31 to TRANSCONTINENTAL & WESTERN AIR, INC., New York, NY. TWA Fleet No. 4. Converted as of 4/14/31 to Model 3 (2 passengers, 1 crew) under ATC Gr. 2-335. Acc. 7/27/31, Winslow, AR. Required new factory wing and extensive repair to underside. Converted as of 9/18/31 to Alpha 4 by factory (with new trousered l/g) under ATC 451. Acc. 1/20/32, Glendale, CA. Again required new left wing and l/g replacement, etc. Acc. 2/19/32, Leupp, AR. Extensive fuselage repairs, new wing and l/g. Converted as of 5/17/32 to Alpha 4a under ATC 461 as single-place ship. Acc. 11/29/33, Indianapolis, IN. Involved fuselage buckling at rear, repaired. Flown to Seattle, WA, for export and sold 7/22/35 to JAMES W. FISHER, Hong Kong, for use of the Chinese Nationalist govt. Reported 1/27/37 as "obsolete and to be disposed of" by Chinese air force.

C/n 6

Type	Alpha
Model	2
Reg.	NC 942Y
Mfg.	12/18/30
Eng.	P&W Wasp C #3206
ATC	381

Seven-place ship lic. NC 1/15/31 to NORTHROP AIRCRAFT CORPORATION, Burbank, CA. Sold 4/13/31 to TRANSCONTINENTAL & WESTERN AIR, INC., New York, NY. TWA Fleet No. 3. Briefly named *Miss St. Louis*. As of 5/7/31 converted to Alpha 3 under ATC Gr. 2-335, and as of 9/18/31 to Alpha 4 under ATC 451. Acc. 1/14/32, Mobeetie, TX. Pilot Ted Hereford suffered injuries. Airplane demolished.

C/n 7

Type	Alpha
Model	2
Reg.	NC 947Y
Mfg.	1/27/31

Eng.	P&W Wasp C #1547
ATC	381

Seven-place ship licensed 1/27/31 to NORTHROP AIRCRAFT CORPORATION, Burbank, CA. Sold, 4/17/31, to TRANSCONTINENTAL & WESTERN AIR, INC., New York, NY. Price $14,220 less engine. TWA supplied own P&W Wasp #1917, installed at factory prior to delivery. TWA Fleet No. 1. Converted as of 4/27/31 to Alpha 3 by factory, under ATC Gr. 2-335, and on 9/18/31 to Alpha 4 under ATC 451. As of 3/26/32 converted by TWA to Alpha 4a under ATC 461. Acc. 10/7/33. Columbus, OH. Repaired. Acc. 12/11/33, near Roaring Springs, PA. Pilot Henry G. "Andy" Andrews left via parachute in storm after de-icing equipment failure. Airplane demolished.

C/n 8

Type	Alpha
Model	2
Reg.	NC 961Y
Mfg.	3/10/31
Eng.	P&W Wasp #3716
ATC	381

Pilot-and-6-passenger ship, lic. 3/20/31 to NORTHROP AIRCRAFT CORPORATION, Burbank, CA. Sold 4/13/31 to TRANSCONTINENTAL & WESTERN AIR, INC., New York, NY. TWA Fleet No. 2. Before sale converted as of 4/9/31 to Alpha 3 under ATC Gr. 2-335 and again converted at factory as of 10/3/31 to Alpha 4 under ATC 451. Acc. 4/14/32, Winslow, AR (minor). Converted as of 11/5/31 to Alpha 4a by TWA under ATC 461. Acc. 5/25/33, Camden, NJ. Wing damage, repaired. Sold 7/22/35 to JAMES W. FISHER, Hong Kong, and exported from Seattle. Acquired for service with the Chinese Nationalist govt. Reported 1/27/37 as "obsolete and to be disposed of" by Chinese air force.

C/n 9

Type	Alpha

Model	2
Reg.	NC 966Y
Mfg.	4/4/31
Eng.	P&W Wasp C #3198
ATC	381

Seven-place ship, licensed 4/13/31 to NORTHROP AIRCRAFT CORPORATION, Burbank, CA. As of 6/16/31 converted by manufacturer to Alpha 3 under ATC Gr. 2-335. Sold 6/20/31 to TRANSCONTINENTAL & WESTERN AIR, INC., New York, NY. Price $14,220 less engine. TWA supplied own engine, P&W Wasp #1444. TWA Fleet No. 6. Briefly named *Miss New York*. Converted by factory as of 9/17/31 to Alpha 4 under ATC 451. Acc. near Steubenville, OH, 3/21/32. Pilot Hal George, forced down by sleet storm, plunged into Ohio River. George and passenger, Dr. Carol S. Cole of St. Louis, MO, killed. Wreckage dragged ashore at Weirton, WV.

C/n 10

Type	Alpha
Model	3
Reg.	NC 985Y
Mfg.	6/16/31
Eng.	P&W Wasp C #1721
ATC	Gr. 2-335

Sold 6/20/31 to TRANSCONTINENTAL & WESTERN AIR, INC., New York, NY. Price $14,220 less engine, which TWA supplied. NC lic. issued to TWA 6/22/31. TWA Fleet No. 7. Converted by factory as of 9/17/31 to Alpha 4 under ATC 451, and to Alpha 4a by TWA as of 9/17/32 under ATC 461. Acc. 2/26/33 near Cross Fork, PA. Pilot Walter W. Seyerle had icing conditions and radio failure, fog. Bailed out safely, airplane demolished.

C/n 11

Type	Alpha
Model	3
Reg.	NC 986Y
Mfg.	6/25/31
Eng.	P&W Wasp #1356
ATC	Gr. 2-335

Pilot-and-2-passenger ship sold 6/24/31 to TRANSCONTINENTAL & WESTERN AIR, INC., New York, NY. Price $14,220 less engine, which TWA supplied. NC lic. to TWA issued 7/3/31. TWA Fleet No. 8. Converted by factory as of 9/17/31 to Alpha 4 under ATC 451 as a single-place ship. Converted by TWA as of 9/1/32 to Alpha 4a under ATC 451. Acc. 9/22/35, 2 miles SW of St. Clairsville, OH. Pilot R. S. Le Roy unhurt. "Lost and ran out of gas." Enough parts salvaged to sell ship "as a wreck" 9/38 to FOSTER HANNAFORD, JR., Minneapolis, MN. Hannaford planned to rebuild airplane and retained registration as late as 1948. Parts probably combined later with c/n 3 (q.v.).

C/n 12

Type	Alpha
Model	3
Reg.	NC 992Y
Mfg.	6/30/31
Eng.	P&W Wasp C #1512
ATC	Gr. 2-335

Three-place airplane sold 6/25/31 to TRANSCONTINENTAL & WESTERN AIR, INC., New York, NY. Price $14,220 less engine, which TWA supplied. NC lic. issued to TWA 7/4/31. TWA Fleet No. 9. Converted as of 9/17/31 by factory to Alpha 4 under ATC 451. Converted as of 8/8/32 by TWA to Alpha 4a under ATC 461. Acc. 1/10/33, Pittsburgh, PA. Pilot Harry J. "Jack" Zimmerman had engine failure after takeoff, crashed and burned. Zimmerman injured but saved by ground crew. Airplane demolished.

C/n 13

Type	Alpha (Army: Y1C-19)
Model	2
Reg.	A.C. #31-516
Mfg.	4/31
Eng.	P&W R-1340-7
ATC	None

First Alpha for USAAC, obtained on ARMY AIR CORPS Contract A.C.

3895 of 3/6/31. Cost, with engine and radio, $15,814.49. First record 5/1/31 at Wright Field, Dayton, OH. Assigned to Bolling Field, Anacostia, DC, 8/2/32. Acc. 6/19/32, Logan Field, Dundalk, MD. Forced landing, pilot Lt. David W. Goodrich. Shipped to Middletown Air Depot, PA, for repairs. Motor changed as of 8/2/32 to P&W R-1340-D, A.C. #31-321. Assigned Selfridge Field, Mt. Clemens, MI, 1/5/33. Assigned Fairfield Air Depot, OH, 1/3/34, reassigned Selfridge Field, MI, 5/23/35, with engine A.C. #31-446 installed. Last duty as part of Flight B of 16th Observation Squadron. Dropped from records 8/22/39 for "fair wear and tear" and given to NATIONAL YOUTH ADMINISTRATION, Algiers Naval Air Station, Algiers, LA.

NOTE: The USAAC acquired three Northrop Alpha Transports in 1931 under contract #3895. It is assumed that they were Northrop c/n 13, 14, and 15, and that their USAAC serial numbers were in the same sequence: A.C. #31-516, #31-517, and #31-518. Army designation for the Alpha was Y1C-19, YC-19, and C-19. The radio-equipped airplanes were built by Northrop under government inspection while under construction.

C/n 14

Type	Alpha (Army Y1C-19)
Model	2
Reg.	A.C. #31-517
Mfg.	4/31
Eng.	P&W R-1340-7
ATC	None

Bought by UNITED STATES ARMY AIR CORPS on Contract A.C. 3895. First record 5/2/31 at Bolling Field, Anacostia, DC. Assigned to Wright Field, Dayton, OH, 10/2/32. Acc. Bolling Field, 7/12/32, pilot Capt. I. H. Edwards. Major replacements included installation of A.C. eng. #31-509. Assigned Bolling Field 12/2/32. To Langley Field, Hampton, VA, 10/18/33. To Olmstead Field, PA, 1/19/34. To Middletown Air Depot, PA, 9/27/37. Assigned to Pope Field

(Ft. Bragg), NC, 3/18/38, with A.C. eng. #31-406. Dropped from records during 9/39, dismantled and shipped by freight 9/1/39 to CASEY JONES SCHOOL OF AERONAUTICS, Newark, NJ, for use as an instructional aircraft.

C/n 15

Type	Alpha (Army Y1C-19)
Model	2
Reg.	A.C. #31-518
Mfg.	1931
Eng.	P&W R-1340-7 A.C. #31-612
ATC	None

Bought by UNITED STATES ARMY AIR CORPS on Contract A.C. 3895. Official performance tests 9/26/31 at Wright Field, Dayton, OH, under pilots L. A. Beery and J. E. Parker. First official record 7/22/32 at Wright Field, OH, with A.C. eng. #31-612 and radio. Assigned Bolling Field, Anacostia, DC, 10/22/32. Engine change 2/33 to A.C. #31-344. Acc. 3/20/33, near Petersburg, VA. Pilot Lt. James A. Willis, Jr., and his passengers Maj. James A. Willis, Sr., and Major John A. Parker, of the Judge Advocate General's Office, killed. Crashed in fog flying from Spartanburg, SC, to Washington, DC. Airplane a "complete washout." Surveyed in USAAC records as of 5/23/33.

C/n 16

Type	Alpha
Model	3
Reg.	NC 993Y
Mfg.	7/10/31
Eng.	P&W Wasp C #1355
ATC	Gr. 2-335

Three-place airplane sold 6/25/31 to TRANSCONTINENTAL & WESTERN AIR, INC., New York, NY. Price $14,220 less engine, which was supplied by TWA. NC lic to TWA 7/13/31. TWA Fleet No. 10. Acc. 9/17/31, Antrim, OH. Damage to wings and l/g. Repaired and converted as of 12/5/31 as Alpha 4 under

ATC 451. Acc. 2/6/32, Robertson, MO. Fuselage damaged. Repaired as of 2/13/32. Acc. 7/3/32, near Alton, IL. Propeller-blade failure led to engine tearing off its mounting. Pilot Harry Campbell left via parachute. Airplane demolished.

C/n 17

Type	Alpha
Model	3
Reg.	NC 994Y, X 994Y
Mfg.	7/15/31
Eng.	P&W Wasp C #2139
ATC	Gr. 2-335

Three-place airplane, last of the Alphas built. Sold 6/25/31 to TRANSCONTINENTAL & WESTERN AIR, INC., New York, NY. Price $14,200 less engine, which was supplied by TWA. NC lic. to TWA 7/21/31. TWA Fleet No. 11. Converted at factory as of 9/8/31 with special type of 1/g installed and briefly lic. X. Again NC as of 9/9/31 as Alpha 4 under ATC G. 2-371 and then 4a under ATC 461. Acc. 11/5/32, Camden, NJ. Repaired. Acc. 1/31/35, Glendale, CA. Pilot Ernest L. Smith, minor injuries. Suffered partial motor failure, hit high-tension wires, and crashed in Los Angeles River. "Complete washout."

C/n 1

Type	Beta
Model	3
Reg.	X 963Y
Mfg.	4/4/31
Eng.	Menasco Buccaneer 6 LAI #6010
ATC	None

First of its design, a new sport monoplane with tandem seating. X lic. 3/31/31 to NORTHROP AIRCRAFT CORPORATION, United Airport, Burbank, CA. Extensively flown and shown for 4 months. Acc. Los Angeles, CA, 8/12/31. Reported "washed out." DOC Inspector Lester J. Holoubek encountered aileron trouble and left via parachute.

C/n 2

Type	Beta
Model	3D
Reg.	X 12214, NC 12214
Mfg.	9/31
Eng.	P&W Wasp, Jr.
ATC	(Gr. 2-401)

Developed by Northrop under chief engineer Don R. Berlin as a single-seat version of the Beta sport airplane, with an engine twice the horsepower. Approved for X lic. 9/1/31, issued to NORTHROP AIRCRAFT CORPORATION, Burbank, CA. Tested for DOC approval under test pilot Edmund T. Allen. Given ATC approval under Gr. 2-401 and lic. NC 2/15/32. Further development and flight tests run by Stearman Aircraft at Wichita, KS, in 1931–32 (Stearman expected to be building both the Northrop Alpha and the Beta). Had 40 hrs. TT and P&W engine #89 installed when sold 2/8/32 to KENYON BOOCOCK, New York, NY. Hangared at Roosevelt Field, L.I. Boocock had single cockpit enclosed with a sliding canopy, and reported speeds up to 212 mph. For sale late 1932 at $5,000 with 129 hrs. TT. Sold 1/16/33 to GEORGE W. HARD, West Sayville, NY. Acc. 1/16/33, Hicksville, NY. Damage to wings, put in storage. Sold 5/3/34 to UNITED AIRPORTS OF CONNECTICUT, East Hartford, CT, and shipped to Stearman in Kansas. Rebuilt as of 5/1/34, lic. X 5/4/34, with P&W eng. #137. Intention was to use plane to test Zap, Fowler and Wright flaps. Acc. 5/5/34, Wichita, KS. Reported "completely destroyed."

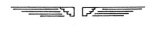

C/n 1

Type	Gamma
Model	2A
Reg.	X 12265, NR 12265
Mfg.	8/32
Eng.	Wright GR-1510 #13648
ATC	None

The first Northrop Gamma, single-seat, built to the order of Lt. Cmdr. Frank M. Hawks, director of the Aviation Dept. of The Texas Company, a major oil producer/distributor. Approved for X lic. 8/22/32 to THE NORTHROP CORPORATION, Los Angeles Municipal Airport, Inglewood, CA, "for development of long-range, high-speed mail transport." Sold 2/14/33 to THE TEXAS COMPANY, New York, NY. Price $40,000, delivery date 12/17/32. Named *Texaco 11* and called *Texaco Sky Chief*. Approved for NR lic. 2/28/33, "for long-distance flight." With Cmdr. Hawks set new nonstop transcontinental record time of 13 hrs. 27 min. flying Los Angeles–New York. Other nonstop records in 1933 such as Los Angeles–Atlanta and Regina, Sask., to Bridgeport, CT. Sold 6/22/34 to GARFIELD ARTHUR "GAR" WOOD, Detroit, Mich. Named *Kinjockety II* and entered in various

The Sky Chief *turned heads wherever it flew, or appeared just sitting on the ground.*

competitions. Acc. 9/4/36, near Stafford, KS. Pilot Joseph Palmer Jacobson. Flying in the Bendix Transcontinental Race of NAR, the airplane "exploded in midair." Jacobson escaped via parachute, unhurt.

C/n 2

Type	Gamma
Model	2B
Reg.	X 12269, NR 12269
Mfg.	8/32
Eng.	P&W Wasp SD-1 #4810
ATC	None

Two-place, tandem-seat, built for explorer Lincoln Ellsworth. Approved for X lic. 8/22/32 to THE NORTHROP CORPORATION, Inglewood, CA, and for R lic. 11/14/32. Restricted to polar explorations. Was first Gamma test-flown, delivery date 11/29/32. Sold 2/14/33 to LINCOLN ELLSWORTH, New York, NY. Price $37,000. Named *Polar Star*. Taken to Antarctic in January 1934 and test-flown on skis by Bernt Balchen. Damaged in unseasonal ice breakup and returned to Northrop factory for repairs and test-flying on floats. Returned to Antarctic in winter of 1934–35 and made one flight. Returned again in fall of 1935. Ellsworth, piloted by Herbert Hollick-Kenyon, made trans-Antarctic flight from Dundee Island to close to Little America between 11/23 and 12/9/35, with 5 stops en route. Returned to the U.S. and presented to the SMITHSONIAN INSTITUTION, Washington, DC, 4/25/36. Part of collection of National Air and Space Museum. The only Northrop Gamma in existence.

C/n 3

Type	Delta
Model	1A
Reg.	X 12292, NC 12292
Mfg.	5/33
Eng.	Wright Cyclone SR-1820 F3 #21122
ATC	(Gr. 2-456)

The first Delta, approved for X lic.

5/13/33 to THE NORTHROP CORPORATION, Mines Field, Inglewood, CA. Approved for NC lic. 8/5/33 under ATC Gr. 2-456. Seating capacity reduced from 8 passengers to 6 and pilot. Leased 8/4/33 to Transcontinental & Western Air, Inc., New York, NY. Put on TWA mail and express runs without passengers. TWA Fleet No. 15. Acc. 10/24/33, Grants, NM. Pilot George Rice made forced landing due to breakage of adjustable propeller blade. Damage to l/g. Repaired and Wright Cyclone engine #21409 installed, with controllable-pitch propeller. Acc. 11/13/33 near Moriarty, NM. Pilot Harlan Hull suffered engine fire at 6,000 feet and left via parachute. Aircraft demolished.

C/n 4

Type	Delta
Model	1B
Reg.	X 236Y, X-ABED
Mfg.	7/33
Eng.	P&W Hornet T-2C-1 #1801
ATC	Gr. 2-458

Pilot-and-8-passenger Delta built for and sold 8/19/33 to PAN AMERICAN AIRWAYS, INC., New York, NY. Delivery date 8/20/33. Approved for export to Mexico with 20 hrs. TT and export certificate E-784 issued 8/19/33. Flown by Pan American subsidiary Aerovías Centrales, S.A., on Mexico City–Los Angeles route. Reported as "destroyed by fire," 5/5/34.

C/n 5

Type	Gamma (Army YA-13, XA-16)
Model	2C
Reg.	X 12291, A.C. #34-027
Mfg.	5/33
Eng.	Wright Cyclone SR-1820 F-2 #21201
ATC	None

Approved for X lic. 5/18/33 to THE NORTHROP CORPORATION, Inglewood, CA, for testing prior to delivery to USAAC at Dayton, OH. Delivered to Wright Field, OH, 7/18/33 by Douglas test pilot Carl Cover. Under evaluation as 2-seat attack light bomber in August 1933. Re-engined 6/9/34 with Wright Cyclone #21368. Purchased by UNITED STATES ARMY AIR CORPS 6/28/34 (under Contract W-535 #A.C.-6811 with price $80,950). Army designation as YA-13 and assigned serial #34-027. Later redesigned with a new vertical fin, 3-bladed propeller, and P&W R-1870-7 950-hp Twin Wasp engine as Army XA-16 or Northrop Gamma Model 2F. Armament consisted of 4 wing-mounted .30 cal. guns, one rear .30 cal. gun, with upper and lower gun ports; 1,100-lb. bomb load could be slung under center section. Eventually became an instructional air frame at aircraft mechanics school at Roosevelt Field, NY.

C/n 6

Type	Gamma (Navy XFT1/XFT2)

Dual-registered Delta 1B flown by Pan American's Mexican subsidiary, Aerovías Centrales, S.A. in 1933–34.

Model –
Reg. Navy #9400
Mfg. 1933–34
Eng. Wright XR-1510-8/ R-1535-72
ATC None

A small single-seat experimental monoplane fighter aircraft, developed by The Northrop Corporation, based on Gamma design experience, Navy contract 31282, delivered to Anacostia Naval Air Station, VA, 2/14/34. Equipped with wing flaps and emergency life raft stowed behind pilot's headrest. Plane tested at Anacostia and Langley Field, VA, in 1934, but deemed too fast for Navy use, in particular carrier landings. Returned to the Northrop factory in California, the plane was re-engined with a P&W Twin Wasp R-1535 engine and designated as an XFT-2 under a new contract, and delivered to Anacostia Naval Air Station, 3/29/36. Slated for return to factory, but reported crashed near Altoona, PA, 7/21/36. Contract closed out.

C/n 7

Type Delta
Model 1C
Reg. SE-ADI, EC-AGC
Mfg. 2/34
Eng. P&W Hornet T1C-1 #2003
ATC Gr. 2-458

Pilot-and-8-passenger plane, sold 2/34 to A.B. AEROTRANSPORT, Stockholm, Sweden, with delivery date of 3/1/34. Exported under export certificate E-946. Given Swedish registration SE-ADI and named *Halland.* Used on Malmö-Gothenburg route and as a mail carrier Stockholm-Malmö-Hannover. Entered in 1934 MacRobertson Race to Australia, with Race #22, to be flown by Marshall Lindholm and Georg Lindow. Entry withdrawn. Made record Stockholm-Paris flight in 4 hrs. 40 min. Engine replaced with P&W Hornet #4518 (?). Reported sold 5/37 to Kenyan long-distance flyer Beryl Markham, with British reg. G-AEXR allotted, but

not taken up. Also reportedly sold to Iraqi Royal Flight as YI-OSF, as of 9/29/37. In actuality, sold 1937 through agents to the militarized Spanish Republican airline LÍNEAS AÉREAS POSTALES ESPAÑOLES (LAPE), and flown during the Spanish Civil War with reg. EC-AGC. Possibly survived the war. Disposition unknown.

C/n 8

Type Gamma
Model 2D
Reg. NR 13757, NC 13757
Mfg. 4/34
Eng. Wright Cyclone SR-1820 F3 #21896
ATC (549)

Single-place Gamma built for and sold 4/30/34 to TRANSCONTINENTAL & WESTERN AIR, INC., New York, NY. Approved for cross-country cargo flights with R lic. Flown by Jack Frye, president of TWA, from Los Angeles to Newark 5/13-14/34 for new, one-stop transport record of 11 hrs. 31 min. TWA Fleet #16. NC lic. approved as 1 PCLM 7/15/34 under ATC 549. Entered by TWA in MacRobertson Race to Australia, 1934, to be flown by Royal Leonard, but withdrawn. Acc. 1/11/35, near Deep Lake, AR. Pilot Jack Frye cracked up in forced landing after motor failure. TWA wrote off $16,208.48, and wreckage sold as of 9/10/35 to CHARLES H. BABB, Glendale, CA. Aircraft broker Babb had the plane trucked to California and later repaired by Aero Industries Technical Institute. Used a right wing from a Northrop Delta (c/n 74?) with a special shim. Re-licensed 10/30/40 with Wright Cyclone engine #21947, for cargo and freight use. Sold 1/3/42 to AIRMOTIVE, INC., New York, NY (Babb's New York division), and with no bill of sale in 1942 to UNITED STATES ARMY ENGINEERS. Later reported as "wrecked in Africa."

C/n 9

Type Gamma
Model 2D

Reg. X 13758, NR 13758, NC 13758, A.C. #42-94140
Mfg. 5/34
Eng. Wright Cyclone SR-1820 F3 #21897
ATC 549 (pend.)

Built for and sold 10/11/34 to TRANSCONTINENTAL & WESTERN AIR, INC., New York, NY. Delivery date 6/11/34. Approved 5/19/34 for X lic. for flight tests. Approved 5/28/34 for NC lic. TWA Fleet No. 17. Approved 1/26/36 for NR lic., to test wing and propeller de-icers, radio, gasoline analyzers, and General Electric turbo-superchargers. Given NX lic. 7/25/36 and 2 observer seats installed. Used as "Experimental Overweather Laboratory," with TWA pilot D.W. "Tommy" Tomlinson and TWA development engineer James Heistand. Substratospheric flights undertaken at from 20,000 to 35,000 feet, with studies of icing, turbulence, engine efficiency, radio performance, etc. Acc. 4/12/38, near Princeton, NJ. Pilot D. W. Tomlinson made forced landing after an error which took plane 150 miles out over the Atlantic Ocean. Repaired by TWA at Kansas City shops. Sold 10/10/40 to THE TEXAS COMPANY, New York, NY. Named *Texaco 36* and flown by pilot Aubrey Keif to test oil temperature and flowage. Sold 10/15/42 to UNITED STATES WAR DEPARTMENT, Washington, DC. Price $11,225. Put in military use as Army UC-100, with USAAC serial #42-94140. Assigned to Duncan Field, TX, 10/26/42. Acc. 1/17/43, Duncan Field, TX. Shortage of parts noted 7/27/43. Surveyed at Kelly Field, TX, 9/11/43.

C/n 10

Type Gamma
Model 2D
Reg. NC 13759, NR 13759, XA-ABJ
Mfg. 6/34
Eng. Wright Cyclone SR-1820 F-3 #21898
ATC 549

Built for and sold 10/10/34 to TRANSCONTINENTAL & WESTERN AIR, INC., Kansas City, MO. Delivery date 7/18/34. TWA Fleet No. 18. Flown by TWA on mail/cargo routes 1934–35. Acquired 10/11/35 (bill of sale 12/10) by THE TEXAS COMPANY, New York, NY. Named *Texaco 20*. Given NR lic., ski attachment fittings installed, and observer's seat placed in mail compartment. Hastily substituted for Gamma c/n 12 (q.v.) and directed by a "Lincoln Ellsworth Rescue Committee" to South America in 1935–36. Flown from Kansas City to Magallanes, Chile, by H. T. "Dick" Merrill, and carried on to Antarctica by ship. Before arrival, Ellsworth and Hollick-Kenyon found safe (see c/n 2). This Gamma put on floats at Gallegos, Argentina, and flown briefly over Antarctica on skis. Returned to U.S. by boat and NC lic. issued. Sold 2/18/37 to FRANK CORDOVA, Hempstead, NY. Flown to San Antonio and sold 2/20/37 to COL. GUSTAVO LEÓN of Mexican air force. In actuality bought for the Spanish Republican govt., but given Mexican reg. XA-ABJ in name of RAFAEL MONTERO. Shipped 12/26/37 on S.S. *Ibai* to France and Spain. Flown with 1A Escuadrilla de Vultee, Grupo 72, in coastal defense patrols for Spanish Republican air force. Reportedly not flown out of Spain at end of war. Disposition unknown.

C/n 11

Type	Gamma
Model	2G
Reg.	X 13761, NC 13761, NR 13761
Mfg.	8/34
Eng.	Curtiss-Wright Conquerer SGV-1570 F-4 #20304
ATC	Gr. 2-489

Built as a 2-place Gamma with in-line, liquid-cooled Curtiss Conqueror engine. Ordered by Jacqueline Cochran for entry in Mac-Robertson Race to Australia to be held in October 1934. Approved for NC lic. 9/29/34 and acquired by Miss Cochran 9/30/34 with lic. to THE NORTHROP CORPORATION, Inglewood, CA. Acc. 10/1/34, Tucumcari, NM, Pilot Wesley Smith. Returned to factory for repair of forward lower half of fuselage and wing section. Eng. change to P&W Twin Wasp, Jr., SAI-G #27, with controllable-pitch propeller. Approved 8/28/35 for NR lic. as 1PCLM, for racing only. A starter in 1935 Bendix Transcontinental Race with Jacqueline Cochran, but made forced landing at Kingman, AR. Finally sold, as of 11/30/35, to JACQUELINE COCHRAN, New York, NY. Leased to Howard R. Hughes, whose Hughes Development Company installed 3 new gas tanks, a

3-bladed propeller, and Wright Cyclone SGR-1820 G-5 eng. #21227. Hughes set new west-east transcontinental speed record, 9 hrs., 26 min., 10 sec., on 1/13-14/36. Reconverted with P&W Wasp, Jr., SAI-G #588 and NR lic. 7/1/36. Acc. 7/10/36, Indianapolis, IN. Pilot Jacqueline Cochran. Motor cut out after takeoff, nosed over in landing and motor torn out. Not rebuilt as c/n 11 (see Gamma c/n 12).

C/n 12

Type	Gamma
Model	2D2 ("2H")
Reg.	NC 2111, NX 2111, NR 2111
Mfg.	12/34
Eng.	Wright Cyclone SR-1820 F-3 #22376
ATC	549

Bought on order of Marron Price Guggenheim, but reg. 12/21/34 in name of Guggenheim personal pilot RUSSELL W. THAW, Garden City, NY. Delivery date 12/20/34. Lic. NX 1/2/35, for testing Sperry automatic pilot. Approved for NR lic. 8/28/35 for use as entry in the Bendix Transcontinental Race of NAR. Flown by Thaw to 3rd place. To NC lic. as of 10/14/35. NR lic. reapproved 11/35 for flight of Thaw to South America for "rescue" of Lin-

---

Vance Breese, who test-flew many Northrop Airplanes.

Jackie Cochran's big Gamma is piloted by Howard Hughes in quest of a new speed mark, January 1936.

coln Ellsworth and Herbert Hollick-Kenyon, thought to be lost in Antarctica. Acc. 12/9/35, Atlanta, GA. Pilot Russell Thaw and mechanic William H. Klenke, Jr., escaped injury. On predawn takeoff, motor cut out and ship grazed trees, skidded 200 feet into ditch. Wing, 1/g, etc. badly damaged. Wrecked aircraft transferred 11/36 to JACQUELINE COCHRAN, New York, NY, but bill of sale dated 2/16/37. It was thought that parts would be used to rebuild the Cochran Gamma (c/n 11), but instead c/n 12 was rebuilt at the Northrop factory during 1-3/37 and NC lic. issued 4/1/37 under ATC Gr. 2-535. Sold as of 7/28/38 to MACFADDEN PUBLICATIONS, New York, NY. Acc. 5/8/38, Bendix, NJ. Pilot Edward F. Gorski. Eng. quit on take off, nosed over in landing. Damage to fuselage, left wing, 1/g, tail, etc. Sold as wreck for $3,000 to CHARLES H. BABB, Glendale, CA, 8/18/39. Rebuilt, sold 4/42 to CONTINENTAL AIR LINES, Denver, CO, for executive use. Sold 10/26/42 to U.S. ARMY ENGINEERS, San Francisco, CA, for use on CANOL PROJECT, Edmonton, Alberta, Canada. Ultimate disposition uncertain.

C/n 13

Type	Gamma
Model	2E
Reg.	K 5053
Mfg.	1934
Eng.	Wright Cyclone R-1820 F-53
ATC	None

Thought to be the 2-place military attack bomber acquired in 1934 by the BRITISH AIR MINISTRY. Utilized for study and comparative evaluation purposes at the Royal Aircraft Establishment at Farnborough. Used to test rubber de-icing equipment by A. E. Clouston. Final disposition unknown.

C/n 14 through 27

Type	Gamma
Model	2E, 2ED, 2EC
Reg.	–
Mfg.	1934
Eng.	Wright Cyclone 750-hp
ATC	None

Purchased by Chinese govt. and shipped to China. First delivery reported as 2/19/34. Used as attack bombers by Chinese air force during hostilities with Japan, 1934–38.

c/n 14 Gamma 2E
c/n 15 Gamma 2ED
c/n 16 Gamma 2ED
c/n 17 Gamma 2EC
c/n 18 Gamma 2EC
c/n 19 Gamma 2EC
c/n 20 Gamma 2EC
c/n 21 Gamma 2EC
c/n 22 Gamma 2EC
c/n 23 Gamma 2ED
c/n 24 Gamma 2ED
c/n 25 Gamma 2ED
c/n 26 Gamma 2ED
c/n 27 Gamma 2ED

C/n 28

Type	Delta
Model	1D
Reg.	NC 13777, N 13777
Mfg.	7/34
Eng.	Wright Cyclone SR-1820 F-3 #21902
ATC	Gr. 2-484

Five-place executive transport built and lic. X to THE NORTHROP CORPORATION, Inglewood, CA, 7/7/34. Sold to RICHFIELD OIL CORPORATION OF NEW YORK, New York, NY. Delivery date 7/21/34. Approved for NC lic. 7/20/34. Bill of sale 10/10/34. Named *The Richfield Eagle*. Sold 12/15/35 to WILLIAM C. M. DUFFIE, as receiver of RICHFIELD OIL CORP. OF CALIFORNIA, Los Angeles, CA. Sold 3/12/37 to RICHFIELD OIL CORP., Los Angeles, CA. Sold 1/7/38 to BAKER OIL TOOLS, INC. Huntingdon Park, CA. Sold 4/3/41 to CHARLES H. BABB, Glendale, CA. Sold 10/16/41 to LE TOURNEAU CO. OF GEORGIA, Toccoa, GA. Sold 10/10/42 to MINNEAPOLIS-HONEYWELL REGULATOR COMPANY, Min-

neapolis, MN. Wright R-1820 F53 engine #25296 installed 4/45. Sold 10/8/46 to MAX A. CONRAD, Hopkins, MN. Sold 5/29/56 to CHRISTLER & AVERY, Greybull, WY. Used as a crop sprayer. Sold 4/6/59 to JACK CUNNINGHAM, Kansas City, MO. Sold 4/23/62 to THE MANUEL CORPORATION, Kansas City, MO. Sold 4/22/63 to EASTERN AERO CORPORATION, Kansas City, MO. Sold 11/28/66 to RICHARD M. DAVIS, Far Hills, NJ, and later Shawnee Mission, KS. Presumed to be the only Northrop Delta still in existence.

C/n 29

Type	Gamma
Model	1E
Reg.	X 13755, NC 13755, SE-ADW
Mfg.	5/34
Eng.	P&W Hornet T2D-1 #2162
ATC	Gr. 2-476

Carried on records as a "Delta 1E." A 2PCLM experimental ship with tandem cockpits, given X lic. 6/1/34 to THE NORTHROP CORPORATION, Inglewood, CA, and approved NC 6/7/34. Sold 6/8/34 to A. B. AEROTRANSPORT, Stockholm, Sweden, and exported under export certificate E-1146. Airplane was to be in night mail plane configuration. Given Swedish reg. SE-ADW and named *Småland*. Flown briefly by A.B. Aerotransport. Acc. 7/6/34, near Almhult, Sweden. Developed aileron flutter and lost a wing. Pilot and radio operator left via parachute. Airplane demolished.

C/n 30 through 37

Type	Gamma
Model	2E
Reg.	-
Mfg.	1934
Eng.	Wright Cyclone R-1820 F53
ATC	None

These 8 airplanes were purchased by

the Chinese govt. and shipped to
China. Used as attack bombers in
the Chinese air force, 1934–38.

C/n 38

Type	Delta
Model	1D
Reg.	NC 14241, 43●5
Mfg.	8/34
Eng.	Wright Cyclone SR-1820 F-3 #21901
ATC	553

Six-place ship, delivered 8/23/34,
NC lic. issued 8/24/34 and bill of sale
10/10/34 to POWEL CROSLEY,
JR., Cincinnati, OH. Flown as executive transport for Crosley and Crosley Radio Corporation. Sold 12/4/36
to THE VIMALERT COMPANY,
LTD., Jersey City, NJ. Under export certificate E-4135, shipped on
the Spanish S.S. *Mar Cantabrico* as
part of a cargo, including aircraft,
assigned to agents of the Spanish
Republic in Bilbao, Spain. Captured
3/8/37 by Spanish Nationalist war-
ship and aircraft incorporated into
Spanish Nationalist air force as part
of Grupo 43 (single-engined transports). Coded 43●5. Reported dismantled during the Spanish Civil
War and later scrapped.
NOTE: At least one of the Northrop
Deltas in either Republican or
Nationalist service survived the
Spanish Civil War. Recoded in 1946,
the Spanish air force lists the Delta
type under "L.12."

C/n 39

Type	Delta
Model	1D
Reg.	X 14242, NC 14242, F-AQAQ
Mfg.	8/18/34
Eng.	Wright Cyclone SR-1820 F-3 #22174
ATC	553 (pend.)

X lic. issued 7/21/34 to THE
NORTHROP AIRCRAFT CORPO-
RATION, Inglewood, CA, for the
purpose of flight testing to obtain an

ATC. Sold 8/18/34 to HAL ROACH
STUDIOS, INC., Culver City, CA.
Price $33,263.31, delivery date
8/23/34. NC lic. approved 11/19/34.
Sold 1/8/35 to ERLE P. HALLI-
BURTON, INC., Los Angeles,
CA. Sold 12/12/36 to CHARLES
H. BABB, New York, NY. Sold
12/14/36 to RUDOLF WOLF,
INC., New York, NY. Exported as
part of export certificate #E-4021, to
a Dutch consignee, but off-loaded at
Le Havre, France. Fuselage ship-
ped on S.S. *President Harding*, and
wings aboard S.S. *Waalhaven*. Air-
plane registered in France as F-
AQAQ. Transferred as of 7/17/37 to
SPANISH REPUBLICAN GOV-
ERNMENT, for use as military
transport. Use and disposition uncertain.

C/n 40

Type	Delta
Model	1D-3
Reg.	NC 14265
Mfg.	9/34
Eng.	P&W Hornet S4D-1 #2381
ATC	Gr. 2-490

Only Model 1D with a P&W engine.
New and approved for NC lic.
9/25/34 to THE NORTHROP COR-
PORATION, Inglewood, CA. Sold
12/5/34 to WILLIAM H. DAN-
FORTH, Boston, MA. Delivery
date 10/7/34. Flown as an executive
transport 1934–38. Engine change
8/8/36 to P&W S9E, #2704. Destroyed in spectacular hangar fire
along with 13 other airplanes on
4/1/38, at Miami, FL.

C/n 41

Type	Delta
Model	1D
Reg.	NC 14266, 43●4
Mfg.	10/34
Eng.	Wright Cyclone SR-1820 F-3 #22199
ATC	553

Approved for NC lic. 10/9/34 to
THE NORTHROP CORPORA-

TION, Inglewood, CA. Delivery
date 10/7/34 and bill of sale 12/5/34
to MORTON MAY, St. Louis, MO.
Transferred as of 3/20/35 to WIL-
BUR D. MAY, Los Angeles, CA.
Used as 6-passenger executive transport by May Department Store officials, 1934–36. Sold 12/14/36 to
THE VIMALERT COMPANY,
Jersey City, NJ. Shipped under export certificate E-4135 as part of cargo of S.S. *Mar Cantabrico*, con-
signed to agents of the Spanish
Republic at Bilbao, Spain. The vessel was intercepted by the Spanish
Nationalist cruiser *Canarias* 3/8/37.
Captured aircraft incorporated into
Spanish Nationalist air force as part
of Grupo 43 (single-engined transports) and coded 43●4. Cracked up
at least once. Reportedly dismantled
during the Spanish Civil War and
eventually scrapped.

C/n 42

Type	Delta
Model	1D
Reg.	NC 14267, NR 14267, VH-ADR, A61-1
Mfg.	8/34
Eng.	Wright Cyclone SR-1820 F-2 #22175
ATC	553

Approved for NC lic. 8/20/34 to
THE NORTHROP CORPORA-
TION, Inglewood, CA. Delivered
10/10/34 to CHICAGO REAL ES-
TATE LOAN & TRUST CO., Chicago, IL. Price $32,959. Bill of sale
7/30/35. Flown as an executive transport 1934–38 for George F. Harding, president of Chicago Real Estate Loan & Trust Co., an Illinois
state senator, flying enthusiast,
and collector of arms and art.
Sold 4/27/38 to LINCOLN ELLS-
WORTH, New York, NY. Approved
for NR lic. 8/14/38, for survey flights
in the Antarctic. Flown on skis during Ellsworth's 4th Antarctic expedition, with extra gas tanks in the
cabin. Made one flight over Antarctic region, 1/14/39, with Ellsworth and pilot J. H. Lymburner.
Sold 2/39 to AUSTRALIAN DE-
PARTMENT OF CIVIL AVIA-
TION and reg. VH-ADR 9/40.

Stored 1941–43. Briefly on charter to U.S. Army and on loan to Royal Australian Air Force for communications duties. Civil reg. kept, but coded A61-1. Used by 34th and 37th Squadrons. Acc. 9/30/43. Damaged in takeoff. Considered uneconomical to repair and scrapped.

C/n 43

Type	(Gamma) Navy XBT-1
Model	-
Reg.	Navy #9745
Mfg.	1935
Eng.	P&W R-1535-66 700-hp
ATC	None

An experimental dive-bomber, tried by U.S. Navy, and designated XBT-1. Basically similar to Army A-17. First flown July 1935 by test pilot Vance Breese. First delivered to Navy 12/35 and Navy-tested as of 4/36. Fifty-four production models ordered and built. These had R-1534-94 engines and redesigned, rounded tail fin. Carried a 1,020-lb. bomb load. Deliveries to Navy began in late 1937.

C/n 44

Type	Gamma (XP-948)
Model	3A
Reg.	-
Mfg.	1935
Eng.	P&W Twin Wasp R-1535 A5G 750-hp
ATC	None

A military version of the Northrop Gamma, but more properly described as a USAAC pursuit adaptation of the experimental Navy XBT-1. Given designation XP-948 and completed in Army colors and finish. A single cockpit forward, with retractable 1/g and split flaps. Built in secrecy and rumored to have a 235-mph speed. Test-flown by Northrop test pilot Arthur H. Skaer 7/30/35. Airplane and pilot completely disappeared and were presumed to have gone down in the Pacific Ocean.
NOTE: The Gamma 3A design was

sold to Chance Vought Aircraft of East Hartford, CT, and a Vought version was built for Army fighter competition trials in 1936, as the Vought V-141. No orders were forthcoming from the USAAC.

C/n 45

Type	(Gamma)
Model	2EC
Reg.	-
Mfg.	1934
Eng.	Wright Cyclone R-1820 F53 750-hp
ATC	None

Purchased by Chinese govt. and shipped to China. Used as an attack bomber in Chinese air force, 1934–38.

C/n 46

Type	Gamma
Model	2E
Reg.	-
Mfg.	Late 1934
Eng.	Wright Cyclone R-1820 F-53
ATC	None

A 2-place military attack bomber purchased by the Chinese govt. and shipped to China. Used by Chinese air force 1934–38.

C/n 47

Type	Gamma
Model	2E
Reg.	X 13760, NC 13760
Mfg.	1/23/35
Eng.	Wright Cyclone R-1820 F-3 #21638
ATC	Gr. 2-503

Lic. X 1/35 to THE NORTHROP CORPORATION, Inglewood, CA. Approved for NC 2/11/35, with pilot-and-1-passenger capacity. Used for South American sales tour, with pilot Frank M. Hawks. Hawks was in Buenos Aires, Argentina, to make demonstration flights for the Argentine navy, but 5/2/35 was called back

"immediately" to the Northrop factory in California. Plane's cowl painted in English and Spanish: "Northrop Gamma 2E, Powered by 716-hp Wright Cyclone Engine." Commander Hawks and Gage Irving, Northrop factory superintendent, made a record flight from Buenos Aires to Los Angeles 5/3–5/35. With 8 stops, they flew 8,090 miles in 39 hrs. 52 min. flying time. Relic. X 8/12/35 to test a Wright SR-1820 F-23 engine of 750 hp. Sold c. 11/20/35 to AMTORG TRADING COMPANY, New York, NY, agent for the UNION OF SOVIET SOCIALIST REPUBLICS. No export certificate or bill of sale filed. Airplane flown to East Coast, dismantled, and shipped to Russia by boat.

C/n 48 through 72

Type	Gamma
Model	2E
Reg.	-
Mfg.	1934–35
Eng.	Wright Cyclone R-1820-F53
ATC	None

These 25 Northrop Gamma 2E airplanes manufactured by Northrop as unassembled parts. Purchased on order by the Chinese govt. and shipped disassembled to China. Assembled by the government-controlled Central Aircraft Manufacturing Company (CAMCO) at Hangchow, Chekiang province, China. Incorporated into the Chinese air force; used as attack bombers during 1934–38 period.

C/n 73

Type	Delta
Model	1D
Reg.	NC 14220, NX 14220
Mfg.	12/34
Eng.	Wright Cyclone SR-1820 F-3 #22377
ATC	553

Approved for NC lic. 12/34 to THE NORTHROP CORPORATION, Inglewood, CA. Sold 2/22/35 to BRUCE DODSON, Kansas City, MO. Pilot-and-6-passenger executive transport. Sold 5/14/35 to SEWARD WEBB PULITZER, Old Westbury, NY. Flown by and for Pulitzer 1935–38. Acc. 7/7/35, Roosevelt Field, NY. S. W. Pulitzer, pilot. Slight buckle in center section, repaired at Northrop factory; reapproved for lic. 6/21/36. Sold 9/23/38 to JOYLAND ENTERPRISES, INC., New York, NY. Had 5-day approval 1/5-10/39 for NX lic., with 48-gal. gas tank replacing two front seats for "a long-distance flight to Miami." Flown by Joyland (Jack Sifka, president) 1938–42. Sold 9/5/42 to CHARLES H. BABB CO., New York, NY. Sold 9/16/42 to UNITED STATES ENGINEERS DEPT., CANOL PROJECT, Edmondton, Alberta, Canada. Used on Canol Project by Bechtel-Price-Callahan Co. Turned over to Hdq. Alaskan Wing of U.S. Army Air Transport Command, Edmondton, Alberta, for operation of "Canol Run." Airplane reportedly scrapped/destroyed at conclusion of project.

C/n 74

Type	Delta, Coast Guard RT-1
Model	1D (1D-7)
Reg.	USCG #382, NC 28663
Mfg.	1/29/35
Eng.	Wright Cyclone R-1820 F-32 #22946
ATC	553

Sold 1/35 to UNITED STATES COAST GUARD, with designation RT-1. Delivery date 2/20/35. Price $41,909.20. Used as executive and staff transport and personal transport of U.S. Treasury Secretary Henry Morgenthau, 1935–40. Sold 10/11/40 to CHARLES H. BABB, New York, NY. Price $1,400 at open-bid sale at USCG station at Floyd Bennett Field, Brooklyn, NY. The airplane had 1,100 hrs. TT and was in damaged condition ("gears, left wing and center section bent, buckled and torn") and less engine, propeller, instruments, and accessories. Repairs made locally (?), another engine in-

stalled and approved 11/17/41 for NC lic. Transferred 12/10/41 to AIRMOTIVE, INC., New York, NY, Babb's subsidiary, as Model 1D-7. No further record. Probably sold to Army Engineers or exported to Latin America.

C/n 75 through 184

Type	(Gamma) Army A-17
Model	(A-17)
Reg.	A.C. #35-051 through #35-160
Mfg.	1935–36
Eng.	P&W R-1535-11 Twin Wasp, Jr., 750-hp
ATC	None

A military attack bomber developed from the Gamma 2C, which was evaluated by the USAAC as the XA-13 and XA-16. The USAAC ordered 110 of the perfected and accepted aircraft, designated A-17, late in 1934. Production A-17s had perforated wing flaps and fixed undercarriage with streamlined teardrop fairings over the inner sides of the wheels. They had four .30 cal. guns in the wings and a fifth in the rear cockpit (upper) for tail protection. Twenty 30-lb. bombs were carried internally. Deliveries to the USAAC ran from December 1935 to January 1937.

C/n 185

Type	Delta
Model	1D (1D-8)
Reg.	(RCAF 667, c/n 177)
Mfg.	1935
Eng.	Wright SR-1820 F52
ATC	None

Built and shipped to Canada as components only. Delivered c. 10/35 to CANADIAN VICKERS COMPANY, Montreal, Quebec, on Department of National Defense specifications. Test flight of first aircraft (RCAF 667) 8/16/36 at Longueuil, Quebec. Twenty built, Vickers c/n 177 through 203, and flown by Royal Canadian Air Force 1936–42. The wreckage of one Canadian Vickers

Delta (RCAF 673) has been salvaged and transported to the National Air Museum at Rockcliffe, Ontario.

C/n 186

Type	Gamma
Model	2J2
Reg.	NC 18148, NX 18148
Mfg.	12/18/35
Eng.	P&W Wasp S3HI-G #6288
ATC	(Gr. 2-553)

A version of the Army A-17, built for use as a demonstrator for the USAAC advanced-trainer competition, with seating for 3 crew. Delivered for testing by USAAC 1/10/36. Rejected, and X lic. issued 12/21/37 to THE NORTHROP CORPORATION, Inglewood, CA. TT: 104:55 hrs. and restricted to flights in the vicinity of factory. Used as a Northrop and Douglas company hack. First approved for NC lic. 7/13/39 under ATC Gr. 2-553 (pend.). Used by Douglas Aircraft Company, Santa Monica, CA, 1937–44. Sold 3/18/44 to DANNY A. FOWLIE, Santa Monica, CA. Sold 9/1/44 to REESE L. MILNER, Los Angeles, CA. Acc. 5/19/45, El Paso, TX. Pilot Aubrey S. Taylor fatally injured and passengers Reese L. Milner and Edward C. Rutherford injured. Engine or propeller trouble on takeoff, "stalled and crashed in attempting to turn back."

C/n 187

Type	Gamma
Model	5A
Reg.	X14997, BXN1
Mfg.	10/35
Eng.	Wright Cyclone SR-1820 F-52
ATC	None

Approved for X lic. 10/4/35 to THE NORTHROP CORPORATION, Inglewood, CA. Exported prior to 10/29/35 with no export certificate or bill of sale. Customer was JAPANESE NAVY, and airplane was to be used for "a study of modern avia-

Northrop 5A military ship, sold in 1935 to the Japanese Navy.

Westover and Sgt. Samuel Hynes were killed in an accident involving #36-349 at Burbank, CA, 9/21/38.

Ninety-three A-17As were released in 1940 for sale to France, and refurbished by the factory (Douglas at El Segundo, CA). Sixty-one ultimately went to England as Nomads. They were given Royal Air Force serial nos. AS 440/462, AS 958/976, and AW 420/438. All but four were released to the South African air force. Thirty-two of the ex-USAAC A-17As went to the Royal Canadian Air Force in October 1940, where, also as Nomads, they were used for training and utility. (RCAF serial nos. 3490 to 3521.)

tion engineering." Coded BXN1 by Japanese navy and given flight evaluation. Destroyed in accident during tests.

C/n 188

Type	Gamma
Model	5B
Reg.	NR 14998, X 14998, XA-ABI
Mfg.	10/35
Eng.	P&W Twin Wasp, Jr., SA1-G #235
ATC	None

A 2PCLM with sliding cockpits forward and a slim rear fuselage. Approved 11/2/35 for R lic. to THE NORTHROP CORPORATION, Inglewood, CA, with intent to make "goodwill foreign tour." X lic. issued 6/15/36 and engine change to Wright Cyclone R-1820 F-52 #23403. TT 26 hrs. and had been in storage with wing and propeller unassembled. Arrived in Buenos Aires, Argentina, 9/36, and demonstrated over a period of 3 months to Fuerza Aérea Argentina by test and demonstration pilot Edmund T. Allen. Reapproved for X lic. at Buenos Aires with Wright Cyclone "G" eng. #23236. TT 126 hrs. Ferry permit issued for Buenos Aires–Mexico City flight "for sale to Lt. Col. Montero," 2/37. Sold c. 3/1/37 to HENRY G. FLETCHER, Mexico City, Mexico. Reg. XA-ABI. Reported flown Mexico City–Vera Cruz 3/17/37 and stored in Pan Am hangar. In actuality bought by agents of Spanish Republic and shipped on S.S. *Ibai* 12/26/37 to Bordeaux with ultimate destination the SPANISH REPUBLICAN AIR FORCE. Flown on coastal patrols. Disposition unknown.

C/n 189 through 290

Type	(Gamma) Army A-17A & A-17AS
Model	(A-17A)
Reg.	A.C.#36-162 to #36-261, #36-349, #36-350
Mfg.	1936–37
Eng.	P&W Twin Wasp 825-hp
ATC	None

An improved Army Model A-17, the A-17A, was ordered from Northrop in December 1935. Ship had similar, but increased, armament and was now equipped with retractable l/g. One hundred A-17As (c/n 189–288) were built by Northrop in 1936–37 and delivered between 8/36 and 12/37. There were also two A-17AS unarmed 3-seat command transports, with P&W Wasp R-1340-41 600-hp engines.

A-17AS A.C. #36-349 was the personal transport allotted to Maj. Gen. Oscar Westover, chief of the USAAC, while A.C. #36-350 was flown by the assistant chief, Brig. Gen. H. H. "Hap" Arnold. Gen.

C/n 291

Type	Gamma
Model	5D
Reg.	X 16091, BXN2, M-506
Mfg.	8/36
Eng.	P&W S3H-1 #6153
ATC	None

Approved for X lic. 9/15/36 to THE NORTHROP CORPORATION, Inglewood, CA. Tail surfaces and interior listed as "Army type" on inspection report. With no ATC, export certificate, or bill of sale recorded, exported in September 1936 to Japan. Customer was JAPANESE NAVY, and coded BXN2. After navy flight testing, the airplane was handed over to the Nakajima Aircraft Manufacturing Company at Koizumi, Japan, for study by engineers. Said to have been "very helpful" in construction of aircraft which led to the Type 97 carrier-based attack bomber, or Nakajima "Kate." Passed on to Manchurian Air Lines, whose photographic division used it for aerial reconnaissance, both over China and above territory of the USSR, through 1939.

C/n 292 through 345

Type	(Gamma) Navy BT-1
Model	-
Reg.	Navy #0590 through #0643

Mfg.	1936–37
Eng.	P&W R-1534-94 825-hp
ATC	None

Fifty-four production models of the BT-1 were built and delivered to the UNITED STATES NAVY in 1936–37. The production model carried a 1,020-lb. bomb load and had a redesigned, rounded tail fin. Deliveries began in late 1937. Of the number, one (Navy #0643) was modified with tricycle l/g, and Navy #0627, with a 1,000-hp Wright engine, was designated XBT-2. BT-1s were the first dive-bombing aircraft assigned to the aircraft carriers *Yorktown* and *Enterprise*.

C/n 346

Type	(Douglas)
Model	1X
Reg.	X 18995
Mfg.	9/30/38
Eng.	P&W Twin Wasp R-1535-94 750-hp
ATC	None

A 2-place airplane with c/n in the Northrop series, but built and registered with X lic. to DOUGLAS AIRCRAFT COMPANY, INC. (El Segundo Division), El Segundo, CA. Called Douglas 1X and approved 10/1/38 "for experimental flight tests with the U.S. Navy." No further record.

C/n 347

Type	Gamma
Model	2L
Reg.	G-AFBT
Mfg.	1937
Eng.	None
ATC	None

Two-place Gamma-type airplane sold to BRITISH AIR MINISTRY, London, England. Delivery date (sans engine) 6/4/37, under export certificate #E-2802 of 6/2/37. Used by Bristol Aeroplane Company as a flying test bed for its new Hercules engine. Successively tested with Hercules Mk 1SM, Mk 1 M(a), Mk 35 M, and Mk 6 SM. Fitted and tested at Filton, Bristol, England. First flight made 9/37 and British reg. G-AFBT applied. Dismantled at Filton during WWII. Scrapped 1/ 46.

C/n —

Type	Flying Wing
Model	N-1M (Northrop Model 1 Mockup)
Reg.	28311
Mfg.	1939–40
Eng.	Two Lycoming O-145, each 4-cyl., 65-hp
ATC	None

Experimental Flying Wing developed by design team of Northrop Aircraft, Inc., Hawthorne, CA. Lic. NX and test-flown at Baker Dry Lake, CA. Named *The Jeep*. First flight 7/3/40. Engines changed to two 117-hp Franklins, with 3-bladed propellers. Test-flown 1940–42. Given to Army Air Forces by Northrop in 1945. Stored. Custody assumed by Smithsonian Institution in 1949. Restored as of 1983, in collections of National Air and Space Museum, Washington, DC.

SUPPLEMENT B
Roster of Canadian Vickers Delta Aircraft

Key:

*	=	Slated to join No. 119 Squadron at Dartmouth, N.S., as of 4/19/40
+	=	Aircraft to be delivered new from factory on wheels and changed to floats after arrival on west coast
IA	=	Instructional airframe (13 Vickers Deltas became instructional airframes)
SOS	=	Struck off strength
GP	=	General Purpose
BR	=	Bomber Reconnaissance
Acc.	=	Accident

c/n	RCAF #	History
177	667*	To RCAF 9/1/36 as Mk.I, with No. 8 GP Squadron. Acc. North Sydney, N.S., 7/13/40. Repaired. At No. 120 BR Squadron, Patricia Bay, B.C., as of 4/27/41/ To IA A143, SOS 4/26/44.
178	668*	To RCAF 10/17/36 as Mk.I with No. 8 GP Squadron. Cargo door plated up 9/39. Acc. 6/28/40. Ocean swell caused buckling. To IA A144, SOS 2/14/45.
179	669*	To RCAF 10/31/36 as Mk.I. Used by No. 6 GP Detachment to 9/39. In storage (on wheels) at Sydney, N.S., 10/20/41. To IA A145, SOS 4/44.
180	670	To RCAF 11/4/37 as Mk.II, with No. 8 BR Squadron. First Delta to be fitted with turtleback gun hatch and plated-over cargo door. Turret removed and new tail cone fitted. To No. 119 BR Squadron at Sea Island, 3/4/40. Acc. Discovery Passage, B.C., 8/8/40. Crashed, crew killed.

Inside the cockpit of a Canadian RCAF Delta.

c/n	RCAF #	History
181	671*	To RCAF 11/5/37 as Mk.II with No. 8 BR Squadron. Coded YO-H. To IA A146, SOS 4/26/44.
182	672*	To RCAF 11/22/37 as Mk. II. With No. 8 BR Squadron as of 10/39, coded YO-C/YO-L. Cargo door plated over. In storage (on wheels) at Sydney, N.S., 10/21/41. SOS 2/7/42.
183	673	To RCAF 11/25/37 as Mk.II, with No. 8 BR Squadron. Acc. 40 miles north of Fredericton, N.B., 9/14/39. Pilot, F/S J. E. Doan, and L/A/C D. A. Rennie were casualties, never found. Wreckage discovered 7/11/58. Incomplete parts of plane recovered and in storage at National Aviation Museum, Rockcliffe, Ontario.
191	674	To RCAF 10/8/38. With No. 8 GP Squadron. Coded YO-D. In storage (on wheels) at Sydney N.S., 10/20/41. To IA A147, SOS 4/20/44.
192	675	To RCAF 10/18/38. Used by No. 1 Fighter Squadron early 1939 for Hurricane pilot training. Thought to have been used later by No. 1 (F) Squadron for communications duties. Coded MX-B. To IA A158, SOS 2/14/45.
193	676	To RCAF 11/4/38 as Mk.II. To No. 8 BR Squadron. Had 2nd turtle-hatch and back gun. Returned to Montreal in late 1939 and given revised gun hatch and new vertical tail, as Mk.III. Used at Ottawa 4/40 for spin tests. Allotted to No. 119 Squadron, Vancouver, B.C. Coded MX-C. To IA A157, SOS 2/14/45.
194	677*	To RCAF 11/12/38 as Mk.II. With No. 8 GP Squadron. Damaged by ocean swell 8/28/40. To IA A148, SOS 2/14/45.
195	682*	To RCAF 1/17/39. With No. 8 BR Squadron. Cargo door plated up. Acc. Cape Dauphin, N.S., 8/16/40. Caught fire and exploded during gunnery practice at Birds Island. Crew killed.
196	683+	To RCAF 6/1/40, as Mk.III (2nd plane with revised tail). To No. 120 BR Squadron at Patricia Bay, B.C. To IA A156, to be stored at Patricia Bay, 3/24/41, SOS 2/14/45.
197	684+	To RCAF 9/10/40, as Mk.III (3rd with revised tail). To No. 120 BR Squadron, Patricia Bay, B.C. In 1941 to No. 3 Training Command. As of 3/24/41 to be stored at Patricia Bay. To IA A142, SOS 4/20/44.
198	685+	To RCAF 6/24/40. To No. 120 BR Squadron, Patricia Bay, B.C. To IA A149, SOS 2/14/45.
199	686+	To RCAF 7/24/40. To No. 120 BR Squadron, Patricia Bay, B.C. As of 3/24/41 to be stored at Patricia Bay. To IA A150, SOS 10/24/44.
200	687+	To RCAF 7/24/40. To No. 120 BR Squadron, Patricia Bay, B.C. As of 3/24/41 to be stored at Patricia Bay. To IA A151, SOS 2/14/45.
201	688+	To RCAF 8/14/40. To No. 120 BR Squadron, Patricia Bay, B.C. Written off 10/10/40 because of engine failure.
202	689+	To RCAF 9/23/40. To No. 120 BR Squadron, Patricia Bay, B.C. Written off 1/16/42 at Lethbridge, Alberta.
203	690	To RCAF 10/28/40. To No. 120 BR Squadron, Patricia Bay, B.C. Being prepared for storage at Patricia Bay as of 3/24/41. In 1941 to No. 13 OTU Squadron. SOS 5/30/42.

SUPPLEMENT C
Roster of Northrop N-3PB Aircraft

c/n	British code	History
301	GS-A (2nd)	First flight, Lake Elsinore, CA, 12/22/40. Lost out of Iceland 4/25/42, with 330 Squadron commander pilot Hans A. Bugge, observer G. Whist, and wireless operator Staale Pedersen.
302	GS-N	Flown at Toronto. Acc. Vattarnes, near Budareyri, Iceland, 9/17/42, with crew killed.
303		Acc. off Vancouver, B.C., 2/21/41. Instructor Harald Kruse and student Erling Jorgensen killed.
304	GS-V	Flown at Toronto. Acc. Akureyri, Iceland, 11/24/42. Crashed on takeoff. No casualties.
305		Acc. Vancouver, B.C., 3/18/41. Crashed on takeoff. Pilot Grenf Riiser and gunner Kaare Kjos killed, observer Erik Bjorneby injured.
306	GS-K (2nd)	Gave full war service. Scrapped in Norway 2/5/49.
307		Flown at Toronto. Acc. Toronto Bay, Ont., 6/20/41. Crashed into ferry boat on takeoff. Instructor Finn Kjos and student Trond Harsvik killed.
308	GS-A (1st)	Withdrawn from service in Iceland 2/42. Used for spares.
309	GS-K (1st)	Withdrawn from service in Iceland 12/7/42. Scrapped.
310	GS-B (2nd)	Withdrawn from service in Iceland 12/42. Scrapped.
311	GS-B (1st)	Acc. Budareyri, Iceland, 9/16/41. Depth charge exploded when dropped during loading.
312	GS-D	Withdrawn from service in Iceland 12/20/42. Scrapped.
313	GS-L (2nd)	Acc. off Skagata, Iceland, 11/4/42. On operations, went into spin and exploded on hitting water. Pilot Qm. Tarnesvik, observer 2/Lt. Gjertsen, wireless operator Qm. Osland killed.
314	GS-E (2nd)	Withdrawn from service in Iceland 3/43. Scrapped.
315	GS-L (1st)	Acc. Akureyri, Iceland, 10/22/41. Crashed on takeoff. No casualties.
316	GS-S	Withdrawn from service in Iceland 1/5/43. Scrapped.
317	GS-M	Acc. Fossvogur Bay, Iceland, 10/22/42. Crashed on landing.
318	GS-T	Made first operational flight of No. 330 Squadron out of Reykjavík, Iceland, 6/23/41. Escorted convoy of 8 vessels from west of Reykjanes to east of Eldey. Pilot Lt. A. Stansberg, nav. Lt. H. O. Rustad, wireless operator Qm. T. Hansen. Withdrawn from service in Iceland 4/43. Scrapped.
319	GS-G (2nd)	Withdrawn from service in Iceland 2/43. Scrapped.
320	GS-U	Gave full war service in Iceland. Acc. River Thjorsa, Iceland, 4/21/43. pilot Wsewolod W. "Sevi" Bulukin, and Qm. Leif Dag Rustad. Forced landing on ferry flight. No injuries. Wreckage recovered 8/79 and flown to California for rebuild by Northrop factory, with volunteer labor. On display at the Norwegian Air Force Museum, Vaernes, Norway.
321	GS-E (1st)	Acc. Budareyri, Iceland, 2/4/42. Crashed on landing. No casualties.

c/n	British code	History	c/n	British code	History
322	GS-F	Gave full war service. Scrapped in Norway 5/26/56.	324	GS-G (1st)	Acc., lost on navigational training flight out of Reykjavík, Iceland, 7/30/41. Pilot 2/Lt. Hanno, observer Anker-Hansen, and wireless operator O. Batalden killed.
323		Acc. Fossvogur Bay, Iceland, 7/24/41. Crashed on landing. No casualties.			

SUPPLEMENT D
Types and Models of Northrop Aircraft

ALPHA 2
ATC 381 (11/22/30)
12 built, 1930–31

The first production airplane from Northrop, a cabin monoplane for pilot and six passengers. The prototype (X 2W) completed, licensed, and destroyed in March 1930. Certification trials with second example (X 127W). Deliveries of Northrop Alpha to TWA began in April 1931, with five Alpha 2s. Between 1931 and 1935 TWA operated eight, six converted to Alpha 3s, then 4s, and six became Alpha 4a's. Three Alpha 2s became USAAC Y1C-19 military transports.

ALPHA 3
ATC Gr. 2-335 (4/14/31)
5 built, 1931, 6 converted, 1931

The balance of the Northrop Alphas, with 420-hp P&W Wasp engines, were finished as Alpha 3s, with pilot and passenger seating reduced to only one or two passengers. Changes included installation of a mirror radio, landing lights, a larger battery, and a large red hazard light attached to the leading edge of the left wingtip. Five of the Alpha 3s were sold directly to TWA (less engines) and the other six in the airline's service were converted Alpha 2s.

ALPHA 4
ATC 451 (9/10/31)
11 converted, 1931

Conversion of both new Alpha 3s and those previously made over from Alpha 2s for TWA was accomplished in the fall of 1931 at the Northrop factory in Burbank. It included the installation of trousered wheel fairings, NACA cowl, battery, electric starter, low-pressure wheels and tires, flares, and new baggage compartments. The resulting pilot-only mail and express planes flew for TWA for four years (1931–35).

ALPHA 4a
ATC 461 (2/25/32)

10 converted, 1932

Eight of the Alpha 4s were further converted with Goodrich De-Icers installed on the leading edges of the wings, radio mast, stabilizers, and vertical fin, to become Alpha 4a's. The work was done in TWA's Kansas City service shops. TWA later purchased two additional Alpha 2s which were also converted to 4a's. All were flown as pilot-only all-weather day-and-night mail ships.

BETA 3
ATC (None)
1 built, 1931

A tandem-seated sport monoplane, powered by an inverted 155-hp six-cylinder Menasco Buccaneer engine. Offered as a "high-speed utility plane and advanced trainer" and priced at $8,500 flyaway Burbank, California. Prototype, used only for experimental and demonstration flying.

BETA 3D
ATC Gr. 2-401 (2/10/32)
1 built, 1931

Single-place model, powered by 300-hp P&W Wasp, Jr., engine. Taken over by Stearman Aircraft Company in Wichita, Kansas, but not put into production.

GAMMA 2A
ATC (None)
1 built, 1932

Especially designed by Northrop to fit the requirements of Lt. Cmdr. Frank M. Hawks. Had single cockpit to the rear and was powered by a Wright Whirlwind R-1510 700-hp engine, the first installation of a fourteen-cylinder, twin-row radial air-cooled engine in an American commercial airplane. Under test for many months and purchased in 1933 by Hawks's employer, The Texas Company, as *Texaco Sky Chief*.

GAMMA 2B
ATC (None)

1 built, 1932

Under development and construction at same time as Gamma 2A. A similar specially designed ship to fit the requirements of Antarctic explorer Lincoln Ellsworth. The 2B had tandem cockpits and a P&W 500-hp Wasp engine. Named *Polar Star* and flown in the Antarctic.

DELTA 1A
ATC Pending, later Gr. 2-456 (8/5/33)
1 built, 1933

First Delta, developed as an alternate to the Gamma, with same basic structure, but pilot's enclosed cockpit directly behind the Wright Cyclone SR-1820 F-3 710-hp engine. Seats in cabin provided for eight passengers. Three months of testing, but for ATC approval passenger capacity reduced to six.

DELTA 1B
ATC Group 2-458 (8/18/33)
1 built, 1933

Built to carry pilot and eight passengers, using 650-hp Pratt & Whitney Hornet engine. Bought by Pan American Airways and put to work on the airline's Mexican subsidiary, Aerovías Centrales, S.A., carrying passengers, mail, and express.

GAMMA 2C
ATC (None)
1 built, 1933

A Northrop Gamma built to the requirements of the USAAC as an experimental model. Delivered 7/33 to Army at Dayton, Ohio, and later purchased as a YA-13 for evaluation by USAAC. Originally equipped with 650-hp Wright Cyclone engine. Became Gamma 2F (q.v.).

DELTA 1C
ATC Gr. 2-468 (2/15/34)
1 built, 1934

An eight-passenger Delta with P&W Hornet 700-hp engine, built to the order of A.B. Aerotransport of Sweden, and exported in 1934.

GAMMA 2d
ATC 549 (8/9/34)
3 built, 1934

Built between April and June 1934 to requirements of TWA for larger, faster mail plane to use on transcontinental routes. Had Wright Cyclone SR-1820 F-3 engines.

GAMMA 2E, 2EC, 2ED
ATC (None)
51 built, 1934–35, with 25 as component parts

A two-place military attack bomber, supplied on order of the Chinese government. Powered by Wright Cyclone R-1820 F53 750-hp engines, they were armed with two .30-cal. machine guns in the wings, and carried an 1,100-lb. bomb load. A semiretractable bomb-aiming panel and gun port was located under the rear cockpit. First delivery date was 2/19/34. Two Gamma 2Es (c/n 14 and c/n 46) were sold, and the parts for an additional twenty-five aircraft (c/n 48 through 72) were crated and shipped to China, where they were assembled at the plant of the Central Aircraft Manufacturing Company (CAMCO).

One Gamma 2E was sold to the British Air Ministry in November 1934 and another was sold to the USSR.

Fifteen Gamma 2EDs (c/n 15, 16, 23–27, and 30–37) also went to the Chinese government in 1934, as did seven Gamma 2ECs (c/n 17-22 and 45). The EC and ED models differed from the basic Gamma 2Es in seating, tailplane configuration, and the use of three-bladed propellers.

GAMMA 2F
ATC (None)
1 converted, 1934

The former Gamma 2C, or Army YA-13, re-engined with an 800-hp P&W R-1830-7 twin-row engine and designated as Army XA-16.

GAMMA 2G
ATC Gr. 2-489 (9/29/34)
1 built, 1934

A special Gamma, built to the order of racing pilot Jacqueline Cochran with two cockpits and an in-line Curtiss Conqueror SVG-1570-F4 liquid-cooled 745-hp engine. Intended for MacRobertson Race, London-Australia, 1934. Re-engined with Pratt & Whitney Wasp with single-pilot configuration for 1935 Bendix Race. Leased to Howard Hughes, who installed a Wright Cyclone and set new nonstop transcontinental speed record 1/36. Back to P&W Twin Wasp engine in June 1936 and washed out in July.

GAMMA 2D-2
ATC 553 (pending), ATC 549 (8/9/34)
1 built, 1934

Company records show this Gamma as a 2H but all FAA records show 2D or 2D-2, with no reference to an H suffix. Built to order for Marron Price Guggenheim, and flown in tests and races by Guggenheim pilot Russell W. Thaw.

DELTA 1D
ATC Gr. 2-484 (8/3/34), Gr. 2-490 (10/2/34), and ATC 553 (8/23/34)
9 built, 1934–35

The Delta Executive aircraft, built for pilot and four to six passengers. All with Wright Cyclone engines except c/n 40, which had a P&W Hornet. A suffix digit was apparently applied in company records for the last seven Delta 1Ds, but appears in FAA records only with c/n 40 (1D-3) and c/n 74 (1D-7). Parts for a pattern aircraft called Gamma 1D-8 went to Canadian Vickers to start its production of Deltas.

"DELTA 1E" (GAMMA)
ATC Gr. 2-476 (6/8/34)
1 built, 1934

Though carried in company and FAA records as a Delta 1E, this airplane was in actuality in Gamma configuration, with two cockpits to the rear and a cargo cabin forward. Engine was P&W Hornet T2D1. This ship was approved for experimental testing, given commercial ATC certification, issued an export license, and sold, all in eight days! Went to A.B. Aerotransport in Sweden for use on European mail routes.

GAMMA 2J
ATC (None)
1 built, 1935

A version of the Army A-17A, built as demonstrator for USAAC advanced-trainer competition, with P&W 550-hp engine and seating three crew. Not chosen and returned to Northrop and used as company hack to 1944.

GAMMA 3A
ATC (None)
1 built, 1935

Special model of the Gamma, developed as a fighter airplane for the Army. Had retractable landing gear and 750-hp P&W Wasp R-1535-A5G engine. A single-seater, with split flaps and designated XP-948 for testing by USAAC. Disappeared on test flight July 1935, and design sold to Vought.

GAMMA 5A
ATC (None)
1 built, 1935

A version of the Northrop Gamma 2E, powered by a 775-hp Wright Cyclone engine with two-place configuration. Exported 1935 to Japanese navy.

GAMMA 5B
ATC (None)
1 built, 1935

A semimilitary version of the Northrop Gamma, with enclosed tandem cockpits forward and slimmer rear fuselage. Originally with P&W 700-hp Twin Wasp engine, but later with a Wright Cyclone "G." Sold for use in Spanish Civil War.

GAMMA 5D
ATC (None)
1 built, 1936

Another semimilitary version of the Gamma, with two-place cockpits, either open or closed. Powered by P&W S3H-1 550-hp engine. Tail surfaces and interior noted as being of "army type." Sold to Japanese navy.

GAMMA 2L
ATC (None)
1 built, 1937

A two-seat Gamma of A-17 military type, sold to British Air Ministry without engine. Used for testing Bristol Hercules engine.

GAMMA 7A
ATC (None)
Not built

This was to have been a twin-engined attack bomber. The design reportedly was completed, but the airplane was never built.

GAMMA 8A
ATC (None)
Built from 1937 on

Though given a Northrop Gamma numerical designation, the 8A and its successors were built and sold by Douglas after the liquidation of The Northrop Corporation.

SUPPLEMENT E
KNOWN CIVIL REGISTRATIONS OF NORTHROP
SINGLE-ENGINED AIRCRAFT, 1929 to 1939

Key:

c/n = Constructor's number (serial number of manufacturer)

U.S. prefixes:

NS	= Federal or state usage
C or NC	= Commercial
R or NR	= Restricted
X or NX	= Experimental

UNITED STATES

NS 1	Alpha	c/n 3	NC 28663	Delta	c/n 74	
NR 2111	Gamma	c/n 12	X 216H	Exper.	c/n 1	
X 12214	Beta	c/n 2	X 2W	Alpha	c/n 1	
NR 12265	Gamma	c/n 1	NC 127W	Alpha	c/n 2	
NR 12269	Gamma	c/n 2			TWA #14	
X 12291	Gamma	c/n 5				
NC 12292	Delta	c/n 3	NC 11Y	Alpha	c/n 3	
		TWA #15			TWA #12	
NC 13755	Gamma	c/n 29	NC 236Y	Delta	c/n 4	
NC 13757	Gamma	c/n 8	NC 933Y	Alpha	c/n 5	
		TWA #16			TWA #4	
NC 13758	Gamma	c/n 9	NC 942Y	Alpha	c/n 6	
		TWA #17			TWA #3	
NC 13759	Gamma	c/n 10	NC 947Y	Alpha	c/n 7	
		TWA #18			TWA #1	
NC 13760	Gamma	c/n 47	NC 961Y	Alpha	c/n 8	
NC 13761	Gamma	c/n 11			TWA #2	
NC 13777	Delta	c/n 28	NC 966Y	Alpha	c/n 9	
NC 14220	Delta	c/n 73			TWA #6	
NC 14241	Delta	c/n 38	NC 985Y	Alpha	c/n 10	
NC 14242	Delta	c/n 39			TWA #7	
NC 14265	Delta	c/n 40	NC 986Y	Alpha	c/n 11	
NC 14266	Delta	c/n 41			TWA #8	
NC 14267	Delta	c/n 42	NC 992Y	Alpha	c/n 12	
X 14997	Delta	c/n 187			TWA #9	
NR 14998	Gamma	c/n 188	NC 993Y	Alpha	c/n 16	
X 16071	Gamma	c/n 291			TWA #10	
X 18148	Gamma	c/n 186	NC 994Y	Alpha	c/n 17	
NX 18995	"Douglas"	c/n 346			TWA #11	
	1X		NC 999Y	Alpha	c/n 4	
NX 28311	N-1M	c/n –			TWA #5	

GREAT BRITAIN

G-AFBT	Gamma	c/n 347

FRANCE

F-AQAQ	Delta	c/n 39

MANCHURIA

M-506	Gamma	c/n 291

MEXICO

XA-ABI	Gamma	c/n 188
XA-ABJ	Gamma	c/n 10
XA-BED	Delta	c/n 4

SPAIN

EC-AGC	Delta	c/n 7

SWEDEN

SE-ADI	Delta	c/n 7
SE-ADW	Gamma	c/n 29

SUPPLEMENT F
TYPICAL NORTHROP SPECIFICATIONS

Key:

P	= Seating places	S	= Seaplane
O	= Open cockpit	M	= Monoplane
C	= Closed cabin	ATC	= Approved Type Certificate
L	= Landplane		

MODEL	DESC.	ORIGINAL ENGINE	HP	WING-SPAN	WING AREA (SQ. FT.)	LENGTH
AXION EXPERIMENTAL 1	2 POLM	MENASCO, 4-cyl.	90	30'6"	20'	20'
ALPHA 2	7 PCLM	P&W Wasp "C"	420-50	41'10"	295'	28'5"
ALPHA 3	1-3 PCLM	P&W Wasp "C"	420-25	41'10"	295'	28'5"
ALPHA 4	1 POLM	P&W Wasp "C"	420-25	43'10"	312'	28'5"
ALPHA 4a	1 POLM	P&W Wasp "C"	420-25	43'10"	312'	28'5"
BETA 3	1-2 POLM	Menasco Buccaneer, 6-cyl.	165	32'	137'	21'8"
GAMMA 2A	1 PCLM	Wright Whirlwind	700	48'	363'	30'
GAMMA 2B	2 PCLM	P&W Wasp	500	48'	363'	29'9"
GAMMA 2D	1 PCLM	Wright Cyclone	710–50	47'10"	363'	31'2"
GAMMA 2E	2 PCLM	Wright Cyclone	710–50	48'	363'	28'10"
GAMMA 2G	2 PCLM	Curtiss Conqueror	745	47'10"	363'	
DELTA 1D	5–7 PCLM	Wright Cyclone	710–35	47'9"	363'	33'1"
GAMMA 3A	1 POLM	P&W Twin Wasp	750	33'6"	187'	22'10"
ARMY A-17	2 PCLM	P&W Twin Wasp	750	47'8½"	362'	31'8¾"
ARMY A-17A	2 PCLM	P&W Twin Wasp	825	47'8½"	362'	31'8¾"
NAVY XFT1	1 POLM	Wright Cyclone	650	32'	177'	21'
NAVY BT-1	2 PCLM	Pratt & Whitney	700–825	41'6"	240'	31'8"
N3PB	3 PCSM	Wright Cyclone	1,200	48'11"	377	38'
N-1M	1 PCLM	2 Lycomings	65 ea.	38'	300'	17'

HEIGHT	WT. EMPTY	GROSS WT.	TOP SPEED	YEAR BUILT	ATC	COMMENTS
5′		1,100		1928–29		Original Northrop "flying wing"
9′	2,679	4,500	170	1930–31	381	TWA & Army Y1C-19
9′	2,679	4,500	170	1931	GR 2–335	TWA & Army Y1C-19
9′	2,800	4,700	177	1932	451	TWA & Army Y1C-19
9′	2,650	5,100	177	1932	461	TWA & Army Y1C-19
6′1″	1,135	1,770	175	1931	GR 2–401	Sport plane
	3,300	7,100	200	1932		*Texaco Sky Chief*
	3,200–3,400	7,100	180	1932		Ellsworth *Polar Star*
9′	4,119	7,350	224	1934	549	TWA
9′1″		7,600	210	1934–35		China military
9′				1934		Cochran racer
10′1″	4,540	7,350	219	1934–35	553	Executive A/C
		4,430	250–75	1935		Army fighter
12′	4,913	7,337	206	1936–37		Attack bomber
12′	5,106	7,550	220	1936–37		Attack bomber
9′6″		7,761	240	1933		Navy fighter
14′		7,000	222	1936–37		Navy dive-bomber
16′10″		10,600	257	1940–41		Norwegian patrol bomber
6′		3,900	200 max	1939–40		Experimental "flying wing"

SUPPLEMENT G
The Successive Northrop Companies

The early Northrop aircraft were the product of four successive companies of which John K. Northrop was the guiding spirit. These were as follows:

1928–29 *The Avion Corporation*, established in a rented shop at 4515 Alger Street, Los Angeles, California. George Randolph Hearst, president; John K. Northrop, vice-president. William Kenneth Jay was associated with the new venture, and financial backing came from Hearst and his mother-in-law, Mrs. Ada Wilbur. The *Experimental No. 1* ("flying wing") was built by Avion. Assets sold to United Aircraft & Transport Corporation in October 1929.

1929–31 *Northrop Aircraft Corporation*, Burbank, California. Though acquired in the fall of 1929, this new company was officially established on January 1, 1930, as a subsidiary of *United Aircraft & Transport Corporation*, a New York–based holding company with manufacturing divisions. William E. Boeing (of United/Boeing Aircraft), chairman of the board; W. Kenneth Jay, president; John K. Northrop, vice-president; Don R. Berlin, chief engineer. A factory was set up in a hangar at United Airport in Burbank, and this company built the Northrop Alpha and Beta airplanes. In September 1931, the Northrop facility was consolidated with another United/Boeing subsidiary, Stearman Aircraft Corporation of Wichita, Kansas. Plans to continue Alpha and Beta production in Wichita were begun, and some machinery and materials transferred. John K. Northrop resigned, and no Northrop planes were built in Wichita. Some modification and repair

John K. Northrop (left) *and chief engineer Don R. Berlin examine half-fuselage of new Northrop Gamma.*

work was carried out in Kansas, leading to the name "Stearman Alpha" being sometimes applied to Northrop Alpha aircraft.

1931–37 *The Northrop Corporation*, Inglewood, California. Founded in January 1932 as a subsidiary of *Douglas Aircraft Company, Inc.* (51 percent of stock). John K. Northrop, president; W. K. Jay, vice-president and general manager; Don. R. Berlin, chief engineer. (Other officers included Gage H. Irving, pilot/salesman; J. C. Garrett, purchasing agent; Arthur Mankey, chief draftsman; and Harry O. Williams, superintendent.) Established at Los Angeles Municipal Airport (Mines Field) in former White Truck/Moreland Aircraft factory. Northrop Gamma and Delta airplanes were first built and put into production here, as well as experimental military aircraft. By 1934 the company had built a hundred planes and employed 1,000 people. Production of military aircraft continued in 1935 at a new factory built a quarter of a mile east, with the address of El Segundo, California. Douglas Aircraft acquired balance of Northrop stock as of September 8, 1937, and the corporation became the El Segundo Division of Douglas. John K. Northrop resigned effective January 1, 1938.

1939–59 *Northrop Aircraft, Inc.*, Hawthorne, California. New company established August 1, 1939. John K. Northrop, president and chief engineer; La Motte Turck Cohu, chairman of the board and general manager; Gage H. Irving, vice-president and assistant general manager; Moye Stephens, secretary and flight chief. New factory and adjacent airport were first occupied in February 1940. The company had subcontracts for aircraft components and then built N-3PB patrol bombers for Norway and the N-1M (flying wing.) It became a division of the present-day NORTHROP CORPORATION, Los Angeles, California, as of February 2, 1959.

Head-on Gamma shot.

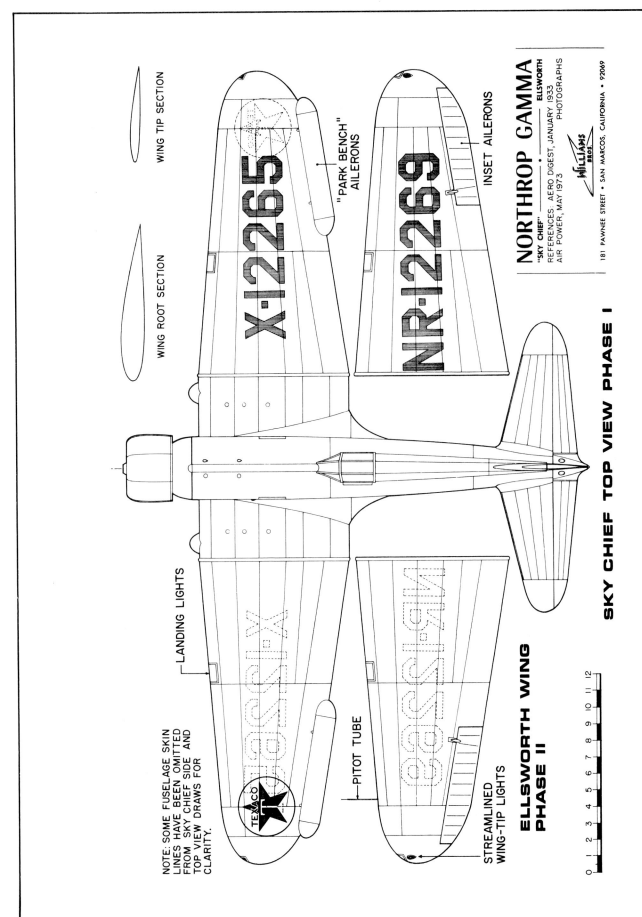

WING TIP SECTION

WING ROOT SECTION

"PARK BENCH" AILERONS

INSET AILERONS

NORTHROP GAMMA

"SKY CHIEF" • ELLSWORTH
REFERENCES: AERO DIGEST, JANUARY 1933
AIR POWER, MAY 1973 PHOTOGRAPHS

WILLIAMS BROS

181 PAWNEE STREET • SAN MARCOS, CALIFORNIA • 92069

SKY CHIEF TOP VIEW PHASE I

NOTE: SOME FUSELAGE SKIN
LINES HAVE BEEN OMITTED
FROM SKY CHIEF SIDE AND
TOP VIEW DRAWS FOR
CLARITY.

LANDING LIGHTS

PITOT TUBE

STREAMLINED
WING-TIP LIGHTS

ELLSWORTH WING
PHASE II

TEXACO

X-12265

NR-12269

0 1 2 3 4 5 6 7 8 9 10 11 12

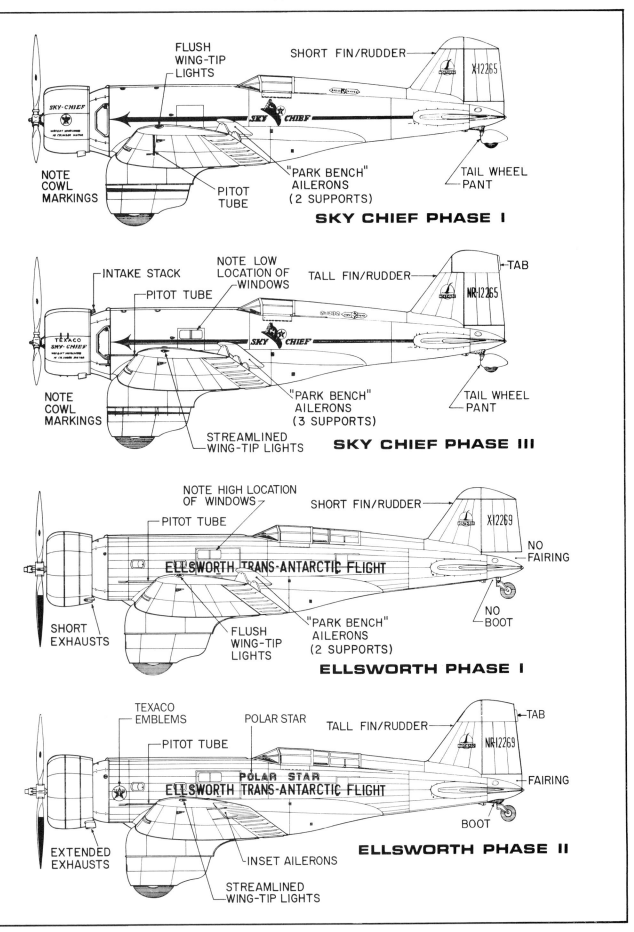

SKY CHIEF PHASE I

FLUSH WING-TIP LIGHTS

SHORT FIN/RUDDER

X-12265

SKY-CHIEF

SKY CHIEF

NOTE COWL MARKINGS

PITOT TUBE

"PARK BENCH" AILERONS (2 SUPPORTS)

TAIL WHEEL PANT

SKY CHIEF PHASE III

INTAKE STACK

NOTE LOW LOCATION OF WINDOWS

TALL FIN/RUDDER

TAB

PITOT TUBE

NR-12265

TEXACO SKY-CHIEF

SKY CHIEF

NOTE COWL MARKINGS

"PARK BENCH" AILERONS (3 SUPPORTS)

STREAMLINED WING-TIP LIGHTS

TAIL WHEEL PANT

ELLSWORTH PHASE I

NOTE HIGH LOCATION OF WINDOWS

SHORT FIN/RUDDER

X12269

PITOT TUBE

NO FAIRING

ELLSWORTH TRANS-ANTARCTIC FLIGHT

SHORT EXHAUSTS

FLUSH WING-TIP LIGHTS

"PARK BENCH" AILERONS (2 SUPPORTS)

NO BOOT

ELLSWORTH PHASE II

TEXACO EMBLEMS

POLAR STAR

TALL FIN/RUDDER

TAB

PITOT TUBE

NR-12269

POLAR STAR

ELLSWORTH TRANS-ANTARCTIC FLIGHT

FAIRING

BOOT

EXTENDED EXHAUSTS

INSET AILERONS

STREAMLINED WING-TIP LIGHTS

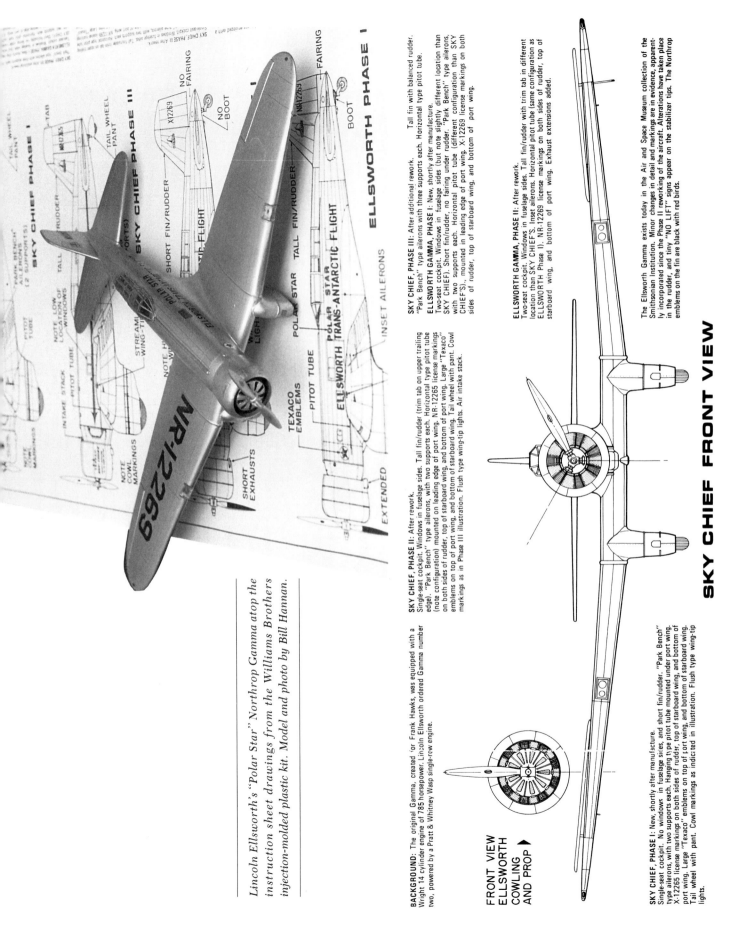

Lincoln Ellsworth's "Polar Star" Northrop Gamma atop the instruction sheet drawings from the Williams Brothers injection-molded plastic kit. Model and photo by Bill Hannan.

SKY CHIEF PHASE I

SKY CHIEF PHASE III

ELLSWORTH PHASE I

ELLSWORTH TRANS-ANTARCTIC FLIGHT

BACKGROUND: The original Gamma, created for Frank Hawks, was equipped with a Wright 14 cylinder engine of 785 horsepower. Lincoln Ellsworth ordered Gamma number two, powered by a Pratt & Whitney Wasp single-row engine.

FRONT VIEW
ELLSWORTH
COWLING
AND PROP ►

SKY CHIEF, PHASE I: New, shortly after manufacture. Single-seat cockpit. No windows in fuselage sides, and short fin/rudder. "Park Bench" type ailerons, with two supports each. Hanging type pitot tube mounted under port wing. X-12265 license markings on both sides of rudder, top of starboard wing, and bottom of port wing. Large "Texaco" emblems on top of port wing, and bottom of starboard wing. Tail wheel with pant. Cowl markings as indicated in illustration. Flush type wing-tip lights.

SKY CHIEF, PHASE II: After rework. Single-seat cockpit. Windows in fuselage sides. Tall fin/rudder (trim tab on upper trailing edge). "Park Bench" type ailerons, with two supports each. Horizontal type pitot tube (note configuration) mounted on leading edge of port wing. NR-12265 license markings on both sides of rudder, top of starboard wing, and bottom of port wing. Large "Texaco" emblems on top of port wing, and bottom of starboard wing. Tail wheel with pant. Cowl markings as in Phase III illustration. Flush type wing-tip lights. Air intake stack.

SKY CHIEF, PHASE III: After additional rework. Tall fin with balanced rudder. "Park Bench" type ailerons with three supports each. Horizontal type pitot tube.

ELLSWORTH GAMMA, PHASE I: New, shortly after manufacture. Two-seat cockpit. Windows in fuselage sides (but note slightly different location than SKY CHIEF). Short fin/rudder, no fairing under rudder. "Park Bench" type ailerons, with two supports each. Horizontal pitot tube (different configuration than SKY CHIEF'S), mounted in leading edge of port wing. X-12269 license markings on both sides of rudder, top of starboard wing, and bottom of port wing.

ELLSWORTH GAMMA, PHASE II: After rework. Two-seat cockpit. Windows in fuselage sides. Tall fin/rudder with trim tab in different location than SKY CHIEF'S. Inset ailerons. Horizontal pitot tube (same configuration as ELLSWORTH Phase I). NR-12269 license markings on both sides of rudder, top of starboard wing, and bottom of port wing. Exhaust extensions added.

The Ellsworth Gamma exists today in the Air and Space Museum collection of the Smithsonian Institution. Minor changes in detail and markings are in evidence, apparently incorporated since the Phase II reworking of the aircraft. Alterations have taken place in the rudder, and tiny "NO LIFT" signs appear on the stabilizer tips. The Northrop emblems on the fin are black with red birds.

SKY CHIEF FRONT VIEW

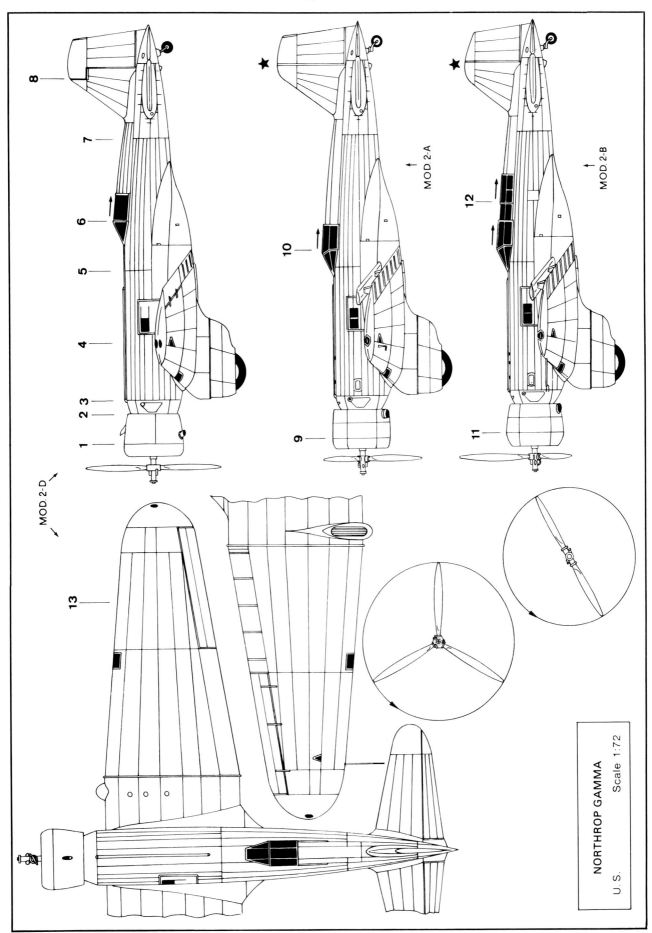

MOD. 2-D

MOD. 2-A

MOD. 2-B

NORTHROP GAMMA

U.S.

Scale 1:72

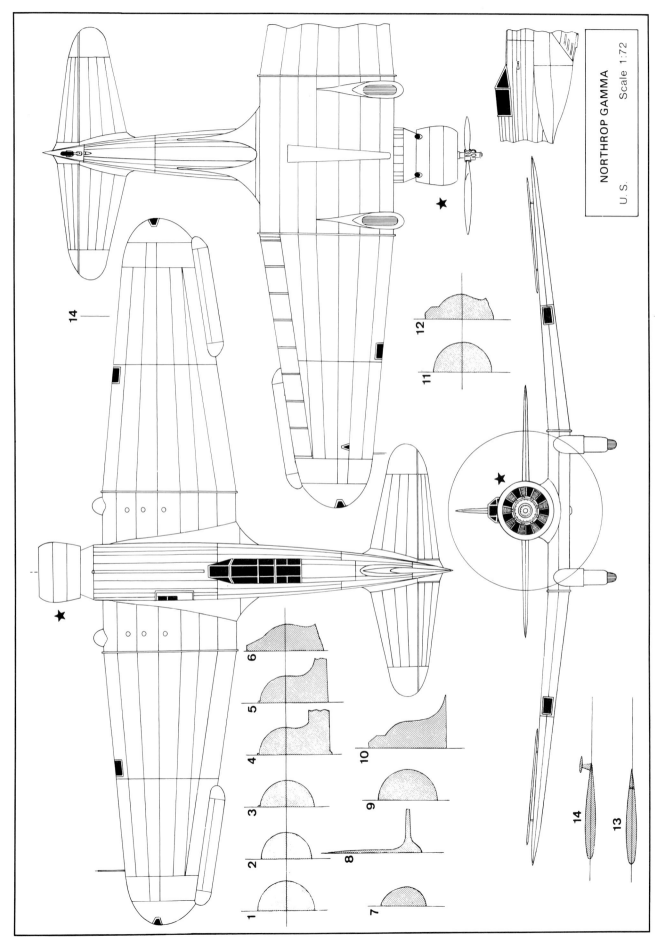

NORTHROP GAMMA

U. S.   Scale 1:72

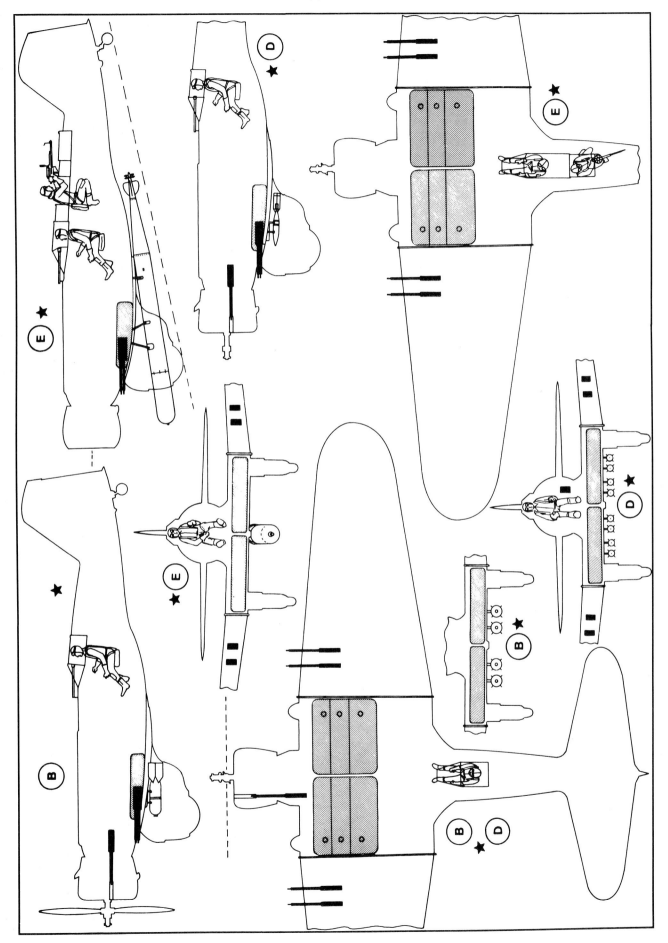

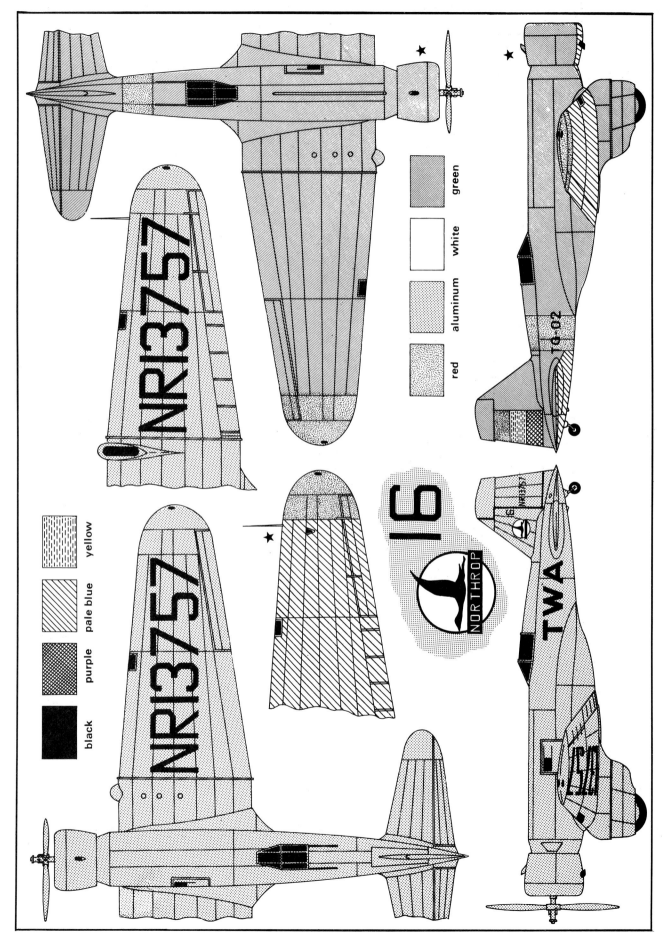

green

white

aluminum

red

yellow

pale blue

purple

black

NR13757

NR13757

NORTHROP

TWA

14-02

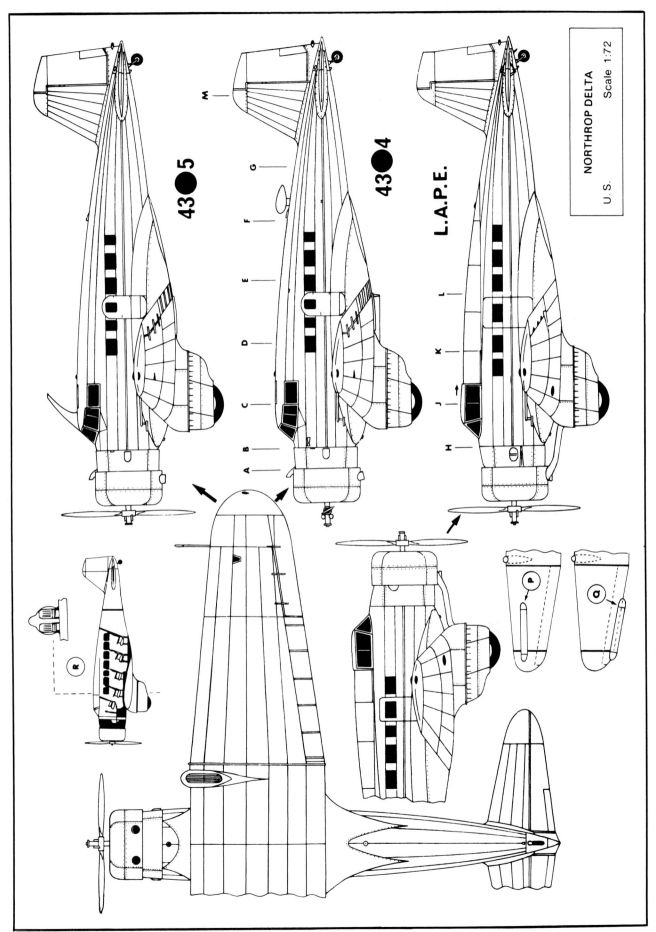

43●5

43●4

L.A.P.E.

NORTHROP DELTA

U. S.　　Scale 1:72

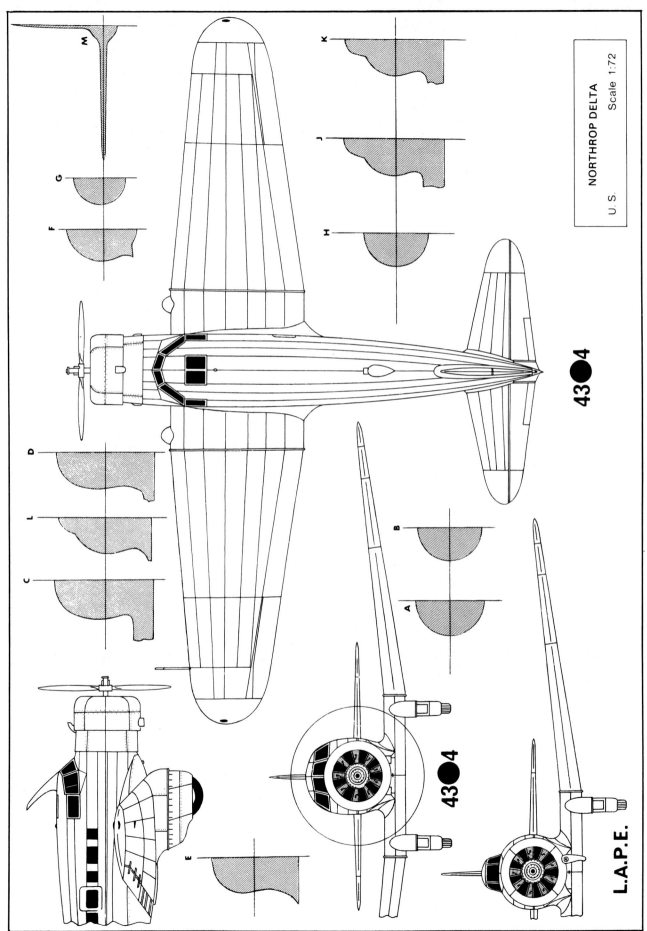

NORTHROP DELTA

U.S.   Scale 1:72

L.A.P.E.

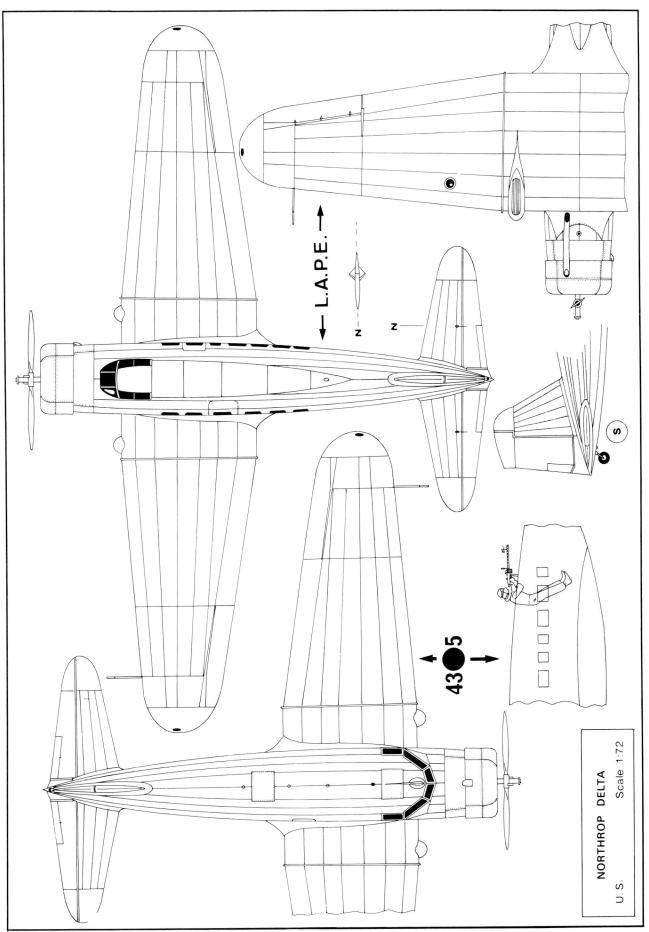

L.A.P.E.

43●5

NORTHROP DELTA

Scale 1:72

U.S.

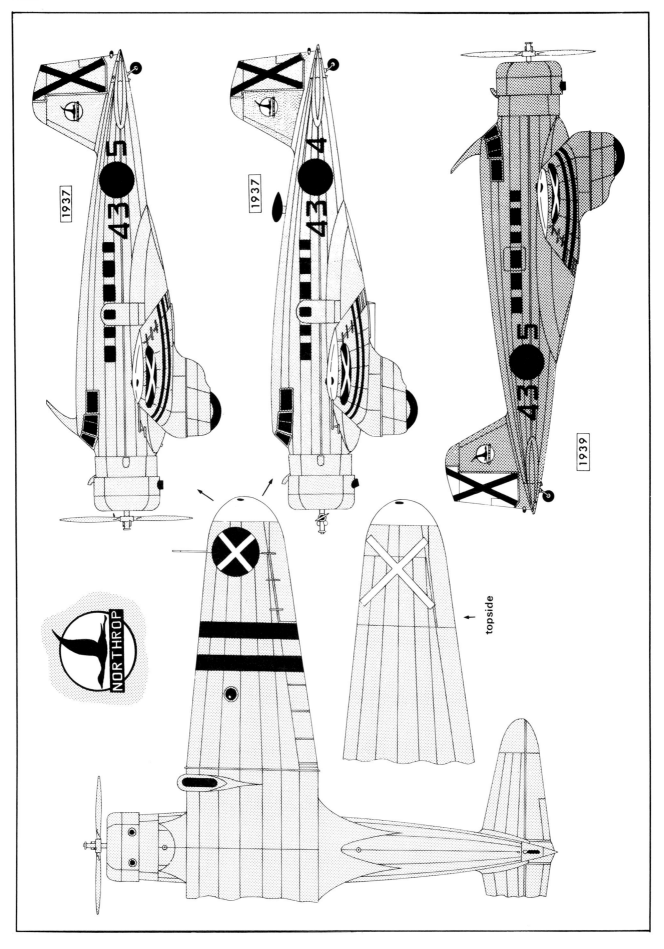

1937

1937

1939

topside

NORTHROP

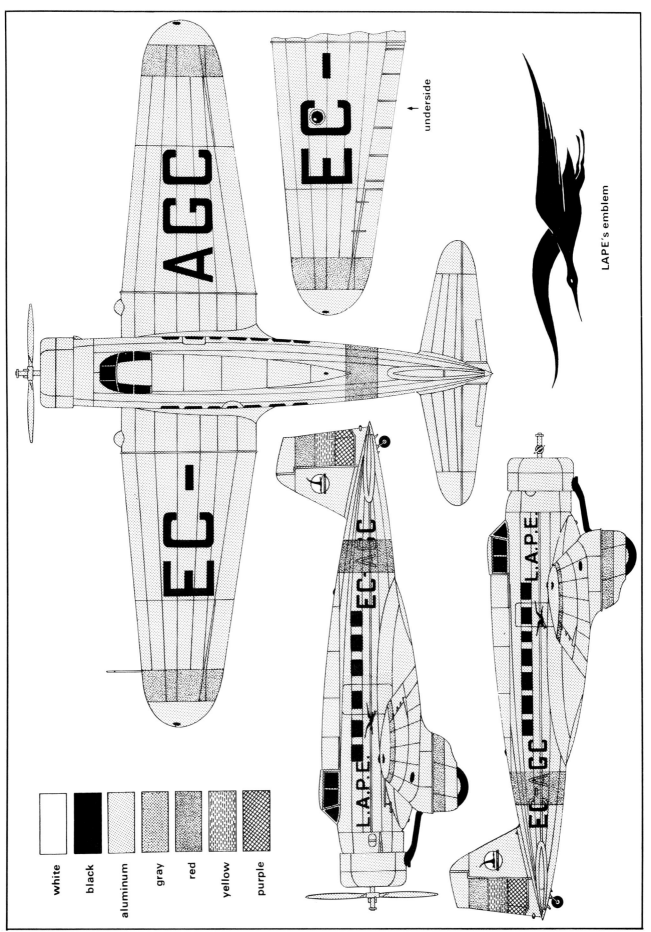

underside

LAPE's emblem

white
black
aluminum
gray
red
yellow
purple

ACKNOWLEDGMENTS

Only unprecedented help and generosity have made this book possible. The many friends and aviation historians to whom thanks is extended include Stafford Acher; Lennart Anderson; Harold Andrews; Juan Arraez; John C. Barbery; Joseph H. Barry; Gerry Beauchamp; Edward G. Betts; Owen S. Billman; Warren M. Bodie; Peter M. Bowers; Walter J. Boyne; Brian J. J. Bridgeman; H. Glenn Buffington; James Carmody; Everett Cassagneres; Ira E. Chart; Jack Cunningham; R. E. G. Davies; John M. Davis; Arthur P. Dowd; Angelo Emiliani; Felipe Ezquerro; Lesley N. Forden; Rene J. Francillon; George A. Fuller; Patricia Groves; Daniel P. Hagedorn; H. Allen Herr; Gerald Howson; Stephen J. Hudek; John L. Johnson, Jr.; T. R. Judge; Joseph P. Juptner; Leo J. Kohn; Mike Kusenda; Willam T. Larkins; Edward Leiser; Harvey H. Lippincott; Charles G. Mandrake; Mitch Mayborn; Paula Mercado; Justo Miranda; Robert Parmerter; Attil A. Pasquini, Sr.; Edward Peck; Edward H. Phillips; Russell Plehinger; Ragnar J. Ragnarsson; Boardman C. Reed; Ross Richardson; Theron K. Rinehart; Matther E. Rodina, Jr.; Irving Rosenberg; Malcolm Rosholt; James A. Ruotsala; Kenn C. Rust; Mauno A. Salo; Thomas Sarbaugh; Milton H. Sheppard; Warren D. Shipp; A. J. Shorrt; Richard K. Smith; Paul L. Stephenson; Emil A. Strasser; Frank Strnad; Robert Taylor; Don Thomas; Noboru Tyoko; John W. Underwood; Jansz Vanderveer; Adolfo Villasenor; Lyman Voelpel; Ray Wagner; Truman C. Weaver; John Wegg; Paul Whelan; William F. Yeager; E. T. Wooldridge, Jr..

The author is grateful to the following companies, individuals, and institutions, past and present, whose generosity made illustrations available for inclusion in this book: Juan Arraez; John C. Barbery; Roger Besecker; Peter M. Bowers; Walter J. Boyne; Canadian Aviation Historical Society; Douglas Aircraft; Warren Eberspacher; Angelo Emiliani; Paddy Gardiner; A. B. Hidy; Gerald Howson; Stephen J. Hudek; Ralph Johnston; Gregory C. Krohn; William T. Larkins; Lockheed Aircraft Corporation; National Air and Space Museum; National Aviation Museum (Canada); Northrop Corporation; Nut Tree Associates; Robert Parmerter; Attil Pasquini; Irving Rosenberg; San Diego Air and Space Museum; Milton H. Sheppard; Warren D. Shipp; Frank Strnad; Texaco, Inc.; TWA; Noboro Tyoko; John W. Underwood; U.S. Air Force; Western Airlines; Wichita Board of Park Commissioners; William F. Yeager.

Also, special thanks to Williams Brothers, Inc., and Justo Miranda and Paula Mercado for permission to reproduce the three-view scale drawings in the Appendix.

SELECTED BIBLIOGRAPHY

Aircraft Year Book. New York: Aeronautical Chamber of Commerce of America, Inc., 1927–41.

Allen, Richard Sanders. *Revolution in the Sky*. New York: 1988.

Anderson, Fred. *Northrop: An Aeronautical History*. Century City, California: 1976.

Balchen, Bernt. *Come North with Me*. New York: 1958.

Bixby, Harold M. "Top Side Ricksha." 1938?.

Cathcart-Jones, Owen. *Aviation Memoirs*. London: 1934.

Cheney, Lindsay, and Michael Cieply. *The Hearsts*. New York: 1981.

Clouston, A. E. *The Dangerous Skies*. London: 1954.

Cochran, Jaqueline. *The Stars at Noon*. Boston: 1954.

Cochran, Jaqueline, and Maryann Bucknum Brinley. *Jackie Cochran: An Autobiography*. New York: 1987.

Coleman, Ted, with Robert Wenkam. *Jack Northrop and the Flying Wing*. New York: 1988.

Davies, R. E. G. *A History of the World's Airlines*. London: 1964.

———. *Airlines of the United States Since 1914*. London: 1972.

———. *Airlines of Latin America Since 1919*. Washington: 1984.

———. *Pan Am: An Airline and its Aircraft*. New York: 1987.

Dwiggins, Don. *They Flew the Bendix Race*. Philadelphia: 1982.

Ellsworth, Lincoln. *Beyond Horizons*. New York: 1937.

Francillon, Rene J. *McDonnell Douglas Aircraft Since 1920*. London: 1979.

Grierson, John. *Sir Hubert Wilkins*. London: 1960.

———. *Challenge to the Poles*. London: 1964.

Hawks, Captain Frank. *Once to Every Pilot*. New York: 1936.

Heinemann, Edward H., and Rosario Rausa. *Ed Heinemann, Combat Aircraft Designer*. Annapolis: 1978.

Heinmuller, John P. V. *Man's Fight To Fly*. New York: 1945.

Hickerson, J. Mel. *Ernie Breech*. New York: 1968.

Hoagland, Roland W., ed. *The Blue Book of Aviation*. Los Angeles: 1932.

Juptner, Joseph P. *U.S. Civil Aircraft*, Vols. 1–9. Los Angeles: 1962–81.

King, Jack L. *Wings of Man*. Glendale, California: 1981.

Knight, Clayton, and Robert C. Durham. *Hitch Your Wagon*. Drexel Hill, Pennsylvania: 1950.

Larkins, William T. *U.S. Navy Aircraft 1921–1941, U.S. Marine Corps Aircraft 1914–1958*. New York: 1989.

Leary, William M., Jr. *The Dragon's Wings*. Athens, Georgia: 1976.

Leonard, Royal. *I Flew for China*. New York: 1942.

Miranda, Justo, and Paula Mercado. *World Aviation in Spain, 1936–1939: American and Soviet Airplanes*. Madrid: 1988.

Molson, K. M., and Taylor, H. A. *Canadian Aircraft Since 1909*. Stittsville, Ontario: 1982.

Pu-Yu, Hu. *A Brief History of Sino-Japanese War 1937–1945*. Taipei: 1974.

Roseberry, C. R. *The Challenging Skies*. New York: 1966.

Simmons, George. *Target: Arctic*. Philadelphia: 1965.

Thomas, Lowell. *Sir Hubert Wilkins*. New York: 1961.

Tunis, John R. *Million-Miler: The Story of an Air Pilot*. New York: 1942.

Underwood, John. *Mapcaps, Millionaires and "Mose."* Glendale, California: 1984.

Vecsey, George, and George C. Dade. *Getting off the Ground*. New York: 1979.

Wilson, Dick. *When Tigers Fight*. New York: 1983.

Wooldridge, E. T. *Winged Wonders: The Story of the Flying Wings*. Washington, D.C.: 1983.

———. *Images of Flight: The Aviation Photography of Rudy Arnold*. Washington, D.C.: 1986.

Also consulted: The files of *AAHS Journal; Aero Digest; Air-Britain Archive; Air-Britain Digest; Air Classics; Air Progress; Air Travel News; Airway Age; American Airman; American Modeler; Antique Airplane News; Aviation; Aviation Quarterly; Aviation Week; CAHS Journal; Flight; Flying; Historical Aviation Album; Los Angeles Times; Model Airplane News; New York Daily News; New York Herald Tribune; New York Times; The Official Aviation Guide; Popular Aviation; Skyways; Sport Aviation; Sportsman Pilot; Texaco Star; The Aeroplane; U.S. Air Services; Western Flying; Wings/Airpower*.

INDEX